Choice and Demand in Tourism

CHOICE AND DEMAND IN TOURISM

Edited by
Peter Johnson and Barry Thomas

MANSELL

First published in 1992 by
Mansell Publishing Limited, *A Cassell Imprint*
Villiers House, 41/47 Strand, London WC2N 5JE, England
387 Park Avenue South, New York, NY 10016-8810, USA

British Library Cataloguing in Publication Data
Choice and demand in tourism.
I. Johnson, Peter   II. Thomas, Barry
339.4891

ISBN 0-7201-2118-3

Library of Congress Cataloging-in-Publication Data
Choice and demand in tourism/edited by Peter Johnson and Barry
Thomas.
    p.   cm.
Includes bibliographical references and index.
ISBN 0-7201-2118-3
1. Tourist trade.   I. Johnson, Peter, 1944-   . II. Thomas, Barry.
E741.C38   1992
338.4'791 – dc20   91-28408
                                                                CIP

Typeset by Colset Pte Ltd, Singapore
Printed and bound in Great Britain by
Biddles Ltd, Guildford and King's Lynn

Contents

Notes on Contributors

Livin Bollaert holds a PhD in Physical Education. He is Director of the Department of Leisure, Future and Policy Planning of the Free University Brussels. Professor Bollaert is Lecturer in Principles of Leisure Sciences and Leisure Theory and Management of Leisure Centres.

Graham Brown is a Senior Lecturer in Tourism at the University of New England, Northern Rivers, NSW, Australia. He gained his PhD at Texas A & M University and was previously a Senior Lecturer in the Department of Tourism at Bournemouth Polytechnic, England. Dr Brown has produced reports for international agencies such as the Pacific Asia Travel Association and the World Tourism Organisation and has been involved in collaborative projects with organizations including Thomson Holidays, American Express (TRS) and Sheraton Hotels. His current research interests focus on the application of consumer behaviour concepts to tourism, particularly the development of techniques to measure tourist 'involvement'.

Barbara Carmichael has an Honours degree in Geography from the University of Bristol, a Master's degree in Management Studies from Durham University Business School, and a PhD from the University of Victoria, BC, Canada. Her research interests are in tourism marketing, tourism management and consumer behaviour. She is a Sessional Lecturer in the Department of Geography and in the School of Business at the University of Victoria.

Ann Clewer has many years' experience of lecturing at the University of Kent on managerial economics, business maths, theory of statistics and forecasting. She is a founder member of the Tourism Research Centre, Canterbury Business School. Her tourism research interests are mainly in the quantitative areas of modelling and forecasting. Her other research interests include the housing market and the visual representation of spatial data.

Chris Cooper graduated from University College London with a doctorate in tourism geography. He then worked for a major tour operator before returning to academic life. He lectures in tourism management at the University of Surrey and his research interests include resort development and tourism education.

Geoffrey Crouch is a Senior Lecturer in Marketing and Strategic Management at the Graduate School of Management, Monash University, Melbourne, Australia. His teaching and research interests are primarily services marketing related. International services marketing, and tourism marketing and management are his special interest. He has published research in these areas and has acted as a consultant to the Australian Tourist Commission on international marketing issues. He was recently a Visiting Assistant Professor in Tourism Management at the University of Calgary.

Adrian Darnell is a Senior Lecturer in Economics at the University of Durham. His main research interest is currently the methodology of econometrics. He has acted as consultant for a number of organizations, and has extensive publications in the form of books and articles.

Peter Johnson is Reader in Economics at the University of Durham. In recent years, his research interests have focused on the economics of small business and on the employment impact of tourism. He has recently completed (in collaboration with Barry Thomas) a substantial project on the effect of a major tourist attraction in the North-East of England on the local economy. He has acted as a consultant to a number of agencies and has published a wide range of books and articles.

Luk Van Langenhove holds a PhD in Psychology. He is a Lecturer in Psychology of Leisure and Consumer Behaviour in Tourism at the Department of Leisure, Future and Policy Planning of the Free University Brussels.

Els Lowyck is a research assistant in the Department of Leisure, Future and Policy Planning of the Free University Brussels. She studied economics at the State University of Ghent and leisure management at the Free University Brussels.

Alan Pack is Lecturer in Economics and founder member of the Tourism Research Centre at the University of Kent, teaching econometrics and economic statistics. His tourism research interests are in the econometric and time series modelling of tourism flows and he has published in this area. Other research interests include the measurement and modelling of house prices.

Richard Prentice lectures in Leisure and Tourism Strategies, and Social Planning in the Geography Department at the University College of Swansea. His present research interests include both heritage tourism and the interrelationship of domestic tourism and internal migration within the British Isles. Dr Prentice has published extensively on Manx and Welsh tourism, and is co-author of *Heritage Sites: Strategies for Management and Development.*

Chris Ryan is Principal Lecturer at the Nottingham Business School, Nottingham Polytechnic. Formerly Head of Tourism and Recreation Studies at the Business School, he was Visiting Professor at the University of Saskatchewan in 1989–90. He is author of *Recreation Tourism – A Social Science Perspective.*

Farouk Saleh is a Professor and Head of the Department of Management and Marketing at the University of Saskatchewan. He has had a number of papers published including articles in the *International Journal of Retailing* and the *Service Industries Journal.* He has held the post of Visiting Lecturer at the Universities of Malaga and Kuwait.

Robin Shaw is Foundation Professor of Marketing at Griffith University, Brisbane, Australia. He holds the degrees of Bachelor of Science from the University of Melbourne; Master of Business Administration from Monash University; and Doctor of Philosophy from Cornell University. His current research areas include: international tourism marketing; services quality in tourism, especially hospitality; methods of assessing attribute importance for tourism products; the role of follow-up in international survey research; and advertising evaluation in tourism.

Thea Sinclair is Director of the Tourism Research Centre and Lecturer in Economics at the University of Kent. Her research and publications examine a wide range of subjects within the economics of tourism and she has undertaken studies for local organizations, the United Nations and the World Bank. She has been involved in tourism development policy in Kenya and is undertaking collaborative research with continental European colleagues.

Barry Thomas is Senior Lecturer in Economics at the University of Durham. His main research interests are in labour economics and in the evaluation of the impact of tourism. He has acted as consultant to local and national government and to European organizations. He has written a number of books and articles on economics.

Christine Witt is Lecturer in Production/Operations Management at the University of Bradford Management Centre. She was formerly Lecturer in Tourism at the European Business Management School, University College of Swansea. Her main areas of research have been forecasting international tourist demand and operations management in the tourism industry. She has published widely, with articles in the *Annals of Tourism Research, Journal of Travel Research, Tourism Management, Service Industries Journal, Journal of Forecasting, Journal of Contemporary Hospitality Management* and the *Tourist Review*. She has also co-authored *Modelling and Forecasting Demand in Tourism*. Dr Witt has worked for KPMG Peat Marwick McLintock, Swansea.

Stephen Witt holds the Lewis Chair of Tourism Studies in the European Business Management School at the University College of Swansea. His research interests centre on tourism demand forecasting, econometric model-building and the economics of tourism. Recent publications include the *Tourism Marketing and Management Handbook, The Management of International Tourism, Modelling and Forecasting Demand in Tourism*. Professor Witt is on the Editorial Boards of *Tourism Management* and the *International Journal of Consumer Marketing*.

Peter Wright is Lecturer in Occupational Psychology at the University of Bradford Management Centre. His main teaching and research interests are in the fields of motivation, job satisfaction, improving work performance, leadership and interpersonal skills. He is the author, with David Taylor, of *Improving Leadership Performance* and *Developing Interpersonal Skills Through Tutored Practice*, and has written numerous articles and chapters for edited textbooks on motivation, job satisfaction and interpersonal skills. He has also carried out interpersonal skills training, particularly in the area of performance appraisal interviewing, for a large number of organizations, both public and private.

Preface

This book, and its sister volume *Perspectives on Tourism Policy*, also edited by us and published by Mansell, grew out of an international conference on tourism research held at Durham University.

The conference was held because it was felt that, although there had been a considerable expansion of tourism research in recent years, the effort was rather fragmented and dispersed. One reason for this is that many tourism researchers usually operate within traditional disciplinary boundaries, with only limited opportunities for contact with others working in similar fields. A primary purpose of the conference was thus to foster contact between researchers, to enable them to present the results of recently completed work and to receive feedback. It was also seen as an opportunity to review the strengths and weaknesses of current research and to identify potentially fruitful avenues for future work. Another objective of the conference was to encourage contact between researchers and users of research.

Nearly 150 delegates, drawn from all over the world and from a variety of disciplines, attended the conference. About two-thirds of the delegates came from academic institutions; the rest were mainly from central and local government and from the tourism agencies.

The conference papers covered a wide range of topics. A number of them were concerned with the analysis of choice and demand.

There is of course already a substantial literature on some aspects of these issues and there is little virtue in adding to this if it is simply replication. However, the present volume adds positively – in some cases by pulling together strands of the literature and taking stock of what is known (for example, by reviewing relevant literature, by attempting generalizations from disparate results and by evaluating the usefulness of existing concepts of models), in other cases by further empirical work which has some novelty in the models used or their application. A book of this scale makes no pretence to be comprehensive, but it does provide a useful range of perspectives on choice and demand in tourism, as well as offering some insights into the preoccupations of researchers and into some of the strengths and weaknesses of current efforts. The book should be of value not only to researchers and policy-makers, but also to those on undergraduate courses on tourism and related subjects.

We owe a considerable debt to a number of organizations and individuals. Sponsorship for the conference was provided by the Bank of England, the Joseph Rowntree Foundation, Newcastle Breweries, British Rail and Peat Marwick McLintock. Our own Department of Economics also gave generous assistance. The help of these organizations is readily acknowledged. Without it, the conference would not have been possible. Particular thanks are due to Dr Janet Lewis, Research Director of the Joseph Rowntree Foundation, who supported this conference from its inception and who was a constant source of encouragement. Thanks are also due to the conference delegates, many of whom contributed vigorously to the seminar discussions.

There is one chapter (apart from the first) that is not based on a paper at the conference: this is Chapter 10 by Darnell *et al*. It originally appeared in *Tourism Management* (volume 11, number 3, 1990) and we are grateful to the editor of that journal for permission to reproduce it here. It has been included in the present book because it fills a gap by presenting an econometric demand model at the level of a *single* tourist attraction. It thus complements the econometric work on demand models in Chapters 11 and 12, which are both concerned with appraising the results of (highly aggregated) demand studies rather than with actually estimating demand models.

We would not have been able to produce this book without the willing and full co-operation of its contributors, all of whom responded so readily to editorial nagging. Julie Bushby, Kathryn

Cowton and Lovaine Ord all provided excellent secretarial services and we are grateful to them.

Peter Johnson and Barry Thomas
Durham 1992

1 The Analysis of Choice and Demand in Tourism

Peter Johnson and Barry Thomas

1.1 INTRODUCTION

1.1.1 The Growth of Tourism

The rapid growth of tourism since the 1960s is well-known. International tourist arrivals worldwide jumped from about 70 million in 1960 to over 400 million by the end of the 1980s (World Tourism Organisation, 1990). The rate of growth has been uneven but there seems little doubt that the tourism industry will continue to grow strongly over the next decade: some forecasters believe that international tourist arrivals will reach half a billion by the year 2000 (Latham, 1991, p. 133). In many developed countries it is one of the fastest-growing sectors of the economy and it is a major source of employment growth. The number of tourist destinations has increased markedly and the range of tourist activities has broadened, giving rise to many different types of tourist.

The definition of a tourist is of course wide-ranging: the purpose of visits includes holidays, business trips, visits to friends and relatives, and miscellaneous visits (for reasons such as study, religion, shopping or sports activities). Taking international tourist activities worldwide, Witt *et al.* (1991, p. 38) note that about 70 per cent of tourist trips are for holiday purposes, about 15 per cent are for business and about 15 per cent for all other reasons. As holidays are by far the most important form of tourist trip many of the issues raised in this chapter will focus on holiday behaviour. This is particularly so in the discussion of choice.

1.1.2 Demand and Supply Considerations

The growth in tourism is to some extent demand-driven. The long-run growth in real incomes in developed economies has brought a more than proportionate increase in demand for tourism and any understanding of the development of and prospects for the tourism industry therefore requires attention to be given to demand and the choices which consumers make. This book brings together a number of contributions bearing on these issues.

The significance of demand in providing an engine of growth for the tourism industry should not be taken to imply that supply elements have not also contributed to this growth. Developments over recent decades, such as the growth of private car ownership and of air travel, together with the development of marketing strategies (which have entailed innovative pricing, packaging and product developments) have certainly played a part in the overall growth of tourism. It would therefore be misleading to suppose that demand and supply can sensibly be separated. While the focus of this book remains on the demand side, the inter-dependence of supply and demand is evident throughout. Supply-side factors, such as the development of marketing strategies, depend on knowledge of consumer types and motivation, which are concerns of early chapters in this book. Supply-related issues are also dealt with in Chapters 7 to 9, which consider aspects of the tourism product and pricing. Even formal economic models, such as those discussed in the later chapters, which are seemingly focused exclusively on demand, do in fact frequently acknow-ledge supply factors. This can be seen from the inclusion of supply-related variables in the demand models: the use of lagged dependent variables, for instance, is often justified on the grounds that demand may be constrained and including the previous actual quantity will capture supply rigidities (as well as habit persistence); and a case is often made for incorporating advertising and marketing variables into demand equations.

1.1.3 Various Perspectives

The purpose of this book is to contribute to a further understand-ing of choice and demand in tourism: most of the chapters do this either by reviewing and appraising the literature on particular topics and suggesting ways forward, or by presenting new research results. This task is of interest from several points of view. Firstly, there is the standpoint of public policy: there is a need to examine trends in and determinants of demand, and also to consider how far tourism demand as expressed through the market-place reflects the extent to which society values, or in some cases perhaps deplores, tourism. (This point is discussed briefly in Section 1.2.) Secondly, there is a strong management interest. Marketing decisions and the strategic planning of tourism provision require knowledge of factors affecting destination choice and type of holiday, and forecasts of tourism flows in the short and longer term. (These management decisions do of course have an influence on tourism behaviour.) The policy and management interests are essentially practical but there is also a need for fundamental insights to underpin these two interests. There is therefore a pure research interest in developing useful analytical frameworks and extending results.

It is evident that there are many perspectives which need to be brought to bear on the analysis of choice and demand. These range from at one extreme, the economist's concern with the estimation of demand relationships, usually at a highly aggregated level (e.g. estimating international flows of tourists), to the concern of psychologists and others with the individual's motivation and the choice of particular holidays at the other extreme. The interest in market segmentation, spatial considerations and tourist roles draws on the work of geographers, sociologists and others.

In the case of the economic models of demand the concern is usually to measure the responsiveness of tourism flows (or sometimes tourism expenditure) to changes in economic variables – notably prices and incomes – and to ignore changes in tastes. The economic approach typically takes tastes to be exogenous and fixed (or they are assumed to change so slowly that they can be ignored in short-run analyses). This is a useful assumption which enables some powerful insights to be developed through economic models, but a more complete understanding of consumers' behaviour obviously requires attention to be given to the formation of preferences and tastes. This is essentially the province of other disciplines, such as psychology.

It is clear from this discussion that the different perspectives based on different subject disciplines tend to be complementary rather than competing. Since all can provide insights which improve our understanding of the tourism industry, whether from a managerial and marketing point of view or from a policy angle, all are worth pursuing. This volume therefore takes a broad-ranging approach and several disciplines (which pose different questions and use different methodologies) are represented in the various chapters.

1.2 SOME SPECIAL FEATURES OF TOURISM CHOICE AND DEMAND

Some of the issues that arise in connection with the study of choice and demand in tourism are of course general in that they apply to any industry. Examples can readily be found to illustrate this point. The basic formulation of the demand models used in the case of tourism is, for instance, similar to that used in other industries. The usual explanatory variables are taken to be prices, the prices of other goods (especially of close substitutes) and disposable income. In addition use is sometimes made of an assortment of dummy variables to account for special factors, time trends and, as noted above, lagged dependent variables. Each of these additional variables can be justified on a variety of *ad hoc* grounds. This approach is as relevant to the demand for goods and services in general as it is to the demand for tourism. A further example of this generality can be found in the analysis of consumer motivation in the tourism industry. Often this draws on generally applicable theories of physiological and psychological needs and goals – the kinds of theories outlined in Chapter 3 by Christine Witt and Peter Wright, for example, are not tourism-specific and have been drawn from applications in other contexts. The same is true of several other contributions to this book, such as Chris Cooper's examination of life cycle models in Chapter 9, and Barbara Carmichael's use of conjoint analysis in Chapter 6.

It might seem that there is little that is distinctive about the analysis of tourism. However, it will be evident from the following chapters that there are indeed some special factors that are relevant for the study of tourism, or at least there are some factors that, while not necessarily exclusive to tourism, are relevant to such an extent that they warrant special treatment.

Two such issues – the nature of the product demanded, and demand as a measure of the social value of tourist activities – are considered here. Taking first the nature of the tourism product, it is apparent that this is unusually complex. Firstly, it is clear, as Goodall (1991, p. 73) notes, that 'holidays comprise bundles of attributes (destination, accommodation type, travel mode, activities, etc.) leading to benefits (and costs) of differential desirability to holiday-makers.' The product ranges from inclusive tours with one price for the composite commodity, to holidays arranged by individuals where all the different elements, such as travel, catering and accommodation, are priced separately. In the analysis of choice and demand it is therefore necessary to be clear whether the focus is the entire holiday experience or some particular component.

A further complication is that the tourism product is often much more than the provision of a collection of services, and as a consequence some aspects of the holiday experience may be marketed in the sense of being used as a selling point, but may not be priced. Part of a holiday experience, for example, may occur at times other than the period of the holiday itself. The planning and anticipation of the trip and the subsequent memories may yield satisfaction over an extended period. And this might last for years if, say, the acquisition of souvenirs or photographs becomes a way of prolonging the experience. The fact that the tourism experience may well persist raises the question of the rate of decay of the experience (or the possible enhancement of the experience with time). This may be relevant in determining the frequency of taking holidays of particular types or, in the case of some particular tourist attraction such as an ancient monument, the frequency of repeat visits.

An allied point is that the tourism product can have significant attitudinal dimensions. How the product is perceived by holiday-makers becomes important and this means that the choice of particular holidays cannot be explained simply in terms of the objective environment. This attitudinal point obviously applies to very many products but it is particularly striking in the case of tourism. Different individuals will seek and derive different things from the same set of services provided, so the social environment and the psychological make-up of individuals (in terms of their needs, perceptions and motivation) become crucial in understanding holiday choices. In the case of visits to museums and galleries, for example, the visitor experience for different individuals may consist of very different bundles of educational and leisure characteristics which satisfy diverse needs. Images become important and symbolic aspects of consumer behaviour thus assume prominence.

Another aspect of the holiday product which makes it distinctive is that it is a relatively large expenditure for most households, yet it is often not easy to know in advance exactly what the product is going to be like; in this sense it is more like medical treatment than, say, car purchase. Moreover, it has been noted by Goodall (1991, p. 71) that the consuming unit is often not a single individual and joint decision making (embracing the views of different adults and, interestingly, sometimes children) may be particularly common where the degree of perceived risk is large (see Moutinho, 1987). This typically large expenditure, together with the presence of strong attitudinal dimensions, means that holiday choice becomes more significant for consumers than is the case with many other products.

Many of these aspects of the product are of direct relevance for marketing. An understanding of the factors which influence holiday choices is crucial for the individual firms providing tourism services and for national and local tourism organizations. Account must also be taken of the fact that the tourism market is clearly segmented in various ways, not only in terms of the demographic characteristics of tourists but also according to their choice behaviour.

The second issue concerning the demand for tourism that is briefly mentioned here is the extent to which measures of tourism demand can be used to measure the contribution of the tourism industry to the economic welfare of society as a whole, and to provide a guide to the efficient allocation of resources. If demand truly reflected the marginal social benefits then it could be taken as a measure of the value which society places on tourism activities; society could then choose, by reference to the social costs of provision of tourism services, how many resources to devote to the industry.

There are in fact several reasons why tourism demand is unlikely to act as a good guide to the socially efficient use of resources. Firstly, the demand as expressed in the market-place may take no account of 'externalities'. These would be positive if, for example, there were spill-over benefits from tourists in an area. Social demand would thus be understated. Perhaps more prominent concerns in recent years have been the cases where social demand is overstated by demand expressed through the market: for example, where tourists cause 'problems' for local communities. Secondly, where a tourist product is jointly produced with other outputs (e.g. museums which produce scholarly output and tourist experiences) then the demand by tourists may not reflect the full demand for all the different components. Thirdly, obviously no account is taken of 'demand' that is not expressed through the market-place. This last point may be of considerable relevance in the case of, say, ancient monuments or special landscapes as tourist attractions. For example, some individuals who do not visit a particular monument may wish to preserve the option of doing so. Similarly, there may be an unmeasured demand for these things by future generations. (In some cases, where there are negative externalities, this option demand concept might more appropriately be applied to the demand for 'unspoilt' tourist-free environments.)

Considerations of the kind just discussed raise fundamental issues for public policy. If one purpose of policy is to look after social interests, and efficient resource allocation is seen as part of this, then there is a prima facie case for intervention if market demand provides 'incorrect' signals. These issues are not explored further here and the contributions of this book do not bear directly on these matters; they are examined a little more fully in the companion volume to this book (Johnson and Thomas, 1992).

1.3 THE STRUCTURE OF THIS VOLUME

The chapters in this volume fall into four groups: the first group (Chapters 2 to 4) deals with types of tourist and the motivation of tourists; the second group (Chapters 5 and 6) looks at aspects of tourism choice and the extent to which these choices are related to other activities or to the image of the destination; the third group (Chapters 7 to 9) examines aspects of the tourism product; and the final group (Chapters 10 to 12) is concerned with the economic modelling of demand.

1.3.1 Tourist Types and Motivation

One approach to understanding tourist behaviour is to identify different types of such behaviour. This has led to a large number of typologies of tourism roles being put forward by various writers. In some cases these are adaptations of typologies that have been developed in other contexts; in other cases they are developed directly for the purpose of classifying tourists. The fact that so many typologies exist indicates that there is little consensus. This is partly because there are varying purposes of classification but it also reflects the fact that they are each subject to limitations which mean that no one typology has become used universally. These typologies do, however, form a useful starting point for the discussions of choice and demand in this book. In Chapter 2, Els Lowyck, Luk Van Langenhove and Livin Bollaert look at some of the attempts which have been made by different authors to develop typologies. Most of the typologies they examine are based on empirical data, usually obtained from questionnaires or personal interviews. It might therefore be supposed that these typologies are all 'realistic' but Lowyck *et al.* raise the question of whether the typologies are in fact simply empty mental constructs of those who propose them. Given the readiness of authors to develop new typologies it is appropriate to question the practical or conceptual value of such typologies in providing insights into tourism behaviour. Lowyck *et al.* offer a critical review and offer some ways forward.

In Chapter 3, Christine Witt and Peter Wright examine the motivation of tourists. There is an ample literature on this subject (and references are still made to very early major contributions such as Maslow's hierarchy of needs approach, e.g. Gilbert, 1991) but as yet there is little agreement or common understanding. Witt and Wright discuss some of the more recent approaches to motivation and in particular consider the relevance of expectancy theory and its possibilities for providing a unifying framework for the analysis of tourist motivation. All products may carry symbolic meaning: that is, consumption may entail a high degree of involvement by the purchaser – it becomes an expressive activity. Issues associated with this perspective on tourism, and in particular the role of tangible objects such as souvenirs in giving the product some life after purchase as a symbol, are dealt with by Graham Brown in Chapter 5. Like the two preceding chapters, Brown's chapter offers a review of the literature on this subject.

1.3.2 Choice

One of the purposes of research on tourism demand is to improve the ability to forecast. This is a theme that is taken up in the later chapters of the book, especially Chapter 12 by Stephen Witt. The models described there are, however, highly aggregated and a particularly useful complementary approach is to recognize explicitly the segmentation of the market for tourism. The different types of tourist (identified according to typologies of the kind discussed in Chapter 2) provide a basis for segmentation. Destinations also provide a basis for segmentation. In Chapter 5 Richard Prentice considers a disaggregated approach to prediction. For particular segments of the market he examines the extent to which patterns of leisure activities by individuals may be used to predict their holiday activities and destinations.

The choice of destination is also the subject of Chapter 6 by Barbara Carmichael. She focuses on the image of different ski resorts and examines the preferences of skiers for hypothetical resort profiles (described in terms of the key attributes of the resort's image). The chapter makes use of conjoint analysis and shows that this technique may have considerable potential for measuring tourist image and thus be of great value in marketing.

1.3.3 The Tourism Product

It is clearly essential for the analysis of tourism choice and demand to consider the object of this choice, i.e. the tourism product. Chapters 7 and 8 present studies of two crucial aspects of the product – its quality and price.

In Chapter 7, Farouk Saleh and Chris Ryan are concerned with product quality. Their study is an application of a statistical model to service provision in hotels: they use the Servqual model to examine consumers' satisfaction as determined by the perception of the service and attention they receive. They discuss the usefulness of this particular model and show the value of identifying gaps between, for example, management's and guests' perceptions of service delivery.

The price competitiveness of inclusive tour holidays in European cities is measured in Chapter 8 by Ann Clewer, Alan Pack and Thea Sinclair. Package holidays are rarely identical, and as individual components of the packages are not given market prices it is difficult to make comparisons of the price competitiveness of such holidays. However, it is possible, by using hedonic pricing models, to find implicit prices of the different components and thus to assess competitiveness. The application of such a model is shown by Clewer *et al.* to provide useful information not only for those involved commercially in the provision of tourism products (to know whether their products are over- or under-priced relative to their competitors) but also for local and national policy-makers who are concerned with the supply of tourist facilities.

A broader view of the tourism product is given in Chapter 9, where Chris Cooper reviews the value of the life cycle approach as a descriptive and analytical tool for understanding tourism products and markets. Cooper shows that some of the claims for life cycle analysis as a guide for strategic planning and forecasting are perhaps exaggerated, but he demonstrates that the idea has considerable value for researchers as a descriptive tool which integrates many aspects of demand and supply.

1.3.4 Models of Demand

The final group of chapters presents formal models (or the results of such models) which use econometric analysis in attempts to explain variations in tourism demand over time. Some of these models are used for forecasting.

In Chapter 10 Adrian Darnell and the editors of this volume develop a model of visitor flows to one particular tourist attraction in the north-east of England. The single equation model is subject to various limitations, which are discussed in the chapter, but the exercise does show that it is possible to provide some robust results at the level of a single tourist attraction on price and income elasticities. These results not only provide a confirmation of basic economic theory but also, and perhaps more importantly, provide helpful management information. Models of the kind used in Chapter 10 can never replace the need for managerial intuition and 'feel' in making pricing and investment decisions, but they can be a useful complement to other sources of information in aiding management's judgements.

Models of the kind presented in Chapter 10 also act as a complement to the broader studies dealt with in the last two chapters, both of which are concerned with international tourism flows. There have been a large number of studies of such flows and it becomes important to take stock from time to time of what is known. It is, however, often difficult to make exact comparisons across different studies (some of the problems of making comparisons have been commented on by Johnson and Ashworth, 1990). Differences in methodologies, purposes and results mean that purely narrative surveys of previous studies often find it difficult to reach generalized conclusions on the size of the principal influences on international tourism flows. However, it is important to try to do so: there is little point in yet further studies of particular sets of estimates if generalizations prove elusive. A potentially fruitful way forward is presented by Geoffrey Crouch and Robin Shaw in Chapter 11. Their statistical analysis of 44 previous studies (which report hundreds of price and income elasticities: the mean income elasticity was $+1.76$ and the mean price elasticity was -0.39) attempts to explain the variation in the elasticities across the different studies.

One of the potentially important uses of demand models is fore-casting. This, of course, is an unavoidable exercise for manage-ment, which necessarily must form some view of the future in taking decisions. In Chapter 12, Stephen Witt examines the track record of two services which provide forecasts of international tourism demand – one dealing with outward tourism from the UK to 12 destinations (countries or country groups) and the other with outward tourism from the USA to various destinations around the world. The forecasting exercises examined are sophis-ticated and their performance is compared with that of very naive models which, for example, take the actual level of the present period's tourism flows as the forecast for the next period's flows. The sophisticated models did not perform well in this comparison and in the light of this finding Witt discusses the value and poten-tial of the sophisticated and costly exercises.

1.4 CONCLUSION

Many of the following chapters indicate ways in which our under-standing of choice and demand can be strengthened and a number of specific research suggestions are made in the concluding parts of these chapters. There is little point in providing, in advance, a detailed presentation of all these suggestions but it is worth noting that there are some common themes. One is that there are potentially fruitful research opportunities in the careful applica-tion of models that attempt serious quantitative measurement (Chapters 6 and 7 provide examples of such applications). A second theme is that, given a burgeoning literature, there is great value in taking stock of the present state of our knowledge in ways which are constructive rather than destructive. This, for example, is the spirit of Chapters 11 and 12, which are concerned with what is known about demand models and forecasting. Throughout many other chapters there is also an emphasis on a search for analytical frameworks that can promote an integration of different disciplines or approaches; this is true, for instance, of the discussion of typologies in Chapter 2, of the use of expectancy theory in Chapter 3 and of the life cycle model examined in Chapter 9.

This volume spells out a number of avenues for research which seem worthwhile in offering genuine additions to the under-standing of choice and demand, and the chapters here take some initial steps along these paths.

References

Gilbert, D.C. (1991) An examination of the consumer behaviour process related to tourism. In Cooper, C. (ed.) *Progress in Tourism, Recreation and Hospitality Management*, Volume 3, pp. 78–105. London: Belhaven in association with the University of Surrey.

Goodall, B. (1991) Understanding holiday choice. In Cooper, C. (ed.) *Progress in Tourism, Recreation and Hospitality Management*, Volume 3, pp. 58–77. London: Belhaven in association with the University of Surrey.

Johnson, P. and Ashworth, J. (1990) Modelling tourism demand: a summary review. *Leisure Studies*, 9, 145–60.

Johnson, P. and Thomas, B. (eds) (1992) *Perspectives on Tourism Policy*. London: Mansell.

Latham, J. (1991) Statistical trends in tourism up to 1989. In Cooper, C. (ed.) *Progress in Tourism, Recreation and Hospitality Management*, Volume 3, pp. 130–9. London: Belhaven in association with the University of Surrey.

Moutinho, L. (1987) Consumer behaviour in tourism. *European Journal of Marketing*, 21(10), 3–44.

Witt, S.F., Brooke, M.Z. and Buckley, P.J. (1991) *The Management of International Tourism*. London: Unwin Hyman.

World Tourism Organisation (1990) *Yearbook of Tourism Statistics*. Madrid: WTO.

2 Typologies of Tourist Roles

Els Lowyck, Luk Van Langenhove and Livin Bollaert

2.1 INTRODUCTION

This chapter explores a number of attempts made by different authors to develop typologies of tourist roles. Most of the authors taken into account base their typology of tourist roles on empirical data, generally obtained from questionnaires and/or personal interviews. Results from such studies are often presented as a typology of life styles.

The objective of this chapter is to gain insight into the different typologies being developed and to analyse how closely the tourist types approach reality. In other words: do these typologies explain tourist recreative behaviour or are they rather a creation of the author who developed the typology?

To answer this question the chapter considers, in Section 2.3, life style as a scientific concept and its importance in tourism research. In Section 2.4 an inventory of typologies of tourist roles is made, though this is not exhaustive. For each typology considered, a short review of the author(s), the publication, the population analysed (who was interviewed, how many people were interviewed and which research method was employed) and the results (the typology itself) is presented. Section 2.5 raises several criticisms of the different typologies and some alternative approaches are presented in Section 2.6.

2.2 TOURISM RESEARCH

Tourism is a composite product that belongs to the tertiary sector. The three most important components of the tourism product are 'transport, stay and attractions' (Theuns, 1984). The core of the tourism product is made up of the tourism attractions, which can be divided into the original existing attractions (climate, nature, culture and shopping facilities) and the attractions particularly designed for tourists. It is well known that tourism is a very fast-growing industry. The enormous growth in the supply of tourist activities is due to government actions which stimulate tourism (planning and development) and to the development of the tourism product by tour operators.

From the academic point of view, tourism is regarded as a subject of study concerned with the motives, expectations and experiences of the tourist and with the economics, socio-cultural and environmental impacts of tourism in the host countries. One of the first steps towards the establishment of an academic approach of tourism research was undertaken by MacCannell (1976). Since then, tourism research has developed into a relatively autonomous academic field (see Smith, 1989).

According to Archer (1989), a basic aim of tourism research is 'to provide a systematic framework to explain and teach the tourism phenomenon in its various forms'. This implies an interdisciplinary approach by which tourism is viewed as an independent domain of study. Different basic disciplines supply theories, concepts, methods and techniques to study in depth some aspect of tourism. Basic disciplines like economics, geography, psychology and sociology, but also new disciplines and research domains like management, marketing and leisure sciences, provide important contributions to tourism research. In economics, for example, most concepts and theories are directly connected with the production industry, but with some modifications these concepts and theories can be applied to the service industry as well. Such transformations of models to make them relevant for tourism research are also applicable to other disciplines, such as statistics, psychology, marketing, and planning.

The increase of international tourism after the Second World War has stressed the economic importance of tourism, and gradually research interests in tourism have grown. A meaningful judgement of tourism amenities can only be made when expected demand is taken into consideration. Analysis of demand can be tackled by a 'socio-economic approach' or by a 'psychological approach' (Theuns, 1984). The socio-economic approach examines correlations between the participation at tourism events and socio-economic characteristics such as income, level of education, age, residence and family situation. The psychological approach on the other hand seeks to discover the motives that stimulate people to travel. In order to optimize the utilization of the realized tourism capacity, a strategic marketing approach is necessary.

2.3 LIFE STYLE AS A SCIENTIFIC CONCEPT

Within the domain of tourism research, much attention is paid to the explanation of choices made by people concerning their holidays. Researchers attempt to explain why people go on holidays, why they choose certain destinations, and so on. Such an interest in tourists' choice behaviour is, in most cases, inspired by the desire to chart tourism demand and supply in a scientific way. In terms of market research, this implies searching for ways in which the heterogeneous holiday market can be segmented into groups of consumers that are as homogeneous as possible (Oppedijk van Veen and Verhallen, 1986). For years, researchers and marketing analysts have tried to picture such homogeneous groups in terms of demographic and socio-economic characteristics of the consumers. However, today demographic and socioeconomic analysis no longer suffices to provide an explanation or understanding of consumer behaviour. The behaviour of people cannot be deduced merely from their social position. On the level of political voting behaviour, for example, it has been shown on the basis of demographic data that in 1965, 40 per cent of the political preferences could still be forecast; in 1981 this percentage had decreased to only 5 per cent (Valen and Aardel, 1983). In response, researchers have made an increasing use of psychological variables, which they connect with responses to products. This research method is often called 'psychographic research', by which researchers attempt to classify people into different groups of life styles. However, the concept of 'life style' is not unproblematic from a scientific point of view. It is conceptually not precisely defined and it is used in different ways. In strict psychographic-oriented research, life styles are regarded as distinctions in people's behaviour which are mapped by means of responses to 'life style items'. The researchers should develop ranges of items which allow them to differentiate between people who will and people who will not buy a product. For the construction of such life style items, the researchers can appeal to (a) their imagination, (b) in-depth interviews or (c) scientific literature. Once a range of life style items has been collected, a group of people can be interviewed. The data obtained can then be categorized by means of factor analysis or hierarchic clustering so that different types of respondents can be visualized. Such life style typologies can then be used as independent variables in research aimed at discovering relationships with other variables or behavioural characteristics.

Most of the psychographic research is conducted with commercial goals and consequently very few results can be found in the public domain: very little is published in scientific professional journals.[1] An overview of some of the studies in which life styles are connected to tourist recreative behaviour is presented in the next section.

2.4 TOURISM AND LIFE STYLE TYPOLOGIES

Six empirically based typologies are presented here according to a fixed scheme which considers: (a) the author or the commissioning organization, (b) the date of publication, (c) the research method used, (d) the respondents and (e) the most important results of the research. The typologies are arranged in chronological order. This overview of six typologies is not exhaustive; it is only meant to give the reader a feel of what kind of typologies exist and to show how they have been developed. In doing so the way is cleared for some critical comments about the idea of tourism typologies. Finally, all this leads to some suggestions for alternative research routes aimed at classifying tourists.

2.4.1 Typology 1

(a) *Author*   Erik Cohen.

(b) *Date of publication*   1972.

(c) *Research method*

Cohen elucidates a general theoretical approach to the phenomenon of international tourism, from which he took his stand on the relation of the tourist to the tourism industry and the host country. Whereas primitive humans only left their residences when forced to by extreme circumstances, modern people are not completely attached to their surroundings any more, and are able to adapt very easily to new environments. They are interested in habits and cultures different from their own. A new value originated: the experience of novelty and strangeness. The tourist seeks these two elements, but shrinks back when the experience becomes too strange. Most tourists need something familiar, something that reminds them of home (e.g. a newspaper or food). The tourists move to another country, but keep relying on the 'environmental bubble' of their own culture. Tourism is directed to combine novelty and familiarity. In other words, the modern tourist wants to join the safety of old habits to the excitement of changes. There exists a continuum of possible combinations of novelty and familiarity. Cohen distinguishes four types of tourist on this uninterrupted line: the organized mass tourist, the individual mass tourist, the explorer and the drifter.

Cohen has also introduced a differentiation between the 'institutionalized' and 'non-institutionalized' forms of tourism. The first two tourist roles may be regarded as institutionalized types, as they tend to deal with the institutionalized tourist system. The latter two tourist roles are categorized as non-institutionalized types, because they do not depend on the services offered by the tourist establishment.

(d) *Respondents* None.

(e) *Results*

The organized mass tourist The organized mass tourist is highly dependent on his or her 'environmental bubble'. These tourists rarely stray from their protection. They buy 'all-inclusive holidays', such as package tours. The itinerary and reservations are well-prepared. Familiarity dominates and the experience of novelty is virtually non-existent.

The individual mass tourist These tourists look like the previous type, but are more autonomous and free from the group. All major travel arrangements are determined before leaving home, but the itinerary and time schedule are subject to possible changes. Familiarity dominates, but the experience of novelty is greater than in the preceding type.

The explorer These tourists explore new areas, and try to get off 'the beaten track' as much as possible. Tending to leave the 'environmental bubble' more than the previous types, the explorers try to associate with the people they visit. If the situation becomes too stressful, however, the explorers opt to step back into comfortable accommodation, reliable transportation and other modern facilities.

The drifter The drifters avoid any kind of 'tourist establishment'. The drifters seek direct contact with the host culture and try to live the way the locals live. They leave familiarity behind and novelty is at its highest.

2.4.2 Typology 2

(a) *Author* Stanley C. Plog.

(b) *Date of publication* 1973 (see Plog, 1987; Gupta, 1984).

(c) *Research method*

At the request of 16 airline and travel companies, Plog analysed what could be done to enlarge the travel market. More specifically, Plog examined how to turn more non-flyers into flyers. A search of the literature showed that there existed a hard core of the population who refused to fly, even when disposable income was sufficient. 'Fear of flying, unfamiliarity with flight, maintenance of old habits' kept these people from flying. The researcher became convinced that there was 'a strong emotional core to the problem and personality-based exploratory research was necessary'.

In order to analyse this problem the researcher gave preference to in-depth interviews with non-flyers who had above average incomes. During the interviews, the reason most non-flyers gave for not flying was that they did not have any reason to fly. After having analysed the interviews, the researcher discovered a common pattern among non-flyers, including 'territory boundness, generalised anxieties and a sense of powerlessness'. Because of the common tendency for these characteristics to appear in each non-flyer, Plog gave them the name 'psychocentrism'. Psychocentrism refers to persons who focus their thoughts on small problem areas. 'Allocentric', on the other hand, refers to a person whose interest patterns are centred on varied activities. Plog classified the US population along a psychographic continuum, ranging from the psychocentric at one extreme to the allocentric at the other. Between these two extremes the 'near-psychocentrics', the 'mid-centrics' and the 'near-allocentrics' are situated.

(d) *Respondents* No data available.

(e) *Results*

The allocentric type   The allocentric type views travelling as a possibility to discover foreign cultures, and prefers exotic destinations. The allocentric tourist seeks satisfaction in strength and freedom (anonymity, flying, travelling by boat, fast trains, etc.) and tries to make friends with the local inhabitants. This type of tourist also likes to gamble.

The near-allocentric type   This type of tourist is sporting, seeks challenges and views the journey as a chance to test a new life style. In this group Plog places the business, conference, meeting and convention tourist. 'Theme tourists' (theatre tours, special entertainment) are also classified in this group.

The mid-centric type   The mid-centric type looks for relaxation and pleasure in a well-known environment with friends and relatives. For this type of tourist, the holiday means an escape from daily routine. Mid-centric tourists like to stay in healthy and beautiful surroundings (sun, spas, forests, lakes, etc.) and choose the most comfortable type of accommodation (car, plane, comfortable trains, etc.) to travel to their holiday destination. They spend a lot of money on souvenirs.

The near-psychocentric and psychocentric types   Both the near-psychocentric and the psychocentric types travel because they think they are indebted to travel for their status. For these types of tourists travelling is a cultural norm, imposed by the legal system of paid holidays. In general they visit famous tourist attraction poles.

2.4.3 Typology 3

(a) *Authors*   W. D. Perreault, D. K. Darden and W. R. Darden.

(b) *Date of publication*   1977.

(c) *Research method*

A questionnaire was mailed to 2000 households. The head of each household was asked to complete the questionnaire, consulting other members of the family when necessary. The questionnaire was composed of three parts: (1) questions about vacation travel behaviour; (2) questions about socio-economic characteristics of the household; and (3) questions about activities, interests and opinions concerning both leisure time and vacation activities and general behaviour predispositions. On the basis of a pre-test (with interviews) of 285 items, 105 items were retained to indicate 28 scales. The items were vacation-specific statements. Respondents had to indicate on a Likert scale in what degree they agreed with the statements.

Each of the households could be characterized by its pattern of scores on the 28 vacation–leisure–life style scales. The analysis proceeded through two major steps. Cluster analysis distributed respondents between groups with a similar profile of activities, interests and opinions. The second stage of the analysis uncovered the nature and extent of among-group differences. Specifically, multivariate analysis of variance procedures were used to analyse and interpret group differences in general behavioural predispositions, socio-economic characteristics, vacation behaviour and vacation information sources.

(d) *Respondents*

Data for this study were collected by a mail questionnaire which was sent to 2000 households. The response rate was over 40 per cent. Eventually 670 of the questionnaires were usable (33.5 per cent). The analysis reported is based on half of the respondents (355). The sample was split so that the study could be cross-validated on the sub-samples. Finally 16.7 per cent of the 2000 questionnaires were used.

(e) *Results*

Cluster analysis of the responses produced evidence of five distinct groups or types of vacation orientation: the budget travellers, the adventurers, the homebodies, the vacationers and the moderates.

Budget travellers People in this group (almost 28 per cent of the respondents) are interested in travel and seek travel information, but their major vacation interests are economy-oriented (a high interest in camping). The budget travellers have medium income.

Adventurers Twenty-four per cent of the respondents exhibit a relatively low desire for relaxing travel and a relatively high disposition for venturesomeness. Adventurers are relatively money-oriented in their travel. They are well educated and next to highest in terms of income. Adventurers are certainly not homebodies.

Homebodies People in this group (20 per cent) enjoy relaxing travel, but have no interest in vacation travel, do not seek travel information and are not venturesome. They do not share vacation talk with others. They currently have good incomes, but are lower than other groups in terms of financial optimism.

Vacationers The vacationers, almost 7 per cent of the total, are the antithesis of the homebodies. They plan ahead more, but are undecided about their vacations. They spend a great deal of time thinking about their vacations. Vacationers are generally active. They are employed in lower-paid jobs and they have less education.

Moderates About 21 per cent of the respondents are rather unremarkable in the main. They do have a high predisposition to travel, but they are not interested in weekend travel or sports. They resemble the vacationers, with the difference that they have no active life style.

2.4.4 Typology 4

(a) *Author* Westvlaams Ekonomisch Studiebureau.

(b) *Date of publication* 1986.

(c) *Research method*

A representative sample of 3000 Belgian adults were interviewed about their demographic and socio-economic characteristics, and about their behaviour and expenditure during their holidays (stay outside the normal living place for at least four successive nights) and during their short holidays (stay outside the normal living place for at least one and less than four successive nights).

The holiday and life typology was made up for potential holiday-makers (2270 persons). Potential holiday-makers were defined as respondents who expected to participate in a holiday in the next five years. The respondents were asked how much importance they attached to 29 possible holiday ingredients, according to a fixed procedure. A set of cards was handed to each of the respondents. On each card, one aspect of the holiday was mentioned. The respondents had to arrange these cards in order of importance by forming four piles. Finally, the most important ingredients had to be ranged in order of importance (maximum five).

(d) *Respondents*

For the part of the research concerned with the holiday and life style typology of the Belgians, questions were put to persons of 18 and over. If the respondent was younger than 18, questions concerning holiday behaviour were put to another person who was at least 18 years old, belonged to the same family and if possible was of the same sex. According to the researchers it does not make sense to question younger people about their holiday

21

appreciation, since their views do not give rise to concrete holiday behaviour.

(e) *Results*

The holiday-makers were grouped on the basis of a cluster analysis. Depending upon the importance that each potential holiday-maker gave to each of the 29 holiday ingredients, seven clusters were formed: the active sea lovers, the contact-minded holiday-makers, the nature viewers, the rest-seekers, the discoverers, the family-oriented sun and sea lovers, and the traditionalists. An overview of each of these types follows.

The active sea lovers This cluster comprises only 5.5 per cent of the potential holiday-makers. The most important factor for these persons is the presence of the sea and a beach. 'Going out' and 'sports' are also very important activities during the holidays.

The contact-minded holiday-makers In this cluster the researchers placed 9.5 per cent of the potential holiday-makers. This group attaches great importance to a hospitable reception, to 'making time for each other' and 'making contact with new people'.

The nature viewers The nature viewers prefer visiting beautiful landscapes, but meeting with a kind reception is indispensable for these people. This cluster contains 12 per cent of the potential holiday-makers.

The rest-seekers For people in this extensive cluster (25.8 per cent of the potential holiday-makers) seeking rest, regaining strength and walking are most important motives for travel.

The discoverers This cluster is different from the previous types because people in this group like to make contact with people, they like cultural holidays, and they like adventure. This group comprises 10.1 per cent of the potential holiday-makers.

The family-oriented sun and sea lovers This is the biggest cluster, with 27.2 per cent of the potential holiday-makers. Rather a lot of different characteristics play an important role for people in this group. In particular, visiting beautiful scenery, making time for each other, a kind reception, good food and 'child-friendly' activities are appreciated by people belonging to this group.

The traditionalists The potential holiday-makers in this cluster draw attention to safety and security, they try to avoid surprises and they like to be in familiar surroundings. Elements such as rest and good food are often mentioned by the people of this group.

2.4.5 Typology 5

(a) *Author* E. Dalen.

(b) *Date of publication* 1989.

(c) *Research method*

A leading marketing and social research company in Norway regularly carries out social change research. A representative sample of about 3000 adults were interviewed in 1987. The interviews lasted more than two hours and consisted of about 750 questions. The emphasis was on information about attitudes: respondents were asked about their beliefs about how to live and their objectives in life. Multi-dimensional correspondence analysis showed that two vectors explain about one-third of the total variance. The first dimension varies from modern to traditional, the second dimension varies from materialistic to idealistic. These two dimensions divide the population into four large segments: the modern materialists, the modern idealists, the traditional idealists and the traditional materialists.

Dalen admits that his research was not directly concerned with travel and tourism, but he asserts that the market segment can be applied to the field of travel and tourism.

(d) *Respondents*

A representative sample of about 3000 Norwegian adults.

(e) *Results*

Modern materialist The modern materialists demand sun to make an impression when they return home. They do not care about skin cancer. They love nightclubs and wild parties, where they can meet new people. The modern materialist is more concerned about beverages than food, and prefers fast foods. Superficial entertainment, sex, action and excitement are important ingredients of a holiday.

Modern idealist The modern idealists also demand excitement and entertainment, but more of the intellectual kind. Atmosphere, ambience and the presence of good friends are part of the menu. Art, culture, new destinations and experiences are a must. Modern idealists do not want mass tourism or fixed programmes. They are willing to pay medium to high prices.

Traditional idealist The traditional idealists demand quality, nature, culture, history, famous places, peace, quiet and safety. They probably choose package tours, but on cultural subjects. Often traditional idealists visit family and relatives.

Traditional materialist The traditional materialists always look for low prices and special offers. They want traditional mass tourism and package tours. They are afraid of being left alone, and have a strong need for personal security.

2.4.6 Typology 6

(a) *Author* Gallup Organisation, commissioned by American Express Travel Related Services Company, Inc. (American Express News Release, 1989).

(b) *Date of publication* 1989.

(c) *Research method*

To develop the traveller classifications, a total of more than 6500 adults in the United States, West Germany, the United Kingdom and Japan were interviewed. These four nations were chosen because they have the highest tourism expenditures and the most international travellers worldwide.

(d) *Respondents*

More than 4000 travellers were identified from the interviews. Travellers were defined as individuals aged 18 or over who had spent at least one night in paid lodgings during the previous 12 months.

(e) *Results*

The study found that there are five distinct groups of travellers, who experience travel differently, regardless of their origin, destination or the frequency of their trips. These five groups are: the adventurers, the worriers, the dreamers, the economizers and the indulgers.

Adventurers Adventurers are independent and confident. They like to try new activities, meet new people and experience different cultures. Generally they are better educated and more affluent than the members of the other groups. For the adventurers travel plays a central role in their lives. They are predominantly male and tend to be younger than other travellers, with 44 per cent of the group between the ages of 18 and 34.

Worriers Worriers experience considerable anxiety from the perceived stresses of travel, have little confidence in their ability to make travel decisions and are generally afraid to fly. Overall, worriers tend to be less educated and less affluent than other travellers in their country. Moreover, this category travels the least of the five groups and, when they do, they are more likely to travel domestically. Worriers are predominantly female and rather older than other travellers, with nearly half over the age of 50.

Dreamers Dreamers are intrigued with the idea of travel and attach great importance to the meaning it can bring to their lives. Despite reading and talking a lot about new destinations, they have travel experiences that are usually less remarkable than their ideas, and more often oriented towards relaxation than adventure. The dreamers belong to the modest income and education categories and they are usually women aged 50 and over. Most dreamers rely on maps and guidebooks when they travel to new places.

Economizers Travel provides economizers with a routine outlet for relaxation and is not perceived as an experience that adds meaning to their lives. The economizers seek value in travel and they do not think it is worth paying extra for special amenities and services, even if they can afford them. Economizers are more likely to be men than women and they are slightly older than their travelling counterparts. These people have an average income level and are slightly below average in education.

Indulgers Indulgers are generally wealthier than other travellers and they are willing to pay for additional comfort and better service when they travel. The indulgers are more likely than other travellers to stay in large hotels because they like to be pampered. This group of travellers is second only to adventurers in the amount they travel and they are equally divided between men and women.

2.5 COMMENTS AND CRITIQUES

The above typologies are not an exhaustive enumeration, but they do allow us to get a picture of how tourist typologies are in general constructed. In this section some critical comments on the available tourism typologies are made from theoretical, conceptual and methodological viewpoints.

First of all, the above-mentioned typologies can be sub-divided into two categories, each of which supposedly has value in predicting tourist behaviour. On the one hand there are the typologies of tourists *per se* and on the other hand there are the typologies of life styles. Neither of them is unproblematic.

One problem with the typologies of tourists is: are they not the result of tautological reasoning? The researcher asks people if they love, say, 'sun, sand and sea', then calls them the 'sun–sand–sea' type and says that those who belong to this type prefer sun, sand and sea. In other words, the results of the research largely depends upon what the researcher has put into it. Most of the typologies reviewed above belong to this category. The approach based on general life style typologies seems preferable: an attempt is made, starting from general personality characteristics, to formulate statements about holiday behaviour. Of the reviewed studies, only Dalen falls into this category and it should be noted that he did not base his work on any empirical research. There do exist a number of general life style studies that refer occasionally to tourist behaviour, but as far as is known these are in the form of detailed presentations of research results concerning tourism. Studies in which tourism consumer behaviour is linked to general life style variables are generally lacking.

The objection that most of the above-mentioned typologies might be an artefact of the researcher is supported by a second critique, which is directed to the results of the typologies: that is, the names given to the different types. In contrast to demographic and socio-economic analysis, there do not exist standard categories for different types of tourists in psychographic research. It is left to the researchers to create the dimensions from their own points of view. A logical consequence of this is that psychographic research gives rise to a very diverse set of names for the different types of tourists. Types resembling each other are hidden behind all these names. Although the above-mentioned typologies represent different numbers of types (from four to seven types of tourist), the same characteristics appear in each of the types described: looking for adventure, discovering new cultures versus accustomed daily habits, the contact-minded attitude, the budget spent on the holiday, the importance attached to nature and authenticity, and seeking rest, sun, sand and sea.

Plog (1987) formulated a similar critique:

> researchers may actually come up with fairly similar dimensions but may label them differently. As it turns out, there probably are a very limited number of psychographic/personality dimensions which have been discussed in travel research. These dimensions may be more clearly defined, or combined in various ways, but they are covered by about eight broad categories.

Plog then created a typology of all tourist typologies. This all-inclusive typology consists of the following eight types:

1 Venturesomeness. This type of tourist is seeking and exploring, and tends to be the first user in terms of travel destinations.
2 Pleasure-seeking. The pleasure-seeking tourist desires a considerable amount of luxury and comfort in all aspects of travel, transportation, hotel services and entertainment.
3 Impassivity. The trip decision of this type of tourist is made very quickly, at the last moment and without planning.
4 Self-confidence. The self-confident person is willing to do very different things. This is reflected in the selection of unusual tour destinations or activities at these destinations.
5 Planfulness. The planful tourist plans the trip well in advance, but looks more for pre-packaged tour programmes than does the previous type.
6 Masculinity. This tourist is action-oriented and seeks the outdoors in a very traditional way (fishing, camping, hunting, etc.). Wives are often forced to participate or they are left at home.
7 Intellectualism. This tourist pays a lot of attention to historic and cultural aspects of the holiday destination.
8 People orientation. The people orientation tourists want to have close contact with the people they visit.

In other words, *it is possible to establish a typology of tourists without it being based on psychographic research*. Thinking only about how the supply side is structured is sufficient to develop a classification.

A third critique can be formulated on the methodological level. Without exception all the studies make use of questionnaire data. However valuable such an approach may be, it has been shown that such a methodology is only suitable when the research problem is precisely defined. This definition of the problem has to be made from the viewpoint of the persons studied and not from the viewpoint of the researchers. At this point it is possible to refer to the *ethogenic method of social science* proposed by Harré (Harré and Secord, 1972; Harré, 1979). It has been argued by Harré that in order to be able to conduct extensive design research (that is, research on large populations) a necessary first step is to conduct intensive design studies (case studies). One has to analyse a few tourists in very great detail. Such case studies

can then provide the researcher with types, from which populations of similar activities can be constructed and the concepts
used can be developed.

A related issue is the question of whether it makes sense at all
to divide people into different types without taking into account
their full life spans. Even if two persons, at a given time, exhibit
the same type of tourist behaviour, it may well be that they are
such different persons that their next tourist experience will
be completely different. In other words, case studies are needed
in which the 'holiday biographies' of people are analysed in
detail.

Finally, the static idea that people have to belong to one type
or another can be questioned. People are complex and it may not
be possible to describe adequately all their behaviour in terms of
a single simple category.

2.6 ALTERNATIVES

However critical these comments may sound towards the available tourist typologies, this does not imply that it is useless to
pay research attention to the questions of how and why people
differ in their tourist behaviour. This chapter concludes by briefly
presenting some suggestions for research.

First of all, there is a basic need within the field of tourism
research for intensive design studies. Before any large-scale questionnaires can be developed much work has to be done on the
individual level: detailed analyses are needed of how people experience tourist settings (following the ideas of MacCannell (1976)
and Urry (1990) who argue for, but have not conducted, such
detailed studies). Moreover, as suggested by Pearce (1982), a
more biographical approach should be introduced. In order to
undertake such research, a theoretical framework is needed in
which different empirical data can be integrated. The ethogenic
approach to social science can be a very useful starting-point for
such an integrative theory. The tenets of such a theory for leisure
have been presented by Harré (1990) and Van Langenhove (in
press).

A second suggestion concerns the issue of how a 'typology' is to
be conceived. Tourist typologies, like most other behavioural
typologies, all present a static and rather simple picture of what
people are. Two alternative forms of typology are presented: one
developed in the context of personality theory, the other in the

context of criminology, which can be formally transposed to questions of tourism behaviour.

2.6.1 The Matrix Typology Approach

The first alternative kind of typology could be called the matrix typology approach. Such an approach was used by the German psychologist Spranger (1928) in his attempt to develop a typology of personality. His starting point was a classic typology of six ideal types of men (e.g. economic men, political men, aesthetic men and so on). The original idea of Spranger was to elaborate each of those basic types by relating its central characteristics to the five other types. For example, the 'economic type of man' is characterized by a number of dominant economic values but this does not imply that such a person would have no aesthetic interests, and so on. But the aesthetic interests are coloured by the dominating economic interests. In this way Spranger succeeded in presenting a far more complex typology than is normally used. The same strategy could be used in designing a complex strategy of tourism behaviour. The eight types introduced by Plog (1987), for example, related to each other. Thus a more complex typology could be constructed. It may also be the case that, within one basic type, sub-types can be established on the basis of the dominance of certain other factors. This is a question to be answered by research and, as noted earlier, only intensive design research can provide the necessarily detailed empirical material.

2.6.2 The 'Processual' Typology Approach

In his seminal study, De Waele (1990) introduced a processual taxonomy of murderers based on biographical data. His method can be summarized as follows: instead of categorizing murders in pre-existing categories (parental murder, murder for robbery etc.), De Waele analysed the lives of murderers in great detail (see De Waele and Harré, 1976, for an outline of the method) and then ordered the biographical data in such a way that several patterns within the life course could be detected. It was found that the same type of murder did not imply the same type of life pattern and the same biographical development did not 'automatically' lead to the same kind of murder. Alongside the biographical typology, De Waele also developed a typology of the criminogenesis that led to the murder. Such a criminogenesis covers the time-span between the intention to murder someone and the actual murder. However dramatic such a study may be for academics dealing with holidays, it would be useful to transpose De Waele's idea of processual typology to tourism consumer behaviour. This would imply the development of a biographical typology of holiday patterns and the development of a typology of holiday choosing patterns. A first step towards the construction of such typologies could be case study research, in which people are asked to tell their stories about all the holidays they have had and about how decisions on such matters as destination and transport were made. It is of course necessary to take into account the fact that people do not make most of their tourism consumer choices alone, but together with their partner and family. Such an approach is similar to that of Pearce (1988), who introduced the concept of a 'tourist's travel career'. However, Pearce started from a pre-existing career model based on Maslowian levels of self-actualization and not from an analysis of the processual developments as such. In that way his approach seems to be more prescriptive than descriptive.

2.7 CONCLUSION

In this chapter a number of tourist typologies have been presented and compared. From the various comments and critiques that have been made about such typologies, it is clear that they can only be of little value for understanding tourism motives and for the analysis of demand. However, there is a convincing case for the usefulness of a (supplementary) psychological approach along with the more classical socio-economic approach in any attempt to understand tourism consumer behaviour. The two alternative typologies presented may open perspectives for such an understanding. Trying to apply the Spranger and De Waele approaches to the study of tourism consumer behaviour is a formidable task which involves collecting lots of detailed life-history data. But if the alternative is working with simple and sterile typologies like the ones presented in this chapter, then it is worthwhile to accept that challenge.

Note

1 An important exception on this subject is the Values and Life Style (VALS) research, based on Maslow, as reported by Mitchell (1983), Holman (1984) and Kahle *et al.* (1986).

References

American Express News Release (1989) *Unique Four Nation Travel Study Reveals Traveller Types*. London: American Express.

Archer, B. (1989) The nature of tourism: its practical importance and its relationship with other disciplines. A paper presented at an open lecture, Vrije Universiteit Brussel.

Cohen, E. (1972) Toward a sociology of international tourism. *Social Research*, **39**, 164–82.

Dalen, E. (1989) Research into values and consumer trends in Norway. *Tourism Management*, **10**(3), 183–6.

De Waele, J.P. (1990) *Daders van Dodingen* (Committing Murder). Antwerp: Kluwer.

De Waele, J.P. and Harré, R. (1976) Personality of individuals. In Harré, R. (ed.) *Personality*, pp. 189–246. Oxford: Basil Blackwell.

Gupta, S. (1984) Types of tourists. In McIntosh, R. and Goeldner, C. (eds) *Tourism Principles: Practices, Philosophies*, pp. 178–85. Columbus, OH: Grid Publishing.

Harré, R. (1979) *Social Being*. Oxford: Basil Blackwell.

Harré, R. (1990) Leisure and its varieties. *Leisure Studies*, **9**(3), 187–96.

Harré, R. and Secord, O. (1972) *The Explanation of Social Behaviour*. Oxford: Basil Blackwell.

Holman, R. (1984) A values and life styles perspective on human behaviour. In Pitt, R.E. and Woodside, A.G. (eds) *Personal Values and Consumer Psychology*, pp. 136–58. Lexington, MA: Lexington Books.

Kahle, L.R., Beatty, S.E. and Homer, P. (1986) Alternative measurement approaches to consumer values: the List of Values (LOV) and Values and Life Styles (VALS). *Journal of Consumer Research*, **13**, 405–9.

MacCannell, D. (1976) *The Tourist. A New Theory of the Leisure Class*. New York: Schocken Books.

Mitchell, A. (1983) *The Nine American Life Styles*. New York: Warner.

Oppendijk van Veen, W.M. and Verhallen, T.W.M. (1986) Vacation market segmentation: a domain-specific value approach. *Annals of Tourism Research*, **13**, 37–58.

Pearce, P.L. (1982) *The Social Psychology of Tourist Behaviour*. Oxford: Pergamon Press.

Perreault, W.D., Darden, D.K. and Darden, W.R. (1977) A psychographic classification of vacation life styles. *Journal of Leisure Research*, **9**, 208–24.

Plog, S. (1987) Understanding psychographics in tourism research. In Ritchie, J.R.B. and Goeldner, C.R. (eds) *Travel, Tourism, and Hospitality Research. A Handbook for Managers and Researchers*, pp. 203–13. New York: John Wiley & Sons.

Smith, S.L.J. (1989) *Tourism Analysis. A Handbook*. Harlow: Longman.

Spranger, E. (1928) *Types of Men. The Psychology and Ethics of Personality*. Halle: Niemeyer Verlag.

Theuns, H.L. (1984) Toerisme als multidisciplinair veld van studie, een systeem- en ontwikkelingsschets. *Vrije Tijd en Samenleving*, **2**(1), 65–92.

Urry, J. (1990) *The Tourist Gaze. Leisure and Travel in Contemporary Societies*. London: Sage.

Valen, H. and Aardel, B. (1983) *Et Valgi Perspectiv: En Studie av Stortingsvalget, 1981*. Oslo: Norwegian Central Bureau of Statistics.

Van Langenhove, L. (in press) *Leisure and social control: a theory of non-everyday life* (under editorial review).

Westvlaams Ekonomisch Studiebureau, Afdeling Toeristisch Onderzoek (1986) *Toeristische gedragingen en attitudes van de Belgen in 1985*. Brussels: Reeks vakantieonderzoeken.

3 Tourist Motivation: Life after Maslow

Christine A. Witt and Peter L. Wright

3.1 INTRODUCTION

Writing about the motivation for travel, Jafari (1987, p. 152) stated: 'There is already a wide range of literature dealing with such motivational propositions, but no common understanding has yet emerged.' Furthermore, much of the work on tourist motivation is based on a content theory approach to the study of motivation, as exemplified by Maslow's theory of needs, and largely ignores more recent developments in motivation theory. In this chapter, we describe some of the major current theories of tourist motivation and then draw on advances made in the study of motivation in other applied areas, particularly the motivation to work, in an attempt to develop a more comprehensive framework for the analysis of tourist motivation.

Most theories of work motivation are partial theories, in that they tend to concentrate on one particular aspect of work motivation, such as the roles of needs, goals, equity beliefs, rewards and so on, to the virtual exclusion of others. However, there is one exception, an approach to the study of work motivation theory known as expectancy theory or VIE (valence–instrumentality–expectancy) theory. The theory is not without weaknesses, but its major advantage is that it can be used to provide a unifying framework within which it is possible to incorporate all other theories of work motivation (Wright, 1989, 1991). Our aim in the present chapter is to show how expectancy theory can provide a similar unifying framework for the study of tourist motivation, in an attempt to get perhaps a little closer to the 'common understanding' of the urge or need to travel to which Jafari refers.

3.2 CONTENT THEORIES OF MOTIVATION

3.2.1 Introduction

Central to most content theories of motivation is the concept of need. Needs are seen as the force which arouses motivated behaviour, and it is assumed that in order to understand human motivation it is necessary to discover what needs people have and how they can be fulfilled. This is what Maslow (1943) attempted to do with his need hierarchy theory, which is probably the best known of all motivation theories. It was originally developed by Maslow in the context of his work in the field of clinical psychology. Nevertheless, it became widely influential, both as a general theory of motivation and as an explanation of motivation in applied areas, such as industrial and organizational psychology, counselling, marketing and tourism.

3.2.2 Maslow's Need Hierarchy

Maslow (1943) identified five main classes of needs: physiological, safety, love (social), esteem and self-actualization. These are shown, together with examples of specific needs of each type, in Table 3.1. Maslow further suggested that these needs form a hierarchy. He argued that if none of the needs in the hierarchy were satisfied, then the lowest needs, the physiological ones, would dominate behaviour. If these were satisfied, however, they would no longer motivate, and the individual would be motivated by the next level in the hierarchy, safety needs. Once these were satisfied, the individual would move up to the next level, continuing to work up the hierarchy as the needs at each level were satisfied. In a later version of the theory, Maslow (1954) added two other sets of needs – aesthetic needs and the need to know and understand – but it is not entirely clear how these needs fit into the original hierarchy.

One of the main reasons for the popularity of Maslow's need hierarchy is probably its simplicity. The convenient five- or seven-level classification system makes it easy to present to non-psychologists, which may explain its wide adoption in applied

Table 3.1 Maslow's need hierarchy

Physiological needs	Hunger, thirst, sex, sleep, air, etc.
Safety needs	Freedom from threat or danger; a secure, orderly and predictable environment
Love (social) needs	Feeling of belonging, affectionate relationships, friendship, group membership
Esteem needs	Self-respect, achievement, self-confidence, reputation, recognition, prestige
Need for self-actualization	Self-fulfilment, realizing one's potential

Source: adapted from Maslow (1943).

areas. Nevertheless, the theory suffers from a number of significant limitations, some of which Maslow himself was well aware of, but which are largely ignored by his popularizers.

The theory was originally developed in the context of clinical psychology, not as a theory of work motivation. Maslow stated:

> My work on motivation came from the clinic, from a study of neurotic people. The carry-over of this theory to the industrial situation has some support from industrial studies, but I would certainly like to see a lot more studies of this kind before feeling finally convinced that this carry-over from the study of neurosis to the study of labor in factories is legitimate. (Maslow, 1965, p. 55)

Presumably, the same considerations would apply in the case of tourist motivation.

In the second part of his 1943 article, Maslow introduced major reservations which considerably diluted the force of the arguments put forward earlier in the article. He identified seven ways of proceeding through the hierarchy apart from a simple step-by-step progression from the lowest level to the highest. He also stated that one did not have to satisfy the needs at one level fully before moving on to the next, and therefore people could be partially satisfied and partially dissatisfied at *all* levels in the hierarchy at the same time. Not surprisingly, these caveats are rarely if ever quoted by Maslow's popularizers, as they would completely undermine the type of conclusions they wish to draw.

Despite Maslow's (1965) claims, his need hierarchy has received little clear or consistent support from the research evidence. Some of Maslow's propositions are totally rejected, while others receive mixed and questionable support at best (Wahba and Bridwell, 1976).

The theory does not include several important needs, perhaps because they do not fit conveniently into Maslow's hierarchical framework. These include such needs as dominance, abasement, play, aggression and so on. These needs are, however, included in a classification scheme developed by a near contemporary of Maslow's, H. A. Murray.

3.2.3 Murray's Classification of Human Needs

On the basis of extensive research, Murray (1938) identified a total of 14 physiological and 30 psychological needs. Space does not permit a full listing of the needs identified by Murray, but some typical examples are given in Table 3.2.

Containing as it does over 40 different needs organized under only two main headings, Murray's classification system does not lend itself as readily as Maslow's need hierarchy to easy presentation to non-psychologists. Furthermore, Murray's theory of human needs is not as easy to apply as Maslow's. Unlike Maslow, Murray envisages needs as varying independently, which means that knowing the strength or degree of satisfaction of one need will not necessarily tell us anything about the strength of others. Thus identifying what motivates people involves measuring the strength of all their important needs, rather than simply working out what level in a hierarchy they have reached.

Probably for these reasons, Murray's work on human needs never became as popular as Maslow's did. Nevertheless, it did stimulate influential research into specific needs, particularly the needs for achievement, affiliation and power, and from the point of view of tourist motivation it does provide a much more comprehensive list of human needs that could influence tourist behaviour. In the case of each need, it would be possible to identify factors which could influence a potential tourist to prefer or avoid a particular holiday. Examples range from acceptable toilet facilities, air conditioning or a preferred average temperature in the case of physiological needs, to conservation holidays (conservance), out-of-the-way holidays (contrariance), 'war game' holidays (aggression), and even a 'Fawlty Towers' holiday (abasement) in the case of psychological needs. Thus Murray's needs would provide a much more useful starting point for research into the types of need which people try to fulfil through tourism than Maslow's better-known need hierarchy.

Table 3.2 Examples of needs from Murray's classification system

Sentience	The inclination for sensuous gratification, particularly from objects in contact with the body: taste sensations and tactile sensations.
Sex	To form and further an erotic relationship. To have sexual intercourse.
Heat and cold avoidance	The tendency to maintain an equable temperature: to avoid extremes of heat and cold.
Activity	To need to expand built-up energy: to discharge energy in uninhibited movement or thought.
Passivity	The need for relaxation, rest and sleep: the desire to relinquish the will, to relax, to daydream, to receive impressions.
Conservance	To collect, repair, clean and preserve things. To protect against damage.
Achievement	To overcome obstacles. To exercise power. To strive to do something difficult as well and as quickly as possible.
Recognition	To excite praise and commendation. To demand respect. To boast and exhibit one's accomplishments. To seek distinction, social prestige, honours or high office.
Exhibition	To attract attention to one's person. To excite, amuse, stir, shock, thrill others. Self-dramatization.
Dominance	To influence or control others. To persuade, prohibit, dictate. To lead and direct. To restrain. To organize the behaviour of a group.
Autonomy	To resist influence or coercion. To defy an authority or seek freedom in a new place. To strive for independence.
Contrariance	To act differently from others. To be unique. To take the opposite side. To hold unconventional views.
Aggression	To assault or injure another. To murder. To belittle, harm, blame, accuse or maliciously ridicule a person. To punish severely. Sadism.
Abasement	To surrender. To comply and accept punishment. To apologize, confess, atone. Self-depreciation. Masochism.
Affiliation	To form friendships and associations. To greet, join and live with others. To co-operate and converse socially with others. To love. To join groups.
Play	To relax, amuse oneself, seek diversion and entertainment. To 'have fun', to play games. To laugh, joke and be merry. To avoid serious tension.
Cognizance	To explore. To ask questions. To satisfy curiosity. To look, listen, inspect. To read and seek knowledge.

Source: adapted from Murray (1938).

3.2.4 Theories of Tourist Motivation

Most attempts to explain tourist motivation take a content theory approach to the problem and, despite its limitations, many show marked similarities to Maslow's need hierarchy in particular. For example, Mill and Morrison (1985) see travel as a need or want satisfier. Basically a person has certain needs, of which he or she may or may not be aware. These then translate into wants. For instance, a person may *need* affection but will *want* to visit friends and relatives. As Mill and Morrison (1985, p. 4) succinctly put it: 'Motivation occurs when an individual wants to satisfy a need.' They then show how Maslow's need hierarchy ties in with travel motivations and the travel literature. For example, those who say they travel to escape or relieve tension can be seen as seeking to satisfy their basic physiological needs, travelling for reasons of health can be seen as a way of attempting to satisfy one's safety needs, and so on.

Similarly, Dann's (1977) identification of anomie and ego-enhancement as basic tourism motivators can be interpreted in terms of Maslow's need hierarchy. According to Pearce (1982) 'Dann's analysis of anomie is an implicit restatement of Maslow's love and belongingness needs' (p. 62), and 'In the terminology adopted by Maslow ego-enhancement could aptly be described by the concept of self-esteem needs' (p. 63). Dann (1977) argued that much of the 'so-called' motivation research did not really address the fundamental question: 'Why do people travel?' He says that basically there are two factors or stages in a decision to travel, the push factors and then the pull factors, in that order.

The push factors are those that make you want to travel. The pull factors are those that affect *where* you travel, *given* the initial desire to travel. They 'pull' you to a certain resort after you have been 'pushed' into wanting to travel. The pull factors are therefore *consequent* on a prior need to travel. So the question 'What makes people travel?' can only relate to push factors.

According to Dann, we live in an anomic society and this fosters a need in people for social interaction which is missing at the home place. Therefore there is a need to travel away from the home environment. Ego-enhancement, on the other hand, derives from the level of personality needs. Just as there is a need for social interaction, so too do people need to be recognized. Analogous to the desire for a bodily tune up is the need to have one's ego enhanced or boosted. At home, one already has a social position, but away from home one can pretend – be waited on – especially in developing countries. The tourist can 'escape' into a world of fantasy on holiday and indulge in kinds of behaviour generally frowned on at home.

> Related to anomie, the fantasy world of travel seeks to over-come the humdrum, the normlessness and meaninglessness of life, with more satisfying experiences. As regards ego-enhancement, travel presents the tourist with the opportunity to boost his or her ego in acting out an alien personality. (Dann, 1977, p. 188)

Crompton (1979) agreed with Dann, as far as the idea of push and pull motives was concerned. However, he identified nine motives – seven classified as socio-psychological or push motives and two classified as cultural or pull motives. The push motives were: escape from a perceived mundane environment; exploration and evaluation of self; relaxation; prestige; regression; enhance-ment of kinship relationships; and facilitation of social inter-action. The pull motives were novelty and education. Crompton identified these motives from a series of in-depth interviews with 39 people. He said the push or socio-psychological motives were rarely overtly identified by respondents in early discussion. However,

> as the interview proceeded it often became apparent that while initial concern and effort had been with selecting a vacation destination, the value, benefits and satisfactions derived from the vacation were neither related to, nor derived from, a par-ticular destination's attributes. . . . In effect, these motives represented a hidden agenda. (Crompton, 1979, p. 415)

Iso-Ahola (see Mannell and Iso-Ahola, 1987) identifies two main types of push and pull factors, personal and interpersonal. He argues that people are motivated to seek leisure activities in order both to leave behind the personal and/or interpersonal problems of everyday life and to obtain personal and/or interpersonal rewards from participation in the leisure activities concerned. The personal rewards consist mainly of self-determination, sense of competence or mastery, challenge, learning, exploration and relaxation; the interpersonal rewards are those arising from social interaction. The interaction of these motivational forces is shown in Figure 3.1.

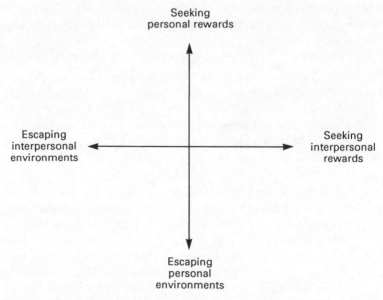

Figure 3.1 The escaping and seeking dimensions of leisure motivation.

Source: Mannell and Iso-Ahola (1987, p. 323).

Pearce (1982) reviewed some of the studies on tourist motivation and presented a typical one done by the Canadian Government Travel Bureau in 1972 – typical insofar as the British Tourist Authority and American market research teams have used this technique extensively. Five thousand Canadians from ten cities participated in 30 to 50 person group discussion evenings. Advertising films and travelogues were used as a basis to stimulate group discussion. This technique was supplemented by market research personnel asking some specific questions of the group participants. The sessions were tape-recorded. Table 3.3 is an example of the data obtained. These are the responses to an open-ended question seeking *all* reasons for the choice of destination. However, note that the reasons relate to *destination* choice and not to why the participants travelled in the first place. As Crompton pointed out, in this kind of situation, people may be reluctant to give the *real* reasons for travel if these are deeply personal or intimate.

Mill and Morrison (1985, p. 2) also make this point. They state that 'Many tourists will not feel comfortable admitting that a major reason for taking a vacation is that they will be able to impress their friends upon their return home.' They also point out

Table 3.3 Canadian vacation travellers: all reasons for choosing last vacation destination (percentages)

All reasons for destination choice	All destinations	Total Canadian	Total USA	Mid-Atlantic region	New England region	North Central	North-West	South-West	South-East/Central	USA (state unspecified)	Total other countries	Total Europe	British Isles	Other Europe	Mexico, Bermuda, Caribbean, Central and South America	All other destinations
To visit friends or relatives	50	53	39	37	37	63	40	53	21	35	59	73	78	71	29	34
Relaxing atmosphere	33	33	31	28	37	18	35	29	41	25	32	22	28	18	62	38
Scenery	41	43	35	30	40	26	29	40	39	38	40	33	34	33	52	55
For oceans and beaches	19	15	33	29	49	4	19	19	57	33	22	11	7	14	57	24
Sports facilities	10	11	8	5	8	9	9	6	12	7	3	1	–	2	8	7
Good camp-sites	11	13	10	7	11	9	10	4	8	19	*	*	1	–	–	2
Good weather there	24	20	37	27	36	15	15	50	68	37	33	18	7	24	76	42
Not too many tourists	10	11	6	5	11	4	5	1	3	7	6	4	6	3	8	13
To get better buys	4	2	9	9	8	15	19	10	5	6	7	8	7	8	2	6
Low cost of vacations	11	12	8	5	8	7	8	11	7	8	11	8	8	8	17	16
Warm, friendly people	22	21	22	20	23	24	20	25	26	20	33	36	38	35	25	30
Good roads	13	13	18	19	16	14	12	15	17	24	1	1	1	*	1	–
Outstanding food	7	6	5	4	2	5	7	5	5	7	16	14	6	19	22	17
Attractive customs, life	7	5	7	9	7	3	5	12	4	9	23	21	21	21	24	34
Foreignness	7	4	13	17	14	7	8	17	14	11	22	19	13	22	22	39
Night-life	6	5	10	13	4	15	5	14	13	5	13	8	5	9	28	19
Easier to have fun there	13	13	10	16	8	6	4	15	9	10	12	8	7	9	22	18
Cultural activities	5	4	5	5	5	2	10	–	8	3	14	15	18	13	4	26
Attractive advertising	5	4	9	15	8	1	2	8	13	7	7	3	2	4	15	14
Don't know much about own province's attractions	2	2	2	4	*	1	–	1	4	1	1	1	–	1	1	4
Don't make fun of English	3	2	5	10	6	2	1	1	8	4	2	1	1	2	6	1
Kicks of getting something back through customs	1	*	3	6	2	1	8	4	3	1	1	1	1	1	–	4
None of above	9	9	7	6	6	7	4	7	5	15	5	6	6	6	3	2

*Less than 1 percent.

Source: Canadian Government Travel Bureau (1972), quoted by Pearce (1982, p. 60).

that 'the tourists themselves may be unaware of the true reasons behind their travel behaviour'.

Krippendorf (1987) points out that there are problems with studies asking tourists what their motives for travel are, partly because there are always several motives that prompt a person to travel, but also because the reasons given are, not surprisingly, reiterations of all the reasons that feature in advertising and are repeated over and over in all tourist brochures and catalogues. Many things remain hidden in the subconscious and cannot be brought to light by simple questions. However, he feels that the results of studies of tourists' motives and behaviour can be very instructive and reports on a German study carried out in 1986–7. The results from the question 'What were the main reasons for your 1986 (main) holiday journey?' are presented in Table 3.4.

Krippendorf also outlines eight theories of travel motivation found in the literature on tourism. Travel is: recuperation and regeneration; compensation and social integration; escape; communication; freedom and self-determination; self-realization; happiness; and travel broadens the mind. Krippendorf sees a thread running through all these theories. Firstly, travel is motivated by 'going *away* from' rather than 'going *towards*' something; secondly, travellers' motives and behaviour are markedly self-oriented: 'Now *I* decide what is good for *me*.'

Schmidhauser (1989) reports some of the findings of research he carried out (with others) in Switzerland, which he says showed that a single trip cannot satisfy all the touristic needs of a person. Each trip can only cover part of the needs. They studied the tourist behaviour patterns of 4331 Swiss people and found that, on average, 90.1 per cent of all adults travelled and that these 90.1 per cent had on average taken 3.5 different types of tours during the period 1973–82. According to Schmidhauser, a further study of the travel motives of 9789 Swiss in 1982 showed that 'participating in tourism fulfils a whole series of important sociological functions that otherwise can only be poorly satisfied, or not at all; this explains, at least in part, the high propensity of the Swiss for travel' (Schmidhauser, 1989, p. 571). He lists four sociological functions:

1 To compensate for the many deficits that everyday life in a working performance society inevitably brings:
   (a) social deficits or deficits in human contact and friendliness;
   (b) climatic deficits (the urge for sun and warmth);

Table 3.4 Answers to question: 'What were the main reasons for your 1986 (main) holiday journey?' (percentages)

To switch off, relax	66
To get away from everyday life, have a change of scene	59
To recover strength	49
To experience nature	47
To have time for one another	42
To get sunshine, to escape from bad weather	39
To be with other people, to have company	37
To eat well	36
To have a lot of fun and entertainment, enjoy oneself, have a good time	35
To do as one pleases, to be free	35
To experience a great deal, to have a lot of change (diversity)	33
To experience something entirely different, see new things	33
Cleaner air, clean water, to get out of the polluted environment	32
To get exercise, to engage in light sports and games activities	30
To experience other countries, to see the world	30
To rest a great deal, do nothing, little exertion	29
To be pampered, go on a spree, enjoy oneself	26
To make new friends	23
To do something for one's beauty, get a tan	23
To travel a great deal, to move around	21
To broaden one's horizons, do something for one's culture and education	20
To pursue one's own interest	19
To do something for one's health, prevent disease	18
To refresh memories	18
To see relatives and friends	16
To have time for introspection, thought	15
To engage actively in sport, to get fit	12
To go on exploration trips, to take a risk, to experience something out of the ordinary	10
To have time for one's hobbies	7

Since the same person could name several reasons, the total percentage is over 100.

Source: Krippendorf (1987, p. 23).

(c) deficits in movement and activity, in sports activities;

(d) deficits in closeness to nature, in the enjoyment of scenery, in outdoor recreation;

(e) deficits in experience and change, repression of the discovery and action urges;

(f) deficits in enjoyment, luxury and prestige;

(g) lack of freedom.

2 Physical and psychological recovery from stress, the pressure of performance and the monotony of everyday life, finding again or keeping physical and mental well-being.
3 Widening horizons, satisfying curiosity, self-realization, increase of the feeling of one's own value.
4 Self-reward, self-indulgence.

3.2.5 Limitations of Content Theories of Motivation

Content theories of motivation undoubtedly serve a useful function in drawing attention to the wide variety of different needs which can motivate human behaviour. Nevertheless, the study of needs can at best provide only a partial explanation of motivated behaviour. As Murray (1938) points out, a need is an emergence from the past, a 'push from the rear' rather than a 'pull from the future'. Thus needs are only a *potential* source of motivated behaviour. They may arouse motivated behaviour in the first place, but a knowledge of people's needs will not necessarily tell us what they will actually do to fulfil such needs, or indeed whether they will do anything at all.

For example, knowing that someone is hungry will not tell us in any precise way how this will affect his or her behaviour. The hungry individual may cook a meal, go out for a take-away, eat in a restaurant, try to get an invitation to eat at a friend's house or simply go without. Which of these the person does will depend on a wide variety of other factors besides the state of hunger, including whether there is food in the house, whether the person can cook, whether the take-away or restaurant is open, how the friends are likely to react to a hungry visitor and so on. However, these things do not influence behaviour directly; rather, it is the individual's beliefs about them. For example, the individual may not go out to a take-away, believing it to be closed when it is in fact open. Thus, predicting the effects of motivation on behaviour requires more than an understanding of human needs. It also requires an understanding of the *processes* whereby these needs are transformed into motivated behaviour and, in particular, of the way in which people's expectations give motivated behaviour its direction. These ideas form the basis of a more recent approach to the study of motivation, known as expectancy theory, and in the next section we will examine its applications to the study of tourist motivation.

3.3 EXPECTANCY THEORIES OF MOTIVATION

3.3.1 Introduction

There are a number of different versions of expectancy theory which vary in detail. However, they all have in common the basic premise that:

> the strength of a tendency to act in a certain way depends on the strength of an expectancy that the act will be followed by a given consequence (or outcome) and on the value or attractiveness of that consequence (or outcome) to the actor. (Lawler, 1973, p. 45)

The ideas on which expectancy theory is based can be traced back to Tolman's (1932) work on learning theory, and they are also implicit in Murray's (1938) work on motivation. However, the first version of expectancy theory specifically intended to explain motivation in an applied setting was Vroom's (1964) theory of work motivation. Vroom put forward two equations. The first is intended to take into account the fact that, while some outcomes may be attractive or desirable for their own sake, others may be attractive, not in themselves, but as a means of attaining other outcomes which are attractive in their own right. The equation states:

$$V_j = f_j \left[\sum_{k=1}^{n} (V_k I_{jk}) \right] \qquad (3.1)$$

where V_j is the valence of outcome j; I_{jk} is the perceived instrumentality of outcome j for the attainment of outcome k; V_k is the valence of outcome k; and n is the number of outcomes.

In other words, the equation states that the valence or attractiveness of any one outcome (j) depends upon the individual's beliefs about its instrumentality for obtaining other outcomes (k) and the valence or attractiveness of these outcomes to the individual. Both valence and instrumentality vary from -1 to $+1$. A valence of $+1$ indicates a strong desire for the outcome, while a valence of -1 indicates a strong aversion to it. Similarly, an instrumentality of $+1$ indicates that the first outcome will always lead to the second, while an instrumentality of -1 indicates that attainment of the first outcome will always prevent the attainment of the second.

45

Vroom's second equation is concerned with the force on a person to perform a particular act. It states:

$$F_i = f_i \left[\sum_{j=1}^{n} (E_{ij}V_j) \right] \qquad (3.2)$$

where F_i is the force on the individual to perform act i; E_{ij} is the strength of the expectancy that act i will be followed by outcome j; V_j is the valence of outcome j; and n is the number of outcomes. That is, the force acting on an individual to perform an act (i) will depend upon the strength of the individual's expectancy that it will be followed by outcome j and the valence of outcome j (as measured by equation 3.1) to the individual. In this equation, valence as before varies from $+1$ to -1. Expectancy, on the other hand, is the individual's perceived probability that behaving in a particular way will lead to certain outcomes. It therefore varies from 0 to $+1$.

Typically, Vroom's first formula has been used to explain or predict occupational preference and job satisfaction, while the second has been used to explain or predict occupational choice, remaining in a job and job effort.

3.3.2 Application of Expectancy Theory to Tourist Motivation

INTRODUCTION
Of the various aspects of employee attitudes and behaviour which expectancy theorists have attempted to explain, occupational preference and occupation choice would seem to have the greatest relevance to the study of tourist motivation. Fortunately, they are also areas in which expectancy theory has received considerable empirical support. Mitchell and Beach (1977) reviewed seven studies that had attempted to account for occupational preference and/or choice in terms of expectancy theory and found 'substantial support' for the model in every case. In this section, therefore, we will examine the applications of expectancy theory to the explanation of holiday preference and choice.

HOLIDAY PREFERENCE
Applied to holiday preference, Vroom's first equation would suggest that the overall attractiveness or valence of a particular holiday to an individual will be determined by the attractiveness or valence of different holiday attributes to the individual and the

instrumentality of the holiday for providing positively valent attributes and avoiding negatively valent ones. The individual's relative preference for different types of holiday or holiday destination will be revealed by their summed valence times instrumentality scores, and the most preferred holiday will be the one with the highest score.

As an illustration, let us take the case of an individual who takes into account only a limited number of factors in choosing a holiday, and is only concerned about whether the resort is warm and quiet, provides a pleasant social life, interesting surroundings, sea bathing and clean air, and how much travelling is involved to get there. Table 3.5 shows the valence of these attributes to the individual and his or her beliefs about the instrumentality of two different holiday resorts for providing these attributes. Expectancy theory would suggest that the individual would prefer to go to holiday destination 2 because it has the higher summed valence times instrumentality score. That is, he or she sees holiday destination 2 as being more likely to have the attributes that he or she values in a holiday.

Vroom's first formula can be used to explain not only *where* people would prefer to go on holiday, but also *why* they would want to go on holiday and indeed *whether* they would want to go on holiday at all. This can be achieved by including 'staying at home' as a possible 'holiday destination'. To illustrate this, let us take as an example two people who consider the same limited set of holiday attributes when considering whether to go on holiday, and ascribe similar valences to them, but have quite different views about instrumentalities. The numeric values of these valences and instrumentalities are listed in Table 3.6. Person A is alienated

Table 3.5 Effects of different valences (V) and instrumentalities (I) on holiday destination preferences

Attribute	Holiday destination 1			Holiday destination 2		
	V	I	V × I	V	I	V × I
Warm	+0.7	+0.3	+0.21	+0.7	+0.7	+0.49
Quiet	+0.8	+0.5	+0.40	+0.8	+0.6	+0.48
Pleasant social life	+0.8	+0.7	+0.56	+0.8	+0.8	+0.64
Interesting surroundings	+0.7	+0.5	+0.35	+0.7	+0.7	+0.49
Sea bathing	+0.6	+0.5	+0.30	+0.6	+0.9	+0.54
Clean air	+0.9	+0.7	+0.63	+0.9	+0.8	+0.72
Travelling	−0.7	+0.6	−0.42	−0.7	+0.6	−0.42
Σ (V × I)			+2.03			+2.94

Table 3.6 Effects of different valences (V) and instrumentalities (I) on decisions whether to take a holiday

Holiday attribute	Home – person A			Home – person B		
	V	I	V × I	V	I	V × I
Warm	+0.7	−0.1	−0.07	+0.7	+0.2	+0.14
Quiet	+0.8	−0.8	−0.64	+0.8	+0.8	+0.64
Pleasant social life	+0.8	+0.5	+0.40	+0.8	+0.8	+0.64
Interesting surroundings	+0.7	−0.8	−0.56	+0.7	+0.7	+0.49
Sea bathing	+0.6	−0.9	−0.54	+0.6	−0.9	−0.54
Clean air	+0.9	−0.9	−0.81	+0.9	+0.8	+0.72
Travelling	−0.7	−1.0	+0.70	−0.7	−1.0	+0.70
Σ (V × I)			−1.52			+2.79

from the home environment. It is cold, noisy and situated in uninteresting surroundings, and the atmosphere is polluted. Person A would therefore be attracted to a holiday destination that would get him or her away from the home environment which he or she actively dislikes. Thus, if person A had valences and instrumentalities like those shown in relation to holiday destination 1 (Table 3.5), then this would be an attractive holiday as far as he or she is concerned. Person B, on the other hand, is lucky enough to come from a relatively pleasant home environment. He or she would certainly not be attracted to a holiday destination that for him or her had valences and instrumentalities like those shown for holiday destination 1. If that was the best that was available, he or she would stay at home. On the other hand, a holiday like that shown in relation to holiday destination 2 would be attractive.

HOLIDAY CHOICE

Mitchell and Beach (1977) note that, while we would expect occupational preference and choice to be related to one another, the chosen occupation may well differ from the preferred one because of such things as family pressure, economic conditions or one's own ability. Similarly, an individual may not be able to take his or her preferred holiday for a variety of reasons. It may be too expensive, other members of the family may not wish to go there, it may not be possible to take the holiday at the appropriate time, and so on.

To account for the actual holiday chosen, therefore, it is necessary to use Vroom's second equation. The overall attractiveness (valence) of each holiday destination (as measured by equation 3.1) would be multiplied by the expectancy of being able to take that holiday and the one chosen would be the one with the highest force (F). Thus, if the individual in our hypothetical example in Table 3.5 has a high expectancy of being able to take holiday 1, say 0.8, but, because of the high cost, an expectancy of only 0.2 of being able to take holiday 2, then the summed expectancy times valence scores from the second formula would be 1.62 and 0.59 respectively, and expectancy theory would predict that the individual would be more likely actually to take holiday 1, even though he or she would prefer holiday 2.

We still need to take into account the home environment. If we assume that people are certain to be able to take a holiday at home, then the F value of a holiday at home would be -1.54 for person A and $+2.79$ for person B (see Table 3.6). Thus, while person A would still choose holiday 1, person B would not go on holiday at all. The holiday which he or she can afford is less attractive than staying at home.

The concepts described in this section are expressed in diagrammatic form in Figure 3.2. It is proposed that the attractiveness of the holiday attributes will be determined in part by the individual's needs, thus allowing the work of needs theorists such as Maslow and Murray to be incorporated into the model. It also assumes that the attractiveness (valence) of holiday attributes, instrumentality and expectancy will be influenced by a variety of sources, including brochures, guide books and other people's experience, and also by the individual's own experience of previous holidays of the same or a similar type; hence the feedback loops built into the model.

3.4 EVALUATION OF THE UTILITY OF AN EXPECTANCY THEORY APPROACH TO THE EXPLANATION OF TOURIST MOTIVATION

One thing that will be immediately apparent about expectancy theory is its complexity. This is one of its major limitations, both as a scientific theory and as a practical tool. With respect to its use as a means of predicting job effort and performance, Lawler and Suttle (1973, p. 502) commented rather sadly that: 'At this point it seems that the theory has become so complex that it has exceeded the measures which exist to test it.' The complexity of expectancy theory also makes it difficult to use the model to predict individual behaviour. In order to use the model to predict which holiday an individual would take, for example, it would be

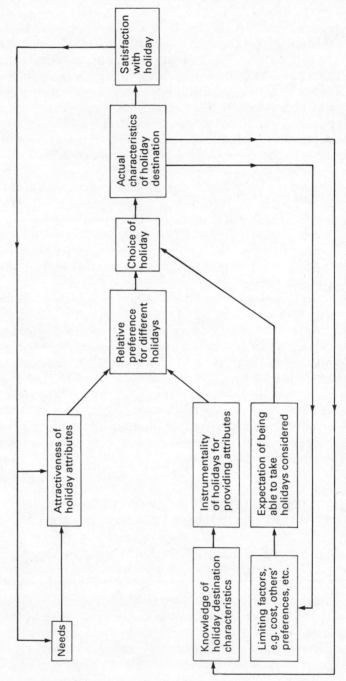

Figure 3.2 An expectancy model of holiday preference and choice.

necessary to identify all the holiday attributes that influence the attractiveness of a holiday to the individual, and then measure the relative attractiveness of these attributes, the individual's instrumentality beliefs about all these attributes in relation to each holiday destination the individual might consider and the individual's expectancy of being able to go on a holiday to each destination. Given the number of possible attributes and the number of possible destinations, this would be a daunting task, and given also the difficulty of assessing intangible things such as valences, instrumentalities and expectancies in any precise manner, even then accurate prediction would be difficult, to say the least.

Nevertheless, the application of expectancy theory to the study of tourist motivation does have a number of significant advantages. At the theoretical level, it enables many of the existing concepts in the study of tourist motivation to be incorporated within a single theoretical framework. For example, by making the assumption that people's needs influence the attractiveness (valence) of holiday destinations, expectancy theory is able to incorporate the work of need theorists, such as Maslow and Murray. This makes it possible to integrate the emotional aspect of tourist motivation – the needs which instigate the desire to travel in the first place – with the cognitive aspect – the decision making involved in choosing whether to go on holiday and, if so, where. Similarly, it can incorporate any of the reasons for travel suggested by writers on tourist motivation, by assuming that they are simply some among the many factors which influence the attractiveness of different holiday destinations.

Furthermore, it provides a way of resolving the problem of push and pull factors, or anomie and ego-enhancement in Dann's (1977) terms, in tourist motivation. According to our approach to tourist motivation, both push and pull factors are important, but it is pointless to argue which is the more important, as some writers do, because which is the more important will depend upon each individual's home circumstances and the type of holiday attributes that he or she considers important.

Because it provides a framework for the analysis of tourist motivation rather than suggesting specific reasons for travel, expectancy theory enables a much more sophisticated and more realistic view to be taken of tourist motivation. Expectancy theory has traditionally placed strong emphasis on individual differences in the valence or attractiveness of different outcomes. Thus taking an expectancy theory approach to tourist motivation would lead to the assumption that: (a) there is a wide variety of different reasons for travel and (b) these reasons vary widely between people. It follows that relatively short lists of reasons for travel which are assumed to apply to all people are likely to be misleading. It is questionable whether they could tell us the reasons why any one individual would want to travel, and they certainly could not tell us with any degree of accuracy which holiday destinations he or she would prefer or actually choose. People's valences, instrumentalities and expectancies with respect to holidays vary so much that the only way to establish what type of holiday would motivate a particular individual is to study that particular individual and find out what his or her preferences, beliefs and circumstances are. Furthermore, even as a general picture of tourist motivation, such short lists of reasons for travel may be misleading. Can it be assumed that all groups of people travel for the same reason? For example, do working-class tourists travel for the same reasons as middle-class tourists, or German tourists travel for the same reason as Japanese tourists? They may, but this is something which needs to be established by empirical research rather than simply being assumed to be the case.

Expectancy theory would provide a good basis for research into tourist motivation. While its complexity may limit its ability to predict individual behaviour in any precise way, it could be used to study the factors which determine holiday-makers' preferences with respect to particular holiday destinations. A set of holiday attributes relevant to these destinations could be generated, and potential holiday-makers' valences and instrumentalities could be measured in relation to these attributes with respect to each destination. At the same time, the holiday-makers' expectations of being able to take a holiday at these destinations could also be measured. The key elements influencing holiday preference and choice could then be identified and further research could be carried out to establish whether holiday preference and choice would change if any of these key elements were to be changed.

A wide variety of different ways of measuring expectancy theory variables has been used in tests of the model, including five, seven, nine and ten point scales, ranking, paired comparisons and forced distributions. Mitchell (1974) suggests that to some extent this adds external validity, but comments that it also adds confusion and some people would argue that different measures constitute different theories. In general, then, it would probably be better to measure expectancy theory variables in ways which approximate as closely as possible to Vroom's original conception of them. Thus, for example, expectancy could be conceptualized as a perceived probability and assessed on, say, a five-point scale, valence could be assessed on a scale from −5 (highly unattractive) to +5 (highly attractive), and instrumentality could also be assessed on a scale from −5 to +5. However, taking into account the numerous comments that in some cases tourists may not know or may be reluctant to admit their reasons for travel, it may be useful to measure certain valences, such as those relating to prestige and status, by more indirect means. A projective test, such as Murray's Thematic Apperception Test (TAT), which has been widely used in the measurement of work motivation, could be used for this purpose. Alternatively, a questionnaire measure designed to counteract the effects of social desirability set, such as the Edwards (1959) Personal Preference Schedule, also based on the work of Murray, might be used.

Finally, expectancy theory would provide a useful format for training those involved in giving advice to potential holiday-makers. Giving useful advice is not simply a matter of having the appropriate information, but is also a matter of asking the right questions to establish what is the appropriate information in the first place. For example, Rackham and Morgan (1977) found that among telephone sales agents working for an airline, there was no evidence of a relationship between sales success and the amount of schedule information, such as information on flights, fares, times, etc., that they gave to potential customers. Two possible reasons for this were suggested. Firstly, overloading passengers with too much information could simply confuse them. Secondly, giving schedule information was often done at the expense of another key agent behaviour, *establishing needs and intentions*. Skilled sales agents

> generally avoided giving schedule information to passengers until they had diagnosed the passengers' needs or intentions by asking questions. By first obtaining a clear picture of the passengers' needs, they were able to concentrate on those areas of schedule information which were relevant. (Rackham and Morgan, 1977, p. 228)

Asking the right questions requires more than simply the desire or intention to do so. The travel adviser also needs to know what questions to ask, and this in turn requires a conceptual framework or mental model of the factors involved in holiday preference and choice. No doubt skilled travel advisers possess such a conceptual framework, at least in an implicit form. This may not be expressed in terms of valences, instrumentalities and expectancies but, nevertheless, he or she will try to find out what holiday attributes the customer finds attractive, which holidays the customer believes would yield these attractive attributes and what constraints (cost, timing, etc.) there are with respect to potential holidays which have these attributes. This information then puts the travel adviser in a position where he or she can correct any misapprehensions that the customer has about the attributes of particular holiday destinations, suggest alternative destinations which may fulfil the customer's requirements, and so on. Thus, in the diagrammatic form shown in Figure 3.2, expectancy theory could provide a useful basis for the training of less experienced travel advisers in the types of questions they need to ask in order to establish what information the customer requires in order to choose the most attractive holiday available.

References

Crompton, J. (1979) Motivations for pleasure vacation. *Annals of Tourism Research*, **6**, 408–24.

Dann, G. (1977) Anomie, ego-enhancement and tourism. *Annals of Tourism Research*, **4**, 184–94.

Edwards, A.L. (1959) *Personal Preference Schedule*, revised edn. New York: Psychological Corporation.

Jafari, J. (1987) Tourism models: the socio-cultural aspects. *Tourism Management*, **8**, 151–9.

Krippendorf, J. (1987) *The Holiday Makers*. London: Heinemann.

Lawler, E.E. (1973) *Motivation in Work Organizations*. Monterey, CA: Brooks/Cole.

Lawler, E.E. and Suttle, J.L. (1973) Expectancy theory and job behavior. *Organizational Behavior and Human Performance*, **9**, 482–503.

Mannell, R.C. and Iso-Ahola, S.E. (1987) Psychological nature of leisure and tourism experience. *Annals of Tourism Research*, **14**, 314–31.

Maslow, A.H. (1943) A theory of human motivation. *Psychological Review*, **50**, 370–96.

Maslow, A.H. (1954) *Motivation and Personality*. New York: Harper.

Maslow, A.H. (1965) *Eupsychian Management.* Homewood, IL: Irwin.

Mill, R.C. and Morrison, A.M. (1985) *The Tourist System.* Englewood Cliffs, NJ: Prentice-Hall.

Mitchell, T.R. (1974) Expectancy models of job satisfaction, occupational preference and effort: a theoretical, methodological, and empirical appraisal. *Psychological Bulletin,* **81**, 1053-77.

Mitchell, T.R. and Beach, L.R. (1977) Expectancy theory, decision theory, and occupational preference and choice. In Kaplan, M.F. and Schwartz, S. (eds) *Human Judgement and Decision Processes in Applied Settings,* pp. 203-25. New York: Academic Press.

Murray, H.A. (1938) *Explorations in Personality.* New York: Oxford University Press.

Pearce, P.L. (1982) *The Social Psychology of Tourist Behaviour.* International Series in Experimental Social Psychology, 3. Oxford: Pergamon Press.

Rackham, N. and Morgan, T. (1977) *Behaviour Analysis in Training.* London: McGraw-Hill.

Schmidhauser, H. (1989) Tourist needs and motivations. In Witt, S.F. and Moutinho, L. (eds) *Tourism Marketing and Management Handbook,* pp. 569-72. Hemel Hempstead: Prentice-Hall.

Tolman, E.C. (1932) *Purposive Behavior in Animals and Men.* New York: Century.

Vroom, V.H. (1964) *Work and Motivation.* New York: Wiley.

Wahba, M.A. and Bridwell, L.G. (1976) Maslow reconsidered: a review of research on the need hierarchy theory. *Organizational Behavior and Human Performance,* **15**, 212-40.

Wright, P.L. (1989) Motivation and job satisfaction. In Molander, C. (ed.) *Human Resource Management,* pp. 96-118. Bromley: Chartwell-Bratt.

Wright, P.L. (1991) Motivation in organizations. In Smith, M. (ed.) *Analysing Organizational Behaviour,* pp. 77-102. Basingstoke: Macmillan.

4 Tourism and Symbolic Consumption

Graham Brown

Entertainment, the arts and leisure activities encompass symbolic aspects of consumptive behaviour that make them particularly fertile grounds for research.

Holbrook and Hirschman (1982, p. 134)

4.1 INTRODUCTION

The focus of this chapter is the relationship between people and their possession of tourism experiences. Tourism is presented as a form of consumptive behaviour which offers a sense of appropriation towards destinations. This may be expressed through the acquisition of tangible souvenirs, which also serve to extend the life of the tourism experience.

The value of this perspective derives from a need to understand the attribution of meaning in tourist behaviour. At the heart of this approach is the interaction between motivation and perception: 'how people's motives lead them to perceive meaning in the objects they encounter and how the meanings of those objects affect their motives . . . how the participants in the marketplace symbolise their lives in the products and brands they consume' (Levy, 1987, p. 16).

The first discipline to be reviewed will be that of consumer behaviour, in which an experiential focus has been adopted in a number of articles, such as those which emphasize 'consumer fantasies, feelings and fun' (Holbrook and Hirschman, 1982). Much of this literature is based on the premise that the consumption of goods may depend more on their social meaning than on their functional utility (Levy, 1981). Other relevant research streams include self-image and product-image congruence (Dolich, 1969; Gardner and Levy, 1955; Grubb and Hupp, 1968; Landon, 1974), the role of products in information and communication (Belk, 1978; Holman, 1981) and consumer aesthetics (Holbrook, 1981).

In a review of the literature devoted to environmental interaction, spatial mobility will be examined in a structural sense, with tourism portrayed as a multi-faceted symbolic act. Reference will be made to the work of phenomenologically oriented geographers who have discussed the experiential quality of spatial activity (Dardel, 1952; Relph, 1985; Tuan, 1980) and to studies by environmental psychologists, which have included the purposive evaluation of place (Canter, 1983), place-identity (Proshansky, 1978) and person–environment compatibility (Kaplan, 1983).

Whenever possible, studies from these disciplines will be related to the way the issues have been addressed within the tourism literature. Other comparisons will be made by referring to interpretations offered in areas such as popular culture. Although the scope of the discussion is broad, the relationship between tourism and symbolism is employed as an integrative theme throughout.

The chapter will conclude with a brief discussion of the epistemology of symbolic behaviour and a proposal for a future research agenda.

4.2 SYMBOLIC CONSUMPTION

It has been accepted for many years that all products may carry symbolic meaning (Veblen, 1925). However, products have traditionally been viewed as responses to, rather than causes of, behaviour. Attention has been focused on the effects of economic, psychological and sociological variables on product choice, rather than on the effects of products on the consumer's experience. Products may also play an *a priori* role as stimuli that are antecedent to behaviour (Solomon, 1983).

Solomon has argued that consumers employ product symbolism to define social reality and to ensure that behaviours appropriate to that reality will ensue. Thus the social actor uses products to clarify patterns of behaviour associated with social roles and often relies upon the social information inherent in products to shape self-image. Goods can act as social tools when their symbolic qualities promote communication between an individual and his or her significant references. For example, a product which has intangible attributes congruent with the self-image a person wishes to convey can be used to express self-identity. For it to convey meaning, the symbolism must be recognized by the group with which the individual is associated (Grubb and Grathwohl, 1967).

A recent example from the leisure literature discussed the symbolic quality of vacations. The study examined the role of leisure in the construction and affirmation of social position by comparing the life styles of two middle-class groups on an English housing estate (Wynne, 1990). The groups were distinguished on the basis of level of education and occupation and it was suggested that, for one group, 'taste in holidays is for à la carte, at a gîte or campsite in France, rather than the tour company construction' (p. 27). For the other group, 'the signs of arrival are the ability to ... holiday abroad in a hotel rather than a tent' (p. 29). An earlier study had found that motives for travel among middle-class Californians included a desire 'to keep up with the Joneses' by visiting prestigious resorts (Smith, 1979).

The consensual interpretation of symbolic meaning is a prerequisite for successful communication. It is therefore important to consider the means by which symbols attain a shared reality. According to a conceptualization proposed by Hirschman (1981), symbols are created and introduced into the consuming sector by a production process which is, in itself, a social phenomenon involving multiple participants. Adopting Hirschman's terminology, those playing 'integral roles' in the introduction of a new tourist destination would include the developer, who may qualify to be regarded as an 'author' of the landscape (Samuels, 1979), and the tour operator, who incorporates the destination within a vacation 'package'. Included among those playing 'tangential roles' in the assignment of symbolic meaning to the destination would be the mass media, advertising agencies and various sectors of the tourism industry. Thus, many people are responsible for physically creating the symbol and providing it with socially significant meaning. 'It is through advertising, retail store display, television shows and magazines that a consumer learns what products currently symbolise youth, prestige, sexuality and conservatism' (Hirschman, 1981, p. 5).

An interesting generalization that can be made concerning symbolic consumption is that it is frequently a longitudinal process. Thus, it is necessary to examine the consumers' perceptions of the symbol not only before and during purchase, but especially after the purchase has been made and during the life of the symbol as it is being consumed.

Attachment to tangible goods may seem to be of little relevance to tourism, where an emphasis would normally be placed on

59

experiential issues. However, this would fail to recognize the symbolic importance of objects associated with the tourism experience. Visitation stamps, such as those issued at National Parks in the United States and at National Trust properties in Britain, represent confirmatory markers and it has been suggested that the message conveyed by postcards may often be 'wish you were here to see us living as upper class' (Gottlieb, 1982, p. 176).

Photographs can perform a similar function and it may be that those which show the tourist at a particular location will duplicate scenes that appeared in brochures used to select the destination. If so, this would symbolically demonstrate satisfactory completion of the tourism process. This perspective finds support in the suggestion that 'An American tourist . . . does more than see the Eiffel Tower. He photographs it exactly as he knows it from posters. Better still, he has someone photograph him in front of it. Back home, that photograph reaffirms his identity within that scene' (Carpenter, 1973, p. 6).

The relationship between tourism and photography has been mentioned in a number of studies (Graburn, 1977; Sontag, 1977 and has been the specific focus of articles which have appeared in the *Annals of Tourism Research* (Albers and James, 1983; Botterill and Crompton, 1987; Chalfen, 1979). Sontag felt that travel could be portrayed as comprising little more than a strategy for accumulating photographs, yet even if this is true, a symbolic interpretation of this behaviour demonstrates an underlying logic: 'The connection between symbol and thing comes from the fact that the symbol – the word or picture – helps give the "thing" its identity, clarity, definition. It helps convert given reality into experienced reality, and is therefore an indispensable part of all experience' (Carpenter, 1973, p. 17). Set in propositional terms, it has been suggested that 'confidence in one's ability to meet role demands may determine the degree to which one must rely upon material symbols to convince others and oneself of this ability' (Solomon, 1983, p. 326). This provides a possible reason why some people, more than others, feel the need to show their holiday photographs.

Many people return from vacations with more than just photographs and memories. A recent study found that when people were asked why they chose a particular object in the house as their favourite, they did not focus on functionally based attributes. For roughly 60 per cent of an American sample, the reasons given reflected attachments based upon personal memories. Selection because the object served as a reminder of a vacation trip featured prominently among responses (Wallendorf and Arnould, 1988).

The sacred quality of souvenirs has been discussed in the *Journal of Popular Culture*. Gordon has suggested that

> People feel the need to bring things home with them from sacred, extraordinary time or space, for home is equated with ordinary, mundane time and space. They can't hold on to the non-ordinary experience, for it is by nature ephemeral, but they can hold onto a tangible piece of it, an object that came from it. . . . When it is taken away and brought into a living room setting, however, it becomes transformed into a significant icon. It becomes sacralised in the new context and is imbued with all the power of associations made with its original environment. (Gordon, 1986, pp. 136, 142)

It is possible to consider attachment to service offerings in the same way as attachment to physical objects. This area of interest has been embraced by a research stream within consumer behaviour under the heading of 'consumer aesthetics', which has been described as 'the study of purchasing situations where involvement is high, where responses are important, and where emotions run deep' (Holbrook, 1981, p. 36).

In an analysis of the behaviour and attitudes of people attending musical performances, Levy *et al.* (1981) found that high culture consumers tended to regard their experiences as necessary to their way of life. This was illustrated with comments such as 'It's extremely important, part of what keeps me going, keeps me happy; I wouldn't survive without it. Music can get into my soul, is a highly emotional experience' (p. 43). Within the leisure literature, attitudes towards activities which are perceived to be central to one's values or life style have been examined in the context of commitment (Buchanan, 1985), ego involvement (Selin and Howard, 1988) and personal meaning (McIntyre, 1989). Much of this work is based in product involvement and a review of this literature and its application in recreation has been provided by Havitz and Dimanche (1990).

Levy *et al.* (1981) suggested that the strength of the high arts product derives partly from a union of pleasure and virtue, and that it has a quality of endurance that contrasts with the ephemeral character of popular art, for which consumers tended to deny the necessity of their affiliation. Although acknowledging the possible influence of elitist attitudes, they suggested that 'High culture is seen to elevate the listener to spiritual realms; middle culture entertains, distracts and diverts; and in the minds of some, low culture (e.g. punk rock) degrades the participants' (Levy *et al.*, 1981, p. 44). The implication of this analysis is that events are symbolically hierarchical, with distinctions between them emphasized by the symbolic quality of settings. For example, the splendour of an opera house symbolically distinguishes its musical products from rock concerts held in utilitarian stadiums. This would seem to be a good example of the way an ability to define a situation assists an understanding of what constitutes an appropriate role performance. It also supports the notion that emotional responses can be seen as socially mediated outcomes which vary according to the symbolism associated with different forms of cultural performance.

There are clearly opportunities to relate this analysis to tourism. For instance, certain types of tourists describe the elevating nature of their experiences whereas others believe their activities to be inadequate to warrant such claims. It is regarded as appropriate to describe the transcendental quality of a wilderness experience, yet hardly suitable to describe sunbathing in the same way. Significantly, there would seem to be a hierarchy of tourism settings, with a visit to the Vatican equivalent to participation in high culture, whereas a day at a theme park would be regarded as a more popular form of cultural experience.

4.3 ENVIRONMENTAL SYMBOLISM

The study of psychological bonds with tangible surroundings has been dominated by an interest in the home environment (Buttimer, 1980; Cooper, 1976; Fried, 1963; Relph, 1976; Seamon, 1979). It has been proposed that these bonds are developed following long-term involvement, as illustrated by Tuan's (1977, p. 179) belief that 'it takes time to get to know a place'. Through the routines of daily life, the home environment becomes a place of familiar and predictable activities, comprising experiences which are, most often, unconscious or taken for granted. The process of attending to and providing interpretations of the home environment means that people not only come to know and have feelings about these places, they also come to know and have feelings about themselves (Feldman, 1990). In this way, the home can come to represent an enduring symbol of the self (Cooper, 1976; Duncan and Duncan, 1976).

It can be argued that social changes have led to a greater role for tourism in the formation of what has been termed 'place-identity' (Proshansky, 1978). Increased mobility has been accompanied by a reduction in identification with a specific place-based community as more individualistic life styles find expression in a dispersed pattern of socio-spatial activities. Tuan (1980) has suggested that 'rootedness' is probably beyond the grasp of most people in a highly mobile, rapidly changing society.

Tourism may be characteristic of what Seamon (1979) has referred to as an 'encounter': an interaction with the environment in a state of heightened consciousness. In this way, tourism destinations become increasingly important as people 'attempt to establish some degree of symmetry between self and external behaviour in space' (Wilson, 1980, p. 145). A destination may be the setting for experiences which render that particular place 'a discrete, temporally and perceptually bounded unit of psychologically meaningful material space' (Godkin, 1980, p. 173).

In an analysis of human ecology from a symbolic interactionist perspective, Ericksen (1980) has suggested that in post-industrial society people have become more assertive. They act as probers of their spatial moorings. Conceptually, a 'referential space' provides a body of perspectives which make possible a critical comparison of spatial anchors. They can be ranked in terms of the extent to which they contribute to an individual's sense of worth or mission. The spatial ideomatic has become less related to place of residence than to the question, 'Have you been there?'

An identification with spatial anchors may be translated into normative expectations, as illustrated by Jakle's observation that, in the 1930s,

> Every British traveler had always been to Harlem, and so every British traveler would always continue to go to Harlem. It was one of the things that was 'done', for when he returned, the first and often the only, question that would be put to him, was 'Did you go to Harlem?' If he faltered, stammered a little and replied, 'Well not exactly', there would be a painful silence and then a painful change of conversation. (Jakle, 1985, p. 261)

Thus, a destination may embody shared meanings as a symbol endowed with cultural significance. The relationship between a tourist and the environment is mediated by the perception of destinations as features within a symbolic landscape (Meinig, 1979). Rowntree and Conkey (1980, p. 461) have suggested that 'the cultural landscape in part functions as a narrative, a symbolic legacy' and Relph (1976) has nominated Red Square, Niagara Falls and the Acropolis as national symbols of common experience which foster a sense of national unity and pride. They have, of course, also become important tourist attractions.

In the United States, 'the National Parks enjoy a special status that is particularly rich in symbolic meaning. They are the nation's crown jewels' (Schreyer *et al.*, 1981, p. 294). Disneyland has been called 'a symbolic American utopia' (Goldberger, 1972). It has been suggested that it has become obligatory for Americans to make 'at least one pilgrimage to Disney Land or World as a popular culture "mecca" of nearly religious importance' (King, 1981, p. 117). Sears (1989, p. 5) has claimed that nineteenth-century tourist attractions in the United States 'provided a means of defining America as a place and taking special pride in the features of its landscape'. Relating this form of interpretation to self-reflection, tourism can be seen as 'a significant means by which modern people assess their world, defining their own sense of identity in the process' (Jakle, 1985, p. xi).

It would seem that the concept of place-identity has evolved from an association with a sense of embeddedness in the home environment to a belief that it may incorporate a more active form of self-maintenance through environmental interaction. Thus, one may develop psychological bonds with places that are spatially dispersed and identity may be related to enhanced geographical awareness.

4.4 FUTURE RESEARCH

> It is not enough to accept the attributes of products as the sources of distinction among them, as conventional marketing analysis is prone to do, resting in such ideas as ingredients, price, size, colour and packaging. The distinctions influencing human action arise from the attributions made by and to persons. (Levy, 1987)

The traditional models that have been used to examine and predict consumer behaviour are inappropriate for the study of tourism as symbolic consumption. Such models, which assume that decision making is a rational process, seek to quantify the influence of variables such as price and distance in destination selection. There is a need to delve deeper, to adopt humanistic modes of enquiry which examine the meaning of human action with the goal of attaining understanding.

An emphasis on the interpretation of meaning is a central feature within many of the studies reviewed in the previous sections. For instance, in a symbolic interactionist perspective people are believed to be creative actors for whom meaning, including self-knowledge, emerges as an outcome of interaction. A humanistic approach seeks to break away from a fragmented, positivistic, view of people and a preoccupation with quantification and to study distinctly human traits, such as meaning, feeling and emotion. It argues that person–environment interaction can best be understood by focusing on the way in which people experience and interpret their surroundings and stresses that a person must be viewed as a complete being with the potential for creativity and individuality (Walmsley and Lewis, 1984). It is suggested that future research should be based on the ontological assumptions of a 'nominalist' and 'voluntarist' position and 'anti-positivistic' and 'ideographic' epistemological assumptions.

In a nominalist orientation, reality is comprised of names and words which are used 'as tools for describing, making sense of and negotiating the external world' (Burrell and Morgan, 1989, p. 4). This position contrasts with that of a 'realist', who believes that the social world is made up of hard, tangible and relatively immutable structures that exist independently of the mind of the individual and operate whether or not the individual is aware of them. A voluntarist views an individual as an active agent who interacts with the environment rather than being controlled by it, as is assumed by 'determinism'. Humans are assumed to be symbol-producing, meaning-seeking creatures who have a certain amount of control over their lives. This is consistent with a symbolic interactionist perspective, which stresses the centrality of the actor's evaluations, with social action premised on how participants subjectively define situations rather than on the basis of objectively measurably features (Sanders, 1987).

The anti-positivist considers that the social world can only be understood from the point of view of the individuals who are, or have been, directly involved in the activities which are to be studied, and the ideographic mode of explanation stresses the importance of particular decisive events in the lives of these individuals. This epistemology is reflected in Sarbin's (1983) conceptualization of place-identity, in which it is contended that people are guided by a desire to create a coherent personal narrative. The origin of the metaphor of the self as story-teller can be traced to the work of American pragmatic philosophers such as William James and George Herbert Mead.

It has been suggested that self-knowledge is achieved through the skilled recollection of one's past and that 'part of an identity project involves a construction directly, or by implication, of an appropriate biography or autobiography' (Harré, 1983, p. 274). This is in accord with a theme advanced by Mead, who proposed that 'remembering is an active process, reconstructive and highly selective' (Strauss, 1956, p. x). More recently, Tuan (1980) has commented that just as nations rewrite history to promote venerable symbols, so individuals project personal biographies. This makes it possible to condense time, to bring the past into the clarity of the present. Thus, symbolically important events can impose an actuality which defies their chronology. An important tourism experience can therefore remain fresh in one's consciousness.

A future research agenda will attempt to enhance understanding of experiential tourism. An emic approach, which focuses on the insider's perception, could incorporate techniques which seek to raise the consciousness of tourists concerning their socio-spatial behaviour.[1] This reflects Buttimer's (1980) advocacy of the need for self-awareness concerning the meaning of our 'expanded horizons'. Forms of co-operative enquiry which concentrate on experiential learning have been advanced under the heading of 'action research' (Reason, 1988).

There is considerable scope to employ an analysis of meaning conveyed by objects such as souvenirs and travel photographs as a way of revealing motives for tourist behaviour. A framework for this area of research has been provided by studies that have examined the role of special possessions (Myers, 1985; Rochberg-Halton, 1984). The symbolic importance of tourism objects may vary according to socio-economic characteristics such as age and gender. Research which seeks to identify the significance of such variables would be valuable. It is also apparent that the materialistic perspective which shapes attitudes towards possessions in Western societies is unlikely to have the same importance in other countries. An examination of cross-cultural differences is required.

Finally, it is proposed that the need to find meaning and a desire for quantification need not be mutually exclusive. An important link between 'involvement' research and place attachment can be forged by attempting to measure the extent to which tourists experience a sense of enduring commitment to different types of leisure environments. Studies of this kind can serve to integrate research conducted in disparate disciplines, which represents one of the advantages that stem from an examination of tourism as symbolic consumption.

Note

1 An emic approach seeks insight by encouraging the participant to provide his or her view of reality. Understanding is based on this perspective rather than the researcher's interpretation of this view.

References

Albers, P.C. and James, W.R. (1983) Tourism and the changing photographic image of the Great Lakes Indians. *Annals of Tourism Research*, **10**, 123–48.

Belk, R.W. (1978) Assessing the effects of visible consumption on impression formation. In Hung, H.K. (ed.), *Advances in Consumer Research*, **5**, pp. 39–47. Ann Arbor, MI: Association for Consumer Research.

Botterill, T.D. and Crompton, J.L. (1987) Personal constructions of holiday snapshots. *Annals of Tourism Research*, **14**, 152–6.

Buchanan, T. (1985) Commitment and leisure behaviour: a theoretical perspective. *Leisure Sciences*, **7**, 401–20.

Burrell, G. and Morgan, G. (1979) *Sociological Paradigms and Organisational Analysis*. London: Heinemann.

Buttimer, A. (1980) Home, reach and the sense of place. In Buttimer, A. and Seamon, D. (eds), *The Human Experience of Space and Place*, pp. 166–85. New York: St Martin's Press.

Canter, D.V. (1983) The purposive evaluation of place. *Environment and Behavior*, **15**, 659–98.

Carpenter, E. (1973) *Oh, What a Blow That Phantom Gave Me!* New York: Holt, Rinehart & Winston.

Chalfen, R.M. (1979) Photography's role in tourism. Some unexplored relationships. *Annals of Tourism Research*, **6**, 435–47.

Cooper, C. (1976) The house as a symbol of self. In Proshansky, H.M., Ittelson, W.H. and Rivlin, L.G. (eds) *Environmental Psychology: People and Their Physical Settings*, 2nd edn, pp. 435–48. New York: Holt, Rinehart & Winston.

Dardel, E. (1952) *L'homme et la terre: nature de la réalité géographique*. Paris: Presses Universitaires de France.

Dolich, I. J. (1969) Congruence relationships between self-images and product brands. *Journal of Marketing Research*, **6**, 80-5.

Duncan, J. S. and Duncan, N. G. (1976) Housing as presentation of self and the structure of social networks. In Moore, G. T. and Golledge, R. G. (eds), *Environmental Knowing. Theories, Research and Methods*, pp. 247-53. Stroudsburg, PA: Dowden, Hutchinson & Ross.

Ericksen, E. G. (1980) *The Territorial Experience*. Austin: University of Texas Press.

Feldman, R. (1990) Settlement-identity. Psychological bonds with home places in a mobile society. *Environment and Behavior*, **22**, 183-229.

Fried, M. (1963) Grieving for a lost home. In Duhl, L. (ed.) *The Urban Condition*, pp. 151-71. New York: Basic Books.

Gardner, B. B. and Levy, S. J. (1955) The product and the brand. *Harvard Business Review*, **33**, 33-9.

Godkin, M. A. (1980) Identity and place: clinical applications based on notions of rootedness and uprootedness. In Buttimer, A. and Seamon, D. (eds) *The Human Experience of Space and Place*, pp. 73-85. New York: St Martin's Press.

Goldberger, P. (1972) Mickey Mouse teaches the architects. *New York Times Magazine*, 22 October, pp. 40-1, 92-9.

Gordon, B. (1986) The souvenir: messenger of the extraordinary. *Journal of Popular Culture*, **20**, 135-46.

Gottlieb, A. (1982) American's vacations. *Annals of Tourism Research*, **9**, 165-87.

Graburn, N. H. H. (1977) Tourism: the sacred journey. In Smith, V. (ed.) *Hosts and Guests*, pp. 17-31. Philadelphia: University of Pennsylvania Press.

Grubb, E. L. and Grathwohl, H. L. (1967) Consumer self-concept, symbolism and market behaviour: a theoretical approach. *Journal of Marketing*, **31**, 22-7.

Grubb, E. L. and Hupp, G. (1968) Perception of self-generalised stereotypes and brand selection. *Journal of Marketing Research*, **5**, 58-63.

Harré, R. (1983) *Personal Being*. Oxford: Basil Blackwell.

Havitz, M. E. and Dimanche, F. (1990) Propositions for testing the involvement construct in recreational and tourist contexts. *Leisure Sciences*, **12**(2), 179-95.

Hirschman, E.C. (1981) Comprehending symbolic consumption: three theoretical issues. In Hirschman, E.C. and Holbrook, M.B. (eds) *Symbolic Consumer Behavior*, pp. 4–6. Ann Arbor, MI: Association for Consumer Research.

Holbrook, M.B. (1981) Introduction: the esthetic imperative in consumer research. In Hirschman, E.C. and Holbrook, M.B. (eds) *Symbolic Consumer Behavior*, pp. 36–7. Ann Arbor, MI: Association for Consumer Research.

Holbrook, M.B. and Hirschman, E.C. (1982) The experiential aspects of consumer behavior: consumer fantasies, feelings and fun. *Journal of Consumer Research*, 9, 132–40.

Holman, R.C. (1981) Apparel as communication. In Hirschman, E.C. and Holbrook, M.B. (eds) *Symbolic Consumer Behavior*, pp. 7–15. Ann Arbor, MI: Association for Consumer Research.

Jakle, J.A. (1985) *The Tourist. Travel in Twentieth-Century North America*. Lincoln, NE: University of Nebraska Press.

Kaplan, S. (1983) A model of person-environment compatibility. *Environment and Behavior*, 15, 311–32.

King, M.J. (1981) Disneyland and Walt Disney World: traditional values in futuristic form. *Journal of Popular Culture*, 15, 116–40.

Landon, E.L. Jr (1974) Self-concept, ideal self-concept, and consumer purchase intentions. *Journal of Consumer Research*, 1, 44–51.

Levy, S.J. (1981) Symbols, selves and others. In Mitchell, A. (ed.) *Advances in Consumer Research*, 9, pp. 542–3. Ann Arbor, MI: Association for Consumer Research.

Levy, S.J. (1987) Semiotician ordinaire. In Umiker-Sebeok, J. (ed.) *Marketing and Semiotics*, pp. 13–20. Berlin: Mouton de Gruyter.

Levy, S.J., Czepiel, J.A. and Rook, D.W. (1981) Social division and aesthetic specialisation: the middle class and musical events. In Hirschman, E.C. and Holbrook, M.B. (eds) *Symbolic Consumer Behavior*, pp. 38–45. Ann Arbor, MI: Association for Consumer Research.

McIntyre, N. (1989) The personal meaning of participation: enduring involvement. *Journal of Leisure Research*, 21, 167–79.

Meinig, D.W. (1979) Symbolic landscapes. In Meinig, D.W. (ed.) *The Interpretation of Ordinary Landscapes. Geographical Essays*, pp. 164–92. New York: Oxford University Press.

Myers, E. (1985) Phenomenological analysis of the importance of special possessions: an exploratory study. In Hirschman, E.C. and Holbrook, M.B. (eds) *Advances in Consumer Research*, 12, pp. 560–5. Ann Arbor, MI: Association for Consumer Research.

Proshansky, H.M. (1978) The city and self-identity. *Environment and Behavior*, **10**, 147–69.

Reason, P. (1988) *Human Inquiry in Action*. London: Sage.

Relph, E. (1976) *Place and Placelessness*. London: Pion.

Relph, E. (1985) Geographical experiences and being-in-the-world: the phenomenological origins of geography. In Seamon, D. and Mugerauer, R. (eds) *Dwelling, Place and Environment*, pp. 15–31. Dordrecht: Martinus Nijhoff.

Rochberg-Halton, E. (1984) Object relations, role models and the cultivation of the self. *Environment and Behavior*, **16**, 335–68.

Rowntree, L.B. and Conkey, M.W. (1980) Symbolism and the cultural landscape. *Annals of the Association of American Geographers*, **70**, 459–74.

Samuels, M.W. (1979) The biography of landscape. In Meinig, D.W. (ed.) *The Interpretation of Ordinary Landscapes*, pp. 51–88. New York: Oxford University Press.

Sanders, C.R. (1987) Consuming as social action: ethnographic methods in consumer research. In Wallendorf, M. and Anderson, P. (eds) *Advances in Consumer Research*, **14**, pp. 71–5. Provo, UT: Association for Consumer Research.

Sarbin, T.R. (1983) Place identity as a component of the self: an addendum. *Journal of Environmental Psychology*, **3**, 337–42.

Schreyer, R., Jacob, G. and White, R. (1981) Environmental meaning as a determinant of spatial behaviour in recreation. *Proceedings of the Applied Geography Conferences*, **4**, 294–300.

Seamon, D. (1979) *A Geography of the Lifeworld*. New York: St Martin's Press.

Sears, J.F. (1989) *Sacred Places. American Tourist Attractions in the Nineteenth Century*. New York: Oxford University Press.

Selin, S.W. and Howard, D.R. (1988) Ego involvement and leisure behaviour: a conceptual specification. *Journal of Leisure Research*, **20**, 237–44.

Smith, V. (1979) Introduction. In Smith, V. (ed.) *Hosts and Guests. The Anthropology of Tourism*, pp. 1–14. Philadelphia: University of Pennsylvania Press.

Solomon, M.R. (1983) The role of products as social stimuli: a symbolic interactionist perspective. *Journal of Consumer Research*, **10**, 319–29.

Sontag, S. (1977) *On Photography*. New York: Farrar, Straus & Giroux.

Strauss, A. (1956) *The Social Psychology of George Herbert Mead.* Chicago: University of Chicago Press.

Tuan, Y.F. (1977) *Space and Place. The Perspective of Experience.* Minneapolis: University of Minnesota.

Tuan, Y.F. (1980) Rootedness versus sense of place. *Landscape*, **24**, 3–8.

Veblen, T. (1925) *The Theory of the Leisure Class.* London: Allen & Unwin.

Wallendorf, M. and Arnould, E.J. (1988) 'My favourite things': a cross-cultural inquiry into object attachment, possessiveness, and social linkage. *Journal of Consumer Research*, **14**, 531–47.

Walmsley, D.J. and Lewis, G.J. (1984) *Human Geography: Behavioural Approaches.* Harlow: Longman.

Wilson, B.M. (1980) Social space and symbolic interaction. In Buttimer, A. and Seamon, D. (eds) *The Human Experience of Space and Place,* pp. 135–47. New York: St Martin's Press.

Wynne, D. (1990) Leisure, lifestyle and the construction of social position. *Leisure Studies*, **9**, 21–34.

5 Market Segmentation and the Prediction of Tourist Destinations

Richard Prentice

5.1 INTRODUCTION

The present chapter evaluates one disaggregated approach to tourism prediction – the use of household survey data collected as case studies in 1989 in the Isle of Man and in south-west Wales. These case studies are discussed with three objectives. The first is to investigate the interrelationship, if any, between leisure activities and activities undertaken on holiday, principally main holiday activities. Two questions are addressed in this regard: firstly, is it appropriate to characterize holiday activities as a sub-set of leisure activities; and secondly, can holiday activities, and possible destination 'regions' of Europe and further away, be predicted from leisure activities? The second main objective of this chapter is to consider whether or not behavioural variables may be usefully included in aggregative models for predicting tourism flows. In particular, in demand prediction how appropriate are attributes of tourist segmentation? The third main objective is to compare, in terms of the characteristics of the holiday-makers they contain, two regional holiday markets in the British Isles. Are these markets essentially the same, or should our predictive models be regionally disaggregated not only in terms of destinations, but also in terms of tourist origins?

5.1.1 Segmentation

In the past the forecasting of international flows of tourists has often depended on analyses of income levels in the countries of origin, costs of reaching the destination, costs to be met at the destination, spatial accessibility and connectivity, substitute prices of holidays elsewhere, 'one-off' events such as wars, demographic changes, popularity expressed as trends over time and promotional activities. Standard texts are now available in the tourism literature on such techniques (e.g. Smith, 1989; Witt and Moutinho, 1989). Such analyses may have 'lagged' dependent variables of holiday taking, to take into account the slowness by which information is assimilated and habits change. Econometric models of this kind are often essentially *aggregative* in character, and therefore tend not to emphasize different kinds of holiday or different kinds of holiday-maker. Such analyses can be supplemented by incorporating the attractiveness of tourism destinations, including such attributes as accommodation and entertainment provisions, the natural landscape, the 'cultural' landscape, the climate and means of travel within the destination region. In Europe in the past two decades tourism has often implicitly become equated both with international tourism and with the 'sun, sea, sand and sex' mass market for holidays. Aggregate analyses may seem intuitively appropriate for studying this market.

The aggregative analyses described above, however, tend not to emphasize the *segmentation* of tourism markets in terms of customers (and non-customers). If one looks beyond the mass international holiday market within Europe into domestic main holidays, specialist markets, markets for additional holidays away and markets for short breaks, then a more disaggregated type of analysis is implied. For example, the volume and location of educational, sports or hobby holidays may be determined by factors different from those relevant for the mass market. As these diverse markets form a disproportionate part of the domestic holiday market in the United Kingdom, disaggregated analyses are particularly appropriate in this case. However, disaggregated approaches to demand prediction may have an enhanced attraction for the analysis of international tourism too, as specialist markets are developed to help counter the effects of the economic downturn of 1990 in international tourism (which was compounded by air travel fears as a result of the Gulf War of 1991).

An example of the kind of segmented analysis which is necessary is provided by the Wales Tourist Board's segmentation of overseas visitors to Wales:

- independent leisure travellers;
- package holiday makers;
- special interest groups concerned with heritage and culture;
- senior citizens;
- the youth market for outdoor activities;
- the ethnic market for involving Welsh communities overseas;
- business travellers (House of Commons, 1987).

Each of these groups may be supposed to have different motivations and propensities to travel, and to perceive different 'benefits' from their holiday taking. Approaches of this kind are of course not new, and in *leisure* studies, more so than in *tourism* studies, statistical clustering of consumers by socio-demographic and behavioural characteristics has a long antecedence (e.g. Tatham and Dornoff, 1971; Romsa, 1973). The development of techniques of this kind in leisure studies is mirrored in Smith's (1989) tourism analysis text; indeed, Smith's presentation of a multi-attribute tourism market segmentation is really a segmentation of leisure and not tourist activities.

5.1.2 The Case Studies

The two case studies discussed in this chapter are now briefly described. They were originally designed by the author as part of the fieldwork programme of the Geography Department of the University College of Swansea. As such, the data were originally collected for applications other than the present discussion, and while many questions asked in the surveys are comparable, this is not fully the case. Nor were all operational definitions consistent between the two surveys. The south-west Wales survey was undertaken in Swansea and the contiguous built-up area, covering parts of the local authority districts of Swansea and Lliw Valley (for brevity it will be termed the Swansea sample). Both the Swansea and Manx surveys were conducted as interviews with adults in their homes. They were chosen randomly within a spatially determined quota of sampling areas of streets and towns or villages respectively. In Swansea 1262 interviews were fully completed; in the Isle of Man 675. Although these sample sizes may appear large, the identification of segments as sub-samples in fact means that only broad segments can be defined, because otherwise the segments would be based on data subject to unacceptable sampling error. This limitation of the data cannot be overcome, but should be an important consideration in the sampling frame of any subsequent research (a point returned to in the research agenda suggested in the conclusion to this chapter). In order to ensure social class comparability between the Swansea and Manx samples (the Isle of Man having a higher proportion of owner-occupied housing tenure than Swansea), the Swansea sampling frame was designed to generate a sample representative only of the owner-occupied areas of 'Greater' Swansea. This removes the potential for differences in holidaying that result from the different social mixes of these two areas of Britain. However, it has the disadvantage of making the sample unrepresentative of the population of 'Greater' Swansea generally. In contrast, the Manx sample may be considered reasonably representative of the island's population and thus of tourists from the island.

One important difference between the Manx and Swansea surveys concerned the questioning about destination areas for holiday-makers. The Swansea survey differentiated between the destination areas of respondents' main holiday, if any, and their additional holiday(s), if any. Likewise, holiday activities were differentiated between main and additional holidays in the Swansea survey. The Manx survey, in contrast, did not differentiate between main and additional holidays off the island. This means that a strict comparison of the samples' holiday making is impossible. Because of the limited size of the sub-sample of the Swansea sample who had taken an additional holiday away from home ($n = 384$), the present analysis only considers main holidays for the Swansea sample, and therefore only main holiday destination areas. As main holidays could not be abstracted from the Manx database for reasons already noted, the Manx sample had to be analysed for all holidays. It is to be expected that the motivations behind destination area choice for main and additional holidays differ, so the modelling of the Manx destination choice profile will produce a less good segmentation than that for the Swansea sample. In effect, in the Manx sample it is not known which activities were pursued where, if more than one holiday was taken by a respondent. However, as many Manx additional holidays are trips to England, the distortions likely in the explanation of trips elsewhere for predominately main holidays are reduced substantially.

By the same token, the importance of England as a holiday destination for the Manx is likely to be inflated beyond that for main holidays only.

Exactly two-thirds of the Swansea sample had taken a holiday away from home in the previous 12 months, and much the same proportion (68 per cent) of the Manx sample had done so; this produces sub-samples of holiday makers of 841 and 459 respectively for Swansea and the Isle of Man. These sub-samples form the basis of the analysis in this chapter.

5.2 HOLIDAY ACTIVITIES

The present analysis assumes that households choose holiday destination areas on the basis, in part, of what these areas have to offer in terms of attractions. The analysis further assumes that the holiday activities of the survey respondents reflect their response to these opportunities. As different destination areas offer different packages of attractions, or potential 'benefits' of holidaying, to holiday-makers, it can be assumed that the market for holiday areas will naturally segment to some degree on the basis of what people wish to do on their holiday. Past holiday destinations and activities are used here to infer this system of expectations.

A comparison of the holiday activities of the Swansea sample for main and additional holidays emphasizes the importance of separating, where possible, the two types of holiday for purposes of demand prediction. In particular, additional (or 'second') holidays involved fewer activities, perhaps because of their generally shorter length. Of 12 activity types investigated in the interviews, all but one – visiting friends or relatives – were more frequently reported as main holiday activities than as additional holiday activities. For certain activities the differences were quite substantial. The attraction of the beach or pool declined markedly between main and additional holidays, being reported by 42 per cent and 14 per cent of the respective groups. Relaxing in the sunshine showed a similarly marked decline: 48 per cent of respondents reported this as a main holiday activity but only 22 per cent of the additional holiday-makers did so. However, the most popular main holiday activities – such as touring, visits to historic sites, towns and villages, and dining – were also popular for additional holidays, although less extensively. As such, additional holidays may not be so distinctive in terms of activities as might be first thought, at least for the mainly middle-class Swansea sample. The Manx sample of holiday-makers did differ in one noticeable way from the Swansea sample: visits to friends and relatives were of greater popularity as activities. This may reflect immigrants to the island visiting friends and relatives across the Irish Sea in England, and the native Manx visiting emigrant friends and relatives from the island, because the island has had a long history of emigration and a post-war history of largely English immigration (Prentice, 1990; Robinson, 1990). It does, however, highlight a regional difference in holiday markets.

Age was highlighted by the interviews as important in the prediction of holiday activities. For example, beach and pool activities were less popular for persons in their fifties and over; clubs and bars were also associated with the young, and particularly so among the Manx sub-sample of holiday-makers. Conversely, visits to friends and relatives increased with age, especially for persons in their sixties or older. These patterns might be thought to be unexceptional, but the broad consistency found between the age groups of the two samples was notable. Analytically, this general consistency is welcome for without it the opportunity to derive comparable market segments based in part on activity patterns from the samples would be forgone.

5.3 HOLIDAY DESTINATION AREAS

5.3.1 Destination Area Popularity

The popularity of holiday destination areas differed, both between Swansea and the Isle of Man and within the Swansea sample. The latter was dependent on whether the main or additional holiday was considered. Half of the Manx sample of holiday-makers had holidayed in England in the 12 months before their interview. In Swansea this proportion was exceeded by those respondents taking a second additional holiday, and nearly equalled by those taking at least one additional holiday. For main holidays, however, the pattern in Swansea was very different: only 26 per cent of main holidays were taken in England and this was exceeded substantially by the combined total for continental Europe and the Mediterranean, at 42 per cent. The latter pattern is of course not unexpected, bearing in mind the social class profile of the Swansea sub-sample and the continued increase in the market penetration of European holidays in the 1980s. Equally, the importance of England as an additional holiday destination for this Swansea sub-sample is significant in terms of domestic holiday development. Bearing in mind the lack of strict comparability of the Swansea and Manx data, the proportion of the Manx population holidaying in continental Europe and the Mediterranean appeared broadly comparable to that of the Swansea sample, with the popularity of these destinations for the Manx falling between that for main and additional holidays for the Swansea sample.

The less popular destinations showed some variation between the samples, notably holidays in Wales, Scotland and Ireland. For example, 7 per cent of all holidays taken by the Manx sample had been taken in Ireland, but only 1 per cent of main holidays by the Swansea sample were taken there. Similarly, Scotland was twice to three times as popular as a holiday destination for the Manx than for the Swansea sample, the exact difference being dependent on whether main or additional holidays are considered. In contrast, Wales as a destination area was more popular with the Swansea sample than with the Manx.

These differences suggest varying regional holiday markets in Britain which cannot be attributed to differing regional social class profiles, but equally some consistency, especially for European holidays. The varying location of destinations is of course to be expected, because of the different geographical locations of the two survey areas, and as such needs to be allowed for in formal segmentations of the market.

5.3.2 Destination Areas and Holiday Activities

The assumption that different destination areas are associated with different profiles of holiday activities is fundamental to the present analysis. This assumption has been discussed above. For the Manx sample of holiday-makers it is not possible to investigate this assumption, as the survey design did not allow for the association of destination areas with holiday activities by holiday type. However, such an analysis is possible for the Swansea sample and confirms this assumption. For example, the beach, swimming pool and relaxing in the sunshine were strongly associated with Mediterranean holidays, including additional holidays to this area. These activities were also associated with holidays in continental Europe, the Channel Islands and outside of Europe. Clubs and discos as activities were particularly associated with Mediterranean holidays. Scotland was distinctive as a destination area for mainly touring and 'heritage' tourism; England for visiting friends and relatives, and for touring; and Wales for its beaches and visiting friends and relatives. The understanding of foreign cultures was clearly associated with travel outside of Europe and the Mediterranean. The distinctiveness of the destination areas found in the Swansea survey is summarized in Table 5.1.

The summary in Table 5.1 has valuable promotional implications. 'Heritage' tourism, touring and visits to historic sites, towns and villages, had a wide popularity across the destination areas, probably reflecting the social composition of the sub-sample (Herbert *et al.*, 1989). 'Heritage' tourism aside, the destination areas were clearly associated with differing packages of activities, implying a basis for segmentation of the market. Because of the universality of 'heritage' tourism to the sample, a segmentation based on other types of holiday activities is implied.

5.3.3 Predicting Destination Area Choice

Because of the association of certain kinds of holiday activities with particular destination areas, the probability of having

Table 5.1 Distinctiveness of destination areas in Swansea survey

	Main holiday	First additional holiday
Wales	Visit friends or relatives	(Not distinctive)
England	Visit friends or relatives	Visit friends or relatives
Scotland	Touring	(Sample small)
Channel Islands	Beach, swimming pool Touring Dining Sports (excluding winter sports)	(Sample small)
Continental Europe (excl. Mediterranean coast)	(Not distinctive)	(Not distinctive)
Mediterranean	Beach, swimming pool Relaxing in the sunshine Dining Discos etc.	Beach, swimming pool Relaxing in sunshine
Outside Europe	Beach, swimming pool Touring Understanding foreign cultures	(Sample small)

selected a main holiday destination will vary by activity undertaken (Table 5.2). Among the Swansea sample, for example, persons who reported beach or pool activities were four times more
likely to have taken their main holiday in the Mediterranean than
in England. Similarly, for winter sports the probability of having
holidayed in continental Europe is 18 times greater than that of
having holidayed in Scotland, although some caution is implied as
the size of the sample for such activities is small. However, as certain destinations are more popular than others, the probabilities
not only reflect those of particular activities but also the popularity of the destination area in general. For example, despite its
association with touring, Scotland is far from the most likely
destination for persons wishing to tour: such holiday-makers are
much more likely to choose England or the Mediterranean. With
a larger sample the activities could be combined to yield condi-
tional probabilities, if further refinement were desired. For the
present analysis the alternative of selecting 'key' activities as
discriminators will be pursued in the segmentation.

Similar probability matrices may be constructed for other
variables to predict destination area choice. The Swansea and
Manx samples allow the prediction of destination choice by, for
example, age group and by social class. Age was found to be a
weak predictor of destination choice. In particular, older persons
were less likely to holiday in continental Europe or the Mediterranean, but more likely to holiday in England. This is a well
remarked feature of the domestic holiday market, but its cause is
disputed: are elderly persons deterred from air travel because of
its perceived inconvenience or cost, or because a significant proportion follow holidaying habits established before mass air
transport? Social class was also found to be a weak predictor of
holiday destinations; however, it was difficult to find clear
patterns in the effects of social class. This is perhaps surprising,
but may reflect the cheapness of foreign holidays in the 1980s,
which removed the constraint of price for many lower social class
households. Other predictors may also be considered. For example, the length of holiday was found to be a destination predictor,
with the probability of having selected a distant destination
increasing with holiday length. However, this variable may be
interpreted as an effect of holiday destination choice as well as a
cause, and as such is of uncertain value as a predictor. Another,
but weak, predictor in the Manx context was immigrant status,
immigrants to the island tending to have taken more distant
holidays, although England remained the most probable holiday

Table 5.2 Swansea sample: probability of having selected a destination area for a main holiday by activities undertaken on holiday (main destinations and persons having taken a holiday away from home only)

	Wales	England	Scotland	Channel Islands	Continental Europe (excl. Mediterranean coast)	Mediter- ranean	Outside Europe
Beach, swimming pool	0.085	0.091	0.011	0.048	0.219	0.403	0.136
Touring	0.079	0.255	0.059	0.050	0.191	0.198	0.151
Visits to historic sites	No statistically significant differences to overall probability						
Visits to towns, villages	No statistically significant differences to overall probability						
Understanding foreign cultures	0.000	0.000	0.000	0.035	0.325	0.303	0.337
Relaxing in sunshine	0.078	0.138	0.020	0.043	0.213	0.365	0.138
Dining	0.093	0.185	0.030	0.060	0.195	0.298	0.123
Sports	0.103	0.145	0.026	0.077	0.179	0.265	0.162
Clubs, pubs, discos, dancing, bars	0.109	0.175	0.031	0.039	0.157	0.341	0.135
Skiing, winter sports	0.000	0.034	0.034	0.000	0.621	0.069	0.241
Course attended, education, skills learnt	0.304	0.217	0.043	0.043	0.130	0.087	0.174
Visit friends or relatives	0.161	0.444	0.054	0.015	0.107	0.049	0.141
Overall probability	0.101	0.264	0.042	0.039	0.202	0.219	0.118

Probabilities would add across the rows to 1.000 if the Isle of Man and Ireland were shown. These destinations are excluded as the samples were small.
As the samples were small for winter sports and courses attended, these probabilities should be treated with caution. *Source*: Sample survey, 1989.

destination for immigrant and native Manx alike. As this variable is unavailable for the Swansea sample and is not critical to the Manx analysis it is not included in the segmentation developed later in this chapter.

5.3.4 Leisure Activities and the Prediction of Destination Area Choice

At the outset of this chapter the usefulness of being able to predict the choice of holiday destination areas from leisure activities was commented upon. It is unknown which, if any, or to what extent leisure activities outside of holiday making reflect activities during holiday making. The worst scenario from the point of view of prediction is that these two forms of leisure activities are wholly independent of each other. Intuitively this would seem unlikely. The present analysis explored the linkages between leisure and holiday taking by reference both to holidays taken specifically to pursue leisure interests and to the broader context of leisure activities in general. The Swansea and Manx samples appeared much the same in their leisure interests. For example, as is to be expected, the passive leisure activities of watching television, listening to music, reading or visiting friends and relatives were generally popular. However, of greater interest to the present analysis is how far leisure interests are translated into holidays taken specifically to pursue these interests.

Over the lifetimes of the persons interviewed in Swansea and on the Isle of Man sports participation and visiting friends and relatives recurred in importance as leisure activities prompting holiday taking. Sixty per cent of the Swansea sample and just under half of the Manx sample claimed to have taken at least one holiday in their lives to visit friends or relatives, and much the same proportions reported having taken a holiday to play sports. However, the samples diverged in that the leisure activities of secondary importance in prompting holiday taking differed. Despite these divergences, the implications of the importance of leisure activities in prompting holiday taking seemed pervasive, if varied. Most categories of leisure activities were reported as having prompted holiday taking by at least a quarter of those persons reporting the leisure activity. Only making or growing things for the home or family, do-it-yourself or house maintenance, watching television, listening to music, reading and shopping were insignificant determinants of holiday taking. Bearing in mind that leisure activities may change over a respondent's lifetime, the actual effect of leisure activities on holiday choice may in fact be greater than that recorded in the surveys, as only current leisure interests were investigated.

As well as the longer-term importance of leisure activities as prompters of holiday taking, the importance of these activities in the shorter term is of importance to the segmentation objective of the present analysis. The pervasive importance of these activities in terms of holiday-making activities was implied by contingency analyses of main leisure activities and holiday activities. An extensive array of positive and negative relationships was found, but the complexity of the array of relationships identified suggested the lack of any clear-cut means of segmenting holiday-makers in terms of their general leisure activities.

Because of the complexity of the relationships identified, leisure activities look unpromising as simple predictors of holiday activities in general – but do they help us in predicting destination areas? This effect was found to be varied. Persons interested in clubs, discos and the like, for example, were more likely than others to holiday in the Mediterranean, but the effect was not strong for either the Swansea or Manx samples. Of the Swansea sample, persons interested in associations, voluntary groups and the church or chapel were more likely than others to holiday in England; but the same was not true of the equivalent Manx sub-sample. Because of this variation between samples it would seem that leisure activities in general are of little help, at least without other variables, as predictors of destination areas. As such, the segmentation of holiday-makers is best undertaken by holiday activities and not by general leisure activities.

5.4 SEGMENTATION OF HOLIDAY-MAKERS

5.4.1 The Segments Derived

As a consequence of the above discussion the two samples of holiday-makers were differentiated into segments using holiday activity, age and social class variables. The segments are described in Table 5.3. In view of the importance of holiday activities in the prediction of destination areas the segmentation is primarily by these activities, secondly by age group and, if the segments are large enough for further subdivision, by social class. To this end it is necessary to include in the analysis those holiday activities discriminating in terms of destination areas. To include a pertinent range of activities defined as categorical variables a composite measure of activities needs to be produced. The present segmentation uses composite measures to show preferences for an 'active resort holiday' and for a 'less active holiday'. The 'active resort holiday' measure is defined by the number of the following activities respondents had given for their main holiday (or for all holidays in the Manx case): beach, swimming pool; relaxing in sunshine; clubs, discos, dancing, pubs, bars; sports; and skiing, winter sports. A respondent had to have reported at least three of these groups of activities to be categorized as pursuing an active resort-style holiday. The 'less active holiday' measure requires a respondent to have reported beach and pool activities or relaxing in the sunshine, but does not include the more active activities of the former group. The latter measure is intended to identify those persons who are not interested in an active resort holiday but are interested in less active resort activities. A problem concerns touring and heritage tourism: these are less discriminating in terms of destination areas, but at the same time they are the main activities of some holiday-makers. Touring and heritage tourism are therefore used to define residual segments for persons who not only do not want an active resort holiday, but who also do not want a less active beach holiday. It is not that other holiday segments do not necessarily pursue these activities, but rather that the residual segments in the classification do not supplement these activities with active resort or beach tourism.

As a minimum, each segment has at least 20 members of the appropriate sample; most of the Swansea segments are in fact around double this minimum size. Where the segments would have been beneath the minimum threshold size they have been combined. Reference to Table 5.3 shows that the Manx segments vary more in size than those of Swansea. For the Swansea sample 12 segments of sufficient size have been delimited, and for the Isle of Man ten. For each sample one additional segment has been disregarded as too small, and inappropriate for amalgamation to another segment. The overall sizes of the samples of course affect the potential for subdivision, as does the extent of compounding non-responses to individual questions by combining individual criteria into composites.

5.4.2 Segmentation and Prediction

The ultimate test of the usefulness of the present segmentation is its success or otherwise in predicting the destination areas of its 'member' holiday-makers. This is achieved for each of the samples. In Table 5.4 the probabilities of having selected a holi-day destination area are defined for the 12 Swansea segments and the ten Manx segments. For example, of the Swansea sub-sample segments, SWAN02, SWAN05 and SWAN11 are most likely to have taken their main holiday in England; and SWAN04, SWAN07 and SWAN10 most likely to have taken their main holi-day in the Mediterranean. The three Swansea segments most likely to take their holidays in England all report neither an active resort-style holiday nor a less active holiday. The three Swansea

Table 5.3 Swansea and Manx samples: description of market segments of holiday-makers

Segment	Description	Proportion of holiday-taking sub-sample (per cent)
Swansea		
SWAN 01	< 31 years; professional/intermediate; not active resort holiday, not beach holiday	5.3
SWAN 02	< 31 years; clerical/manual; not beach holiday	4.2
SWAN 03	< 31 years; not active resort holiday; beach holiday	8.6
SWAN 04	< 31 years; active resort holiday	6.3
SWAN 05	31–50 years; professional/intermediate; not active resort holiday; not beach holiday	10.3
SWAN 06	31–50 years; professional/intermediate not active resort holiday; beach holiday	13.5
SWAN 07	31–50 years; professional/intermediate; active resort holiday	8.8
SWAN 08	31–50 years; clerical/manual; not active resort holiday; not beach holiday	7.8
SWAN 09	31–50 years; clerical/manual; not active resort holiday; beach holiday	8.4
SWAN 10	31–50 years; clerical/manual; active resort holiday	6.1
SWAN 11	> 50 years; not active resort holiday; not beach holiday	8.6
SWAN 12	> 50 years; not active resort holiday; beach holiday	9.4
SWAN 13	> 50 years; active resort holiday	2.7[a]
Isle of Man		
MANN 01	< 31 years; not active resort holiday	8.5
MANN 02	< 51 years; active resort holiday	8.5

Table 5.3 *continued*

Segment	Description	Proportion of holiday-taking sub-sample (per cent)
MANN 03	31–50 years; professional/intermediate; not active resort holiday; not beach holiday	15.9
MANN 04	31–50 years; professional intermediate; not active resort holiday; beach holiday	4.8
MANN 05	31–50 years; clerical/manual; not active resort holiday; not beach holiday	7.0
MANN 06	31–50 years; clerical/manual; not active resort holiday; beach holiday	6.8
MANN 07	> 50 years; professional/intermediate; not active resort holiday; not beach holiday	19.4
MANN 08	> 50 years; professional/intermediate; not active resort holiday; beach holiday	7.2
MANN 09	> 50 years; clerical/manual; not active resort holiday; not beach holiday	14.8
MANN 10	> 50 years; clerical/manual; beach holiday	6.1
MANN 11	> 50 years; active resort holiday	1.1[a]

[a] Sample too small for further analysis.

Source: Sample survey, 1989.

segments most likely to take their main holidays in the Mediterranean are, in contrast, those reporting active resort-style activities.

The segmentation for the Isle of Man is less discriminating in terms of holidays in England, probably as a result of the location of additional holidays included in the Manx data, as discussed above. Two Manx segments are more likely than not to have holidayed in England, namely MANN05 and MANN03. These two segments contain Manx residents reporting neither active resort-style activities nor less active activities, and in this sense are comparable to the Swansea segments already noted. However, only one group of each set may be paired together in terms

Table 5.4 Swansea and Manx samples: probability of having selected a destination area by market segment (main destinations and persons having taken a holiday away from home or off the island only)

Segment number	Wales	England	Scotland	Ireland	Channel Islands	Continental Europe (excl. Mediterranean Coast)	Mediterranean	Outside Europe
Swansea								
SWAN 01	0.143	0.250	0.071	–	*	0.357	0.036	0.143
SWAN 02	0.136	0.409	0.045	–	*	0.182	0.045	0.182
SWAN 03	0.044	0.111	*	–	0.111	0.289	0.267	0.178
SWAN 04	*	0.091	*	–	0.030	0.121	0.606	0.152
SWAN 05	0.093	0.407	0.074	–	0.037	0.241	0.056	0.093
SWAN 06	0.085	0.127	*	–	0.028	0.310	0.338	0.113
SWAN 07	*	0.087	*	–	0.043	0.087	0.500	0.239
SWAN 08	0.195	0.268	0.171	–	0.024	0.146	0.049	0.049
SWAN 09	0.136	0.205	0.045	–	0.068	0.205	0.227	0.114
SWAN 10	0.219	0.063	0.031	–	0.094	0.125	0.438	0.031
SWAN 11	0.067	0.422	0.067	–	0.044	0.222	0.111	0.067
SWAN 12	0.143	0.143	0.020	–	0.061	0.286	0.286	0.061

Isle of Man

MANN 01	0.043	0.468	0.106	0.106	–	0.170	0.043	0.064
MANN 02	0.020	0.216	0.098	0.039	–	0.137	0.314	0.176
MANN 03	0.063	0.526	0.053	0.053	–	0.063	0.116	0.126
MANN 04	0.034	0.310	0.034	0.034	–	0.310	0.241	0.034
MANN 05	0.055	0.556	0.139	0.167	–	*	0.028	0.055
MANN 06	0.054	0.351	*	0.081	–	0.216	0.135	0.162
MANN 07	0.067	0.466	0.108	0.033	–	0.142	0.067	0.117
MANN 08	0.043	0.304	0.065	*	–	0.130	0.261	0.196
MANN 09	0.096	0.482	0.181	0.048	–	0.060	0.036	0.096
MANN 10	*	0.310	0.103	*	–	0.103	0.276	0.207

Probabilities would add across the rows to 1.000 if all destination areas were included.

Segments form substantial sub-samples of the fuller sub-samples taking holidays as defined by age and social class.

* No respondent in the segment indicated the destination area.

Source: Sample surveys, 1989.

of age and social class characteristics, suggesting that the comparability is not great. Of the Manx segments only one is notably more likely than the others to contain people holidaying in the Mediterranean, MANN02. This is the active resort-style segment for all adults aged under 51 years, and as such is comparable to the Swansea segments SWAN04, SWAN07 and SWAN10 already identified. As this Manx segment is smaller than the comparable Swansea ones, it cannot be further disaggregated without a larger sample. Table 5.4 also shows some other segments that are more likely to holiday in certain destination areas. For example, SWAN01 and MANN04 are disproportionately likely to holiday in continental Europe. These are professional and intermediate segments not reporting an active resort holiday, but there the similarity ends.

The lack of extensive comparability between the segments from the two samples in terms of destination areas suggests the need for attention to regional holiday markets to supplement an aggregative national perspective. Equally, the relatively simple segmentation system used here has drawn out segments distinctive in terms of their destination location, and has thus successfully combined attributes. However, this success does not extend into describing the segments in terms of leisure activities comparable between the two areas of survey. The segments were further analysed in terms of the leisure activities disproportionately reported by respondents classified into the segments. It was clear that the segments identified had different leisure patterns in the two areas of the British Isles. This further frustrates any attempt to take the analysis one stage further, to predict holiday destinations from leisure activities, and in effect further confirms the independence of leisure activities in general and holiday activities as a subset of them.

5.5 CONCLUSIONS AND RESEARCH AGENDA

The present analysis yields no support for the idea that leisure activities may be useful as predictors of holiday activities or destinations. From the two samples of holiday-makers discussed in this paper the opportunity to enhance our predictions of tourist destination area choice by including leisure activities in the basis of prediction would seem to be minimal. Holiday activities (or at least main holiday activities) as a subset of leisure activities would seem in most cases to be independent of leisure activities in general. This has particular implications for the development of activity holidays in the domestic market, for such holidays depend upon linking holidays into more general leisure activities. The present analysis may imply limitations, not previously recognized, to the size of this market for main holidays. The market for such holidays may well be much more limited than the population of participants in the particular activity, through constraints not only of time and money, but also, at least in the case of main holidays, of choice. Analysis of the kind undertaken here needs to be replicated for additional holidays, for which leisure activities may have a greater importance in holiday and destination selection.

In terms of holiday activities the regional destinations of tourists would appear to be strongly segmented. In part, this reflects the success of product development by the major tour companies in Britain during the past three decades, especially in developing holiday products in the Mediterranean. For short- and medium-term planning the failure to include behavioural variables in demand modelling for broad destination regions is acceptable, segmentation now being so strong. However, the present analysis says nothing about destinations and activities within the broad destination areas used. Elasticities of demand are potentially greater for more specific destinations, and behavioural variables may be important in more specific destination demand modelling. Therefore, research is needed into segmentation within the major destination regions, implying much larger samples of holiday-makers than surveyed for this research, to enable more specific analysis.

In the short term, the strength of the relationship between the segmentations of destination areas and of activities when on holiday calls into question strategies to diversify tourism products in response to sudden changes in market conditions. The present analysis has demonstrated a degree of 'natural' segmentation of holiday markets in terms of holiday styles and destination areas. This finding might be thought to be unexceptional. However, the clear distinction in terms of market segments between Mediterranean holidays and holidays in England, shown by both samples, is important. It has implications for the development of heritage tourism in Mediterranean destinations, which are seeking to diversify their holiday products away from resort tourism, and also for the domestic market in Britain, where resorts are trying to regain lost markets by provision of facilities to produce an active resort style holiday of the Mediterranean type. As the markets appear segmented it is arguable that both developments have limited potential, at least in the short term.

The present chapter has also demonstrated the need to investigate regional holiday markets supplying holiday-makers, to take account of the origin regions of tourists, and to base our predictive models on disaggregated regions of tourist supply. In part, the present analysis minimized differences between the two markets studied by standardizing through house tenure profiles the social class profile of the residents interviewed. Regionally, such differences may be important, and would compound the market differences suggested here.

References

Herbert, D.T., Prentice, R.C. and Thomas, C.J. (1989) *Heritage Sites: Strategies for Marketing and Development*. Aldershot: Avebury.

House of Commons (1987) *Committee on Welsh Affairs, First Report Session 1986–87*, Tourism in Wales, House of Commons paper no. 256. London: HMSO.

Prentice, R.C. (1990) The Manxness of Mann: renewed immigration to the Isle of Man and the nationalist response. *Scottish Geographical Magazine*, **106**, 75–88.

Robinson, V. (1990) Social demography. In Robinson, V. and McCarroll, D. (eds) *The Isle of Man. Celebrating a Sense of Place*, pp. 132–59. Liverpool: Liverpool University Press.

Romsa, G.H. (1973) A method of deriving outdoor recreational activity packages. *Journal of Leisure Research*, **5**, 34–46.

Smith, S.L.J. (1989) *Tourism Analysis*. Harlow: Longman.

Tatham, R.L. and Dornoff, R.J. (1971) Market segmentation for outdoor recreation. *Journal of Leisure Research*, **3**, 5–16.

Witt, S.F. and Moutinho, L. (eds) (1989) *Tourism Marketing and Management Handbook*. Hemel Hempstead: Prentice-Hall.

6 Using Conjoint Modelling to Measure Tourist Image and Analyse Ski Resort Choice

Barbara Carmichael

6.1 INTRODUCTION

Product positioning and product planning are important aspects of proactive marketing management for the tourism industry. Without a clear understanding of product image and product appeal to potential consumers, industry is at a disadvantage in an increasingly competitive market. Therefore, research that focuses on the image evaluation of resorts by potential visitors leads to greater marketing effectiveness and is vital to industry success. As Davidson (1985, p. 106) states,

> If we are going to influence a decision, a change in behaviour, we need to know how that decision is made. There must be an increasing focus in the research and planning in our industry (travel and tourism) on how decisions are made. The terrain is in the buyer's mind; not in just who he or she is.

In this chapter, a case study is described in which the focus of interest was consumer decision making and destination choice. The area of study was the tourist image and destination choice conditions for a sample of downhill skiers who were residents of Victoria, British Columbia (BC), Canada and who were in the anticipation stage of planning an overnight skiing holi-day in the 1989–90 ski season. This chapter is organized into three parts:

1 Tourist image and the key attributes used in ski resort measurement will be defined.

2 The preference structure for skiers evaluating hypothetical resort profiles described on those key attributes will be examined using conjoint analysis. This is a method that has been widely used in marketing but rarely applied in tourism studies.

3 The relative contribution of the key attributes to the overall preference for resorts will be discussed and interpreted in terms of marketing management implications for the ski industry.

6.2 TOURIST IMAGE

6.2.1 Definition of Tourist Image

Tourist image has been defined as the expression of 'all objective knowledge, impressions, prejudice, emotional thoughts an individual or group have of a particular object or place' (Lawson and Baud-Bovy, 1977, p. 10). This is a broad definition and not easy to operationalize. Crompton's definition of image is perhaps more measurable: 'An image may be defined as the sum of beliefs, ideas and impressions that a person has of a destination' (Crompton, 1979, p. 18).

Gradually, a potential tourist builds up an image of a destination. The image may be stereotyped and vary greatly from reality but it reflects an individual's personal evaluations and expectations of place. Hunt (1975, p. 1) has stated that 'it seems likely that images perceived by individuals in the travel market may have as much to do with the area's tourist development success as the more tangible recreation and tourist resources.'

To measure a multi-variable concept like image presents a methodological challenge. Aesthetics and qualitative aspects like sense of place defy numerical representation. Measurable quantities are those variables over which management have more quality control, such as variety of slopes, crowding and service. Image, as Crompton states, should be measured on more than one dimension, but what are the salient attributes for skiers in ski resort evaluations? Furthermore, how should these image variables be collected and combined to provide an overall image attractiveness index of a ski resort?

6.2.2 Choice of Key Attributes

For skiers from Victoria, local BC resorts will be those of primary consideration, but how are these resorts perceived and compared? They may be grouped in terms of accessibility into three types: island location, coastal mainland location and interior mainland location. They may vary in physical, social, economic and experiential characteristics. The choice of attributes for inclusion in decision models is an area that requires careful consideration and often qualitative research (focus groups, open-ended exploratory questions, repertory grid analysis). However, for the skier market in BC there is already a good reserve of secondary data sources and on the basis of past studies and content analysis of ski brochures six attributes were chosen for inclusion in this study: (1) variety of runs; (2) snow conditions; (3) lift lines; (4) value for money; (5) staff friendliness; (6) access to home.

All six attributes were described on four levels: excellent, good, average and poor. The number of levels was kept even since it has been found that specifying attributes on differing numbers of levels may have some influence on the importance values obtained within the conjoint method (Wittink *et al.*, 1982).

6.3 CONJOINT ANALYSIS

6.3.1 Definition of Conjoint Analysis

Conjoint analysis was first developed in the field of mathematical psychology by Luce and Tukey (1964) and introduced by Green and Rao (1971) into consumer research. The method allows a researcher to begin with simple rank orders, such as expressed order of preference for a series of vacation packages, and to analyse these choices to determine the weights the individual traveller appears to assign to each quality.

Conjoint measurement has been used in choice situations to provide an index of the relative value of attributes or part worths of attributes in influencing preference. Since revealed preference through choice may be the only reliable observable phenomenon accessible to the researcher, this decompositional approach may have a high degree of validity. Separate part worths are estimated for each level of each attribute. These values represent the relative importance of each attribute and its associated level in terms of its contribution to the overall attractiveness of any particular choice (Smith, 1989).

To predict the attractiveness of a product the combination rule for part worths is most often assumed to be additive (Cattin and Wittink, 1982). In this type of model, preference for an object is assumed to be an additive function of the values (part worths) of its components (attribute levels). This model also assumes a compensatory process for attributes; i.e. respondents will trade off low levels on one attribute for high levels of another.

The conjoint measurement decompositional preference model for i attributes with each attribute defined at M_i levels can be formulated as:

$$U(x) = \sum_{i=1}^{i} \sum_{k=1}^{M_i} V_{ik} X_{ik}$$

where $U(x)$ is an overall utility of preference measure; V_{ik} is the part worth contribution associated with the kth level of the ith attribute; and X_{ik} is the presence or absence of the kth level of the ith attribute (based on Timmermans, 1984, p. 203).

6.3.2 Data Collection for Conjoint Measurement

Data collection in this study followed a full profile approach. This is the most common method of data collection today for conjoint studies (Wittink and Cattin, 1989). One hundred skiers were selected for personal interviews and asked to evaluate 29 cards which showed full concept profiles for hypothetical ski resorts. A minimum of 25 profiles was needed to estimate the main effects of six attributes on four levels. In addition, four cards were evaluated but held out from model development. The choices could be predicted for the four hold-out cards to evaluate the predictive validity of the conjoint model.

The 25 profiles were generated by an OPLAN program of the SPSS *Categories* statistical package so that respondents were presented with an orthogonal fractional factorial design that represented a range of profiles with combinations of attributes at different levels (see Table 6.1). Respondents were asked to sort the cards into three sets to simplify the ranking task (those they would really like to visit, those they would possibly visit, those they had no interest in visiting). The cards were then ranked within each group and an overall ranking was produced for cards 1 to 29.

Respondents had no difficulty with the preliminary sorting of cards into the three sets. They knew which places they liked and

Table 6.1 Card profiles for ski resort ranking task

Variety	Snow	Lift	Value	Staff	Access	Status	Card number
1.00	2.00	1.00	1.00	4.00	1.00	0	1
2.00	2.00	4.00	2.00	1.00	3.00	0	2
1.00	1.00	1.00	1.00	1.00	1.00	0	3
4.00	3.00	1.00	1.00	3.00	3.00	0	4
4.00	1.00	4.00	3.00	4.00	1.00	0	5
3.00	1.00	1.00	1.00	2.00	3.00	0	6
1.00	4.00	3.00	3.00	1.00	3.00	0	7
2.00	1.00	1.00	3.00	3.00	4.00	0	8
1.00	3.00	4.00	4.00	2.00	4.00	0	9
2.00	3.00	3.00	1.00	4.00	2.00	0	10
3.00	3.00	2.00	3.00	1.00	1.00	0	11
1.00	3.00	1.00	2.00	1.00	1.00	0	12
3.00	2.00	3.00	4.00	3.00	1.00	0	13
1.00	1.00	2.00	2.00	3.00	2.00	0	14
4.00	1.00	3.00	2.00	2.00	1.00	0	15
1.00	1.00	2.00	4.00	4.00	3.00	0	16
3.00	4.00	1.00	2.00	4.00	4.00	0	17
1.00	4.00	4.00	1.00	3.00	1.00	0	18
4.00	2.00	2.00	1.00	1.00	4.00	0	19
4.00	4.00	1.00	4.00	1.00	2.00	0	20
3.00	1.00	4.00	1.00	1.00	2.00	0	21
2.00	4.00	2.00	1.00	2.00	1.00	0	22
1.00	1.00	3.00	1.00	1.00	4.00	0	23
1.00	2.00	1.00	3.00	2.00	2.00	0	24
2.00	1.00	1.00	4.00	1.00	1.00	0	25
4.00	4.00	4.00	3.00	4.00	4.00	1	26
3.00	1.00	1.00	4.00	3.00	2.00	1	27
4.00	3.00	3.00	3.00	4.00	2.00	1	28
2.00	4.00	2.00	2.00	3.00	4.00	1	29

Levels: 1.00 = poor; 2.00 = average; 3.00 = good; 4.00 = excellent.

Status: 0 = cards used in model estimation; 1 = hold-out cards.

could easily rank order their best set. However, when asked to rank order the medium and worst packs the task got progressively more difficult and confusing. Some individuals found the task easier than others: for example, older skiers tended to have more difficulties. Respondents who felt that the attributes were similar in importance also took longer and found the ranking more difficult.

In choosing the number of attributes and levels, there was a trade-off to be made between information overload and oversimplification of the factors involved. Green and Shrinivasan (1978) suggested that individuals had difficulty in evaluating more than six attributes at a time because of information overload. For some individuals, six attributes at four levels may have been difficult. The task could have been simplified by reducing the number of levels of each attribute. However, this would have led to poorer description and comparison with actual products.

Instead of ranking the cards, rating is often used since it can provide interval data. However, with 29 resorts, it was felt that ranking offered a more realistic task and that it would be difficult to be consistent on a rating scale. The cards enabled the respondents to make a preliminary sorting and to simplify the task. In future, researchers could experiment with preliminary sorting and then ratings within each group. Ratings do, however, have the problem of routinized responses, which may be difficult to avoid especially towards the end of the task.

Claxton (1987, p. 466) recommended that in parallel with conjoint analysis respondents should be asked to provide a direct ranking of the importance of each attribute. This direct ranking acted as a validity check, when compared with the rankings of overall importance from conjoint analysis. Kendall's coefficient of concordance test found that the two ranking methods produced very similar results.

6.3.3 Data Analysis for Conjoint Measurement

Ordinary least squares, as operationalized in the SPSS *Categories* package, was used to estimate the separate part worths for each level of each attribute. These values represent the relative importance of each attribute and its associated level in terms of its contribution to the overall attractiveness of a particular choice. In this analysis the six attributes varied over similar description levels poor, average, good and excellent (see Tables 6.2 and 6.3).

Strictly speaking, ordinary least squares analysis should use data at the interval or ratio scale. However, simulation studies by Cattin and Wittink (1976) and Carmone *et al.* (1978) have found that ordinary least squares regression applied to integer ranks (the rank ordered dependent variable is defined as a pseudo-interval scaled variable taking values $1, 2, \ldots, n$, depending on the rank given to that stimulus) produces solutions that are very close in terms of predictive validity to those obtained by more expensive non-metric algorithms like Monanova (Green and Shrinivasan, 1978). Least squares estimates for conjoint analysis have become increasingly used over the past five years (Wittink

Table 6.2 Sub-file summary data from conjoint analysis for 88 skiers considering a short ski trip (1–3 days' skiing)

Attribute	Attribute level	Part worth utility	Regression coefficient	Importance
Variety	Variety of runs:			16.65
	poor	1.8035	$B = 1.8035$	
	average	3.6070		
	good	5.4104		
	excellent	7.2139		
Snow	Snow conditions:			33.17
	poor	3.5936	$B = 3.5936$	
	average	7.1872		
	good	10.7801		
	excellent	14.3743		
Lift	Lift lines:			11.55
	poor	1.2510	$B = 1.2510$	
	average	2.5020		
	good	3.7530		
	excellent	5.0040		
Value	Value for money:			13.95
	poor	1.5114	$B = 1.5114$	
	average	3.0227		
	good	4.5341		
	excellent	6.0455		
Staff	Staff friendliness:			4.59
	poor	0.4973	$B = 0.4973$	
	average	0.9947		
	good	1.4920		
	excellent	1.9893		
Access	Access to home:			20.08
	poor	2.1755	$B = 2.1755$	
	average	4.3509		
	good	6.5264		
	excellent	8.7019		
Constant		−10.072		

Pearson's $R = 0.948$, significance $= 0.0000$.
Pearson's $R = 0.950$ for 4 hold-outs, significance $= 0.0248$.

Kendall's tau $= 0.793$, significance $= 0.0000$.
Kendall's tau $= 1.000$ for 4 hold-outs, significance $= 0.0208$.

Table 6.3 Sub-file summary data from conjoint analysis for 82 skiers considering a longer ski trip (4 or more days' skiing)

Attribute	Attribute level	Part worth utility	Regression coefficient	Importance
Variety	Variety of runs:			
	poor	2.2491	$B = 2.2491$	21.15
	average	4.4983		
	good	6.7474		
	excellent	8.9966		
Snow	Snow conditions:			
	poor	3.6304	$B = 3.6304$	34.14
	average	7.2608		
	good	10.8912		
	excellent	14.5217		
Lift	Lift lines:			
	poor	1.3625	$B = 1.3625$	12.81
	average	2.7250		
	good	4.0874		
	excellent	5.4499		
Value	Value for money:			
	poor	1.9984	$B = 1.9984$	18.79
	average	3.9968		
	good	5.9953		
	excellent	7.9937		
Staff	Staff friendliness:			
	poor	0.4073	$B = 0.4073$	3.83
	average	0.8146		
	good	1.2220		
	excellent	1.6293		
Access	Access to home:			
	poor	0.9859	$B = 0.9859$	9.27
	average	1.9717		
	good	2.9576		
	excellent	3.9435		
Constant		−9.6296		

Pearson's $R = 0.948$, significance < 0.0001.
Pearson's $R = 0.933$ for 4 hold-outs, significance $= 0.0335$.

Kendall's tau $= 0.793$, significance $= 0.0000$.
Kendall's tau $= 1.000$ for 4 hold-outs, significance $= 0.0208$.

and Cattin, 1989). The details of the model used to estimate part worths may be generally described by the following equation:

$$V_h \simeq \sum_{i=1}^{6} \sum_{k=1}^{4} V_{ik} X_{ik}^{(h)}$$

where V_h represents the evaluation of profile h ($h = 1, 2, \ldots,$ 25); V_{ik} is the part worth (regression coefficient) associated with level k ($k = 1, 2, 3, 4$) of attribute i ($i = 1, 2, \ldots, 6$); $X_{ik}^{(h)}$ is the variable of level k of attribute i that corresponds to profile h; and $\simeq$ denotes a least squares approximation. The attributes are: variety of runs; snow conditions; lift lines; value of money; staff friendliness; access to home. The levels are: excellent; good; average; poor.

Sets of part worth utilities were estimated on an individual basis and an aggregate basis for two scenarios: the short break (up to three days) and the longer trip (four to seven days). As a linear model was assumed, part worth scores were computed for the lowest level of each attribute and the part worths for other levels were found by multiplying the lowest level by 2, 3 or 4. The sub-file summary data given in Table 6.2 show the group values for all skiers in the sample who evaluated a short trip (88 skiers) and Table 6.3 shows the group values of all skiers who evaluated a long trip (82 skiers). Figures 6.1 and 6.2 show the range of importance of the part worth utilities for these grouped results. As a result of the orthogonal design matrix for the independent variables the computed part worth scores (raw regression coefficients) were all expressed in a common unit. This meant that the part worth scores, representing the contribution of attribute levels to preference data, could be added together to give the total utility or image of a particular combination of attributes within a ski resort profile. In this way predictions were made of skier's evaluations on four hold-out cards (see Tables 6.2 and 6.3). The high Pearson's R values between actual and predicted rankings showed a high goodness of fit for the conjoint models ($R = 0.95$, significance 0.02, for short trips; $R = 0.93$, significance 0.03, for longer trips). Predictions were also made for skiers' evaluations of the image of the actual resorts they were considering in their evoked sets. Data had already been gathered about the skiers' beliefs about such resorts in terms of their rating on the six attributes. For example, a skier who was considering a weekend's skiing at Mount Washington, and who perceived this resort as having average variety of runs, excellent snow conditions, average lift lines, good value for money, excellent staff friendliness and good access to home, had an estimated overall utility or image of Mount Washington of:

$$3.6070 + 14.3743 + 2.5020 + 4.5341 + 1.9893 + 6.5264 = 33.5331$$

6.4 DISCUSSION

Using the aggregate and individual part worth utilities computed from conjoint analysis it was possible to measure and compare tourist images for the resorts that skiers were considering in their evoked sets. In addition, comparisons could be made with image scores developed through other forms of measurement (multi-

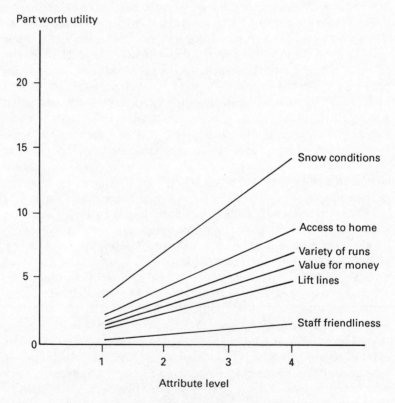

Figure 6.1 Group average part worth functions (1–3 days' skiing).

Part worth utility

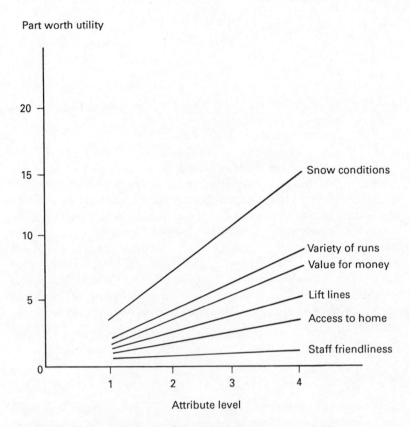

Figure 6.2 Group average part worth functions (4 or more days' skiing).

attribute models, hybrid models). Choice models based on Luce's choice model (Luce, 1959) could also be used to predict the destination choice behaviour of skiers, in comparison with their actual choice decisions. Models of this type are useful in an analytical way as predictive tools but they also give a descriptive indication of processes, i.e. how ideas about a place are combined in a perceptual sense to give a preference value to a tourist destination product.

The overall importance of each attribute in its contribution to preference is shown in Tables 6.2 and 6.3. These importance values were standardized scores. They were found by examining the range in the part worth utilities for each attribute and standardizing the value by dividing by the total range in value for all part worths. This procedure is summarized by:

$$W_i = \frac{\max_k (V_{ik}) - \min_k (V_{ik})}{\sum_{i-1}^{6} \max_k (V_{ik}) - \min_k (V_{ik})}, \text{ for each } i$$

where W_i denotes the relative importance of attribute i ($i = 1, 2, \ldots, 6$) and k is the level of each attribute; and V_{ik} is the part worth utility for attribute i, level k.

Inspection of the data reveals that snow condition is the key variable for skiers in both contexts and much more important than other variables. Using a method like conjoint analysis, which differentiates between attributes to such a fine level, may be preferable to using ranking and rating scales, which assume even intervals between all levels for all importance scales. As 'snow' is such an important variable (to quote one interviewee, 'If it's not snowing, I'm not going') it is worth investigating the introduction of snow-making equipment to exercise more control for this variable. Conjoint analysis is a useful tool in that it suggests areas for product modification and improvement that will best meet skiers' needs.

6.5 CONCLUSION

This chapter has described the potential of conjoint measurement as a way to measure tourist image. The example chosen of skiers from Victoria, BC, showed how the methodology was operationalized within a tourism context. The analysis provided information on the relative importance of attributes that skiers sought in ski destinations. Collection of image data for resorts in this way can form a preliminary step in model building and the prediction of tourist movements. The study could be further extended to an analysis of resort positioning using analysis of variance and multi-dimensional scaling techniques. The challenge facing the skiing industry in British Columbia today is to understand skier needs and effectively to market and position the ski product. This is very important in the increasingly competitive marketing environment as the ski industry matures. It is suggested that consumer perception and behaviour studies, as well as being conceptually challenging, are vitally needed areas of tourism research in the 1990s. Conjoint analysis offers a sound methodological tool for meeting this challenge in future research applications.

References

Carmone, F.J., Green, P.E. and Jain, A.K. (1978) The robustness of conjoint analysis: some Monte Carlo results. *Journal of Marketing Research*, **15**, 300–3.

Cattin, P. and Wittink, D.R. (1976) A Monte Carlo study of metric and non metric estimation methods for multi attribute models. Research Paper No. 341, Graduate School of Business, Stanford University.

Cattin, P. and Wittink, D.R. (1982) Commercial use of conjoint analysis: a survey. *Journal of Marketing*, **46**, 44–53.

Claxton, J.D. (1987) Conjoint analysis in travel research: a manager's guide. In Ritchie, J.R.B. and Goeldner, C.R. (eds) *Travel Tourism and Hospitality Research*, pp. 459–69. New York: John Wiley & Sons.

Crompton, J.L. (1979) An assessment of the image of Mexico as a vacation destination and the influence of geographic location upon that image. *Journal of Travel Research*, **17**(4), 18–23.

Davidson, T.L. (1985) Strategic planning: a competitive necessity. In Travel and Tourism Research Association, *The Battle for Market Share: Strategies in Research and Marketing*, pp. 103–8. Salt Lake City: Graduate School of Business, University of Utah.

Green, P.E. and Rao, V. (1971) Conjoint measurement for quantifying judgemental data. *Journal of Marketing Research*, **8**, 355–63.

Green, P.E. and Shrinivasan, V. (1978) Conjoint analysis in consumer research issues and outlook. *Journal of Consumer Research*, **5**, 103–23.

Hunt, J.D. (1975) Image as a factor in tourism development. *Journal of Travel Research*, **18**(3), 1–7.

Lawson, F. and Baud-Bovy, M. (1977) *Tourism and Recreation Development*. London: Architectural Press.

Luce, R.D. (1959) *Individual Choice Behaviour*. New York: John Wiley & Sons.

Luce, R.D. and Tukey, J.W. (1964) Simultaneous conjoint measurement: a new type of fundamental measurement. *Journal of Mathematical Psychology*, **1**, 1–27.

Smith, S.L.J. (1989) *Tourism Analysis: A Handbook*. Harlow: Longman.

Timmermans, H. (1984) Decompositional multi-attribute preference models in spatial choice analysis: a review of some recent developments. *Progress in Human Geography*, **8**(2), 189–221.

Wittink, D.R. and Cattin, P. (1989) Commercial use of conjoint analysis: an update. *Journal of Marketing*, **53**, 91–6.

Wittink, D.R., Krisharmurthi, L. and Nutter, J.B. (1982) Comparing derived importance weights across attributes. *Journal of Consumer Research*, **8**, 471–4.

7 Conviviality – A Source of Satisfaction for Hotel Guests? An Application of the Servqual Model

Farouk Saleh and Chris Ryan

7.1 INTRODUCTION

One of the conventional distinguishing features between the marketing of services and the marketing of products has been the notion that the provider and user of the service are in close proximity (Booms and Nyquist, 1981). An implication of this relationship is that consumer satisfaction is, at least in part, determined by the consumers' perceptions of the service and attention they receive from the representative of the service company with whom they are dealing. Bitner *et al.* (1990) refer to a critical incident in the sequence of events that make up the service. These events are categorized as being employee response to service delivery system failures, employee response to customer needs and requests, and finally unprompted and unsolicited employee actions. For each of these categories there may be a positive or negative experience.

The critical incident occurs within a context of expected service and within a physical space, both of which aim to achieve a desired end. In short, the critical incident may reinforce and occasionally change the existence of a positive or negative gap between that which is expected and that which is delivered. Laws (1986, 1990) argues that it is the direction of this consumerist gap that is the determinant of satisfaction. On the other hand, the Servqual model proposed by Parasuraman *et al.* (1988) is based on the notion that this is but one of a number of potential gaps, and

that others, as noted below, have to be taken into account.
This chapter seeks to:

- review briefly some of the issues relating to service provision, and to do so with specific reference to hotels;
- utilize the gaps envisaged by the Servqual model as a means of measuring client satisfaction;
- assess the relative contribution of each of the gaps to client satisfaction;
- report and comment upon findings of a study undertaken by the authors using the Servqual model approach.

7.2 REVIEW OF THE ISSUES

Services have generally been characterized as being intangible, heterogeneous, susceptible to decay in the sense that they cannot be stocked and requiring the presence of the supplier (Zeithaml *et al.*, 1985). Such lists have as their purpose a distinction between services and products, with the implication that the nature of the marketing task differs between the two. In practice, it is sometimes difficult to distinguish the difference. Marketing personnel will use geo-demographic and psychographic databases to identify potential customers for both services, such as holidays, and products, such as water softeners. The problem of devising advertising schedules to optimize the reach and frequency of viewing is possibly independent of whether it is a product or a service that is being sold. Fast-moving consumer goods (FMCG) products are advertised in such a way as to generate added values that confirm a sense of well-being or status for the user, in the same way as services such as debit cards. None the less, the characteristics of services as generally listed do prove useful in beginning an analysis of the consumer's experience of use, and hence of the potential sources of satisfaction or dissatisfaction.

From a general viewpoint, the components of a service may be divided into three. Gronroos (1978) describes these variables as being of a technical, functional or image creation nature. Lehtinen and Lehtinen (1982) propose a similar classification into physical, interactive and corporate qualities. With reference to a hotel, its physical or technical features would include the tangibles of reception area, bedrooms, restaurants, etc., while the functional, interactive processes relate to the expressive performance or usage of the tangibles. Courtesy, promptness of attention and empathy are features identified by Lewis and Klein (1987) as being, arguably, the core of the interactive process. Any image that clients possess of a hotel will be determined by a mix of marketing messages to which they have been exposed, the tangible components they view, the interactions they have experienced with staff and the degree of familiarity they have with a specific hotel, chain of hotels or competitors. In short, the factors identified by Lehtinen and Lehtinen (1982) and Gronroos (1978) are not independent variables, but are interacting variables that define a dynamic process.

The nature of this dynamic process is illustrated by the concept of the critical incident. Bitner *et al.* (1990) indicate how failure of components of the technical process of the service can be offset by corrective action by representatives of the service provider. Rapid and courteous action can generate customer satisfaction, overcome the potential dissatisfaction caused by service failure and perhaps even enhance corporate image. Laws (1990), in his analysis of airline service, also refers to the importance of management blueprints indicating structured reactions designed for quick response to customer needs in the event of technical failure. In such situations, the quality of the interaction between customer and the representative of the service provider is of paramount importance. This interaction should comprise at least three components: corrective action, information to the customer and a correct form of personal approach. The expressive performance of the action is not, of course, important only in cases of technical failure. As referred to above, for many authors it is the key distinguishing feature between products and services. Consequently it is pertinent to examine the nature of this expressive service or interaction between client and provider. Parasuraman *et al.* (1985) identified ten components. Briefly, these are reliability, responsiveness, competence, courtesy, communication, credibility, security, knowledge and understanding of the customer and his or her needs, and finally tangibles representing the physical evidence of service. A tangible might be the appearance of staff. Subsequently, in 1988, the same authors tested these variables and reduced them to five factors: tangibles, reliability, responsiveness, assurance and empathy.

Martin (1986) introduced another viewpoint when adopting a systems approach. In the interaction between guest and service provider there exists a procedural element. There are a number of functions that need to be performed. For example, in the hotel there is the registration of guests, completing the formalities, directing them to their room and so on through to the departure of the client. Secondly, there is the manner in which the procedures are carried out – the conviviality that attends the procedure.

7.3 THE DESIGN OF THE RESEARCH

We sought to integrate much of the above into our research design, which attempted to measure customer satisfaction generated by a stay in a hotel. Reviewing specific literature relating to service quality in hotels generated a list of factors that had been identified as being of importance in determining customer satisfaction. Lewis and Pizam (1981), Lewis (1983a, b), Lewis and Klein (1987), Nightingale (1985) and Cadotte and Turgeon (1988) were among the authors referred to and a list of 37 items was identified. Indicative of the listing were factors such as actual price, price–value relationships, the prestige of the hotel, its location, safety, decor, the comfort of the beds, aesthetics, the quality of its food, the availability of additional facilities such as sauna, swimming pool, exercise equipment and valet parking, staff friendliness and professionalism. Of the 37 items, 28 related to physical characteristics, two to price, two to intangibles such as reputation and prestige, and only three to the actual performance of the staff from the viewpoint of their empathic and convivial skills. It is recognized that this process of classification is 'fuzzy' and the literature search incomplete, but it was striking just how few of the variables being identified were explicitly concerned with either procedures or the means in which procedures were being carried out. From the perspective of the importance of the expressive component of services as described above, or the stance of multi-attribute attitudinal theory (Ajzen, 1988), whereby varying degrees of affective evaluation would be attached to the different variables, it was thought important that the expressive component should be measured.

In addition, the performance of the service occurs within a context not only of a physical environment, but of an environment that is managed. It is therefore possible that a service may be carefully conceived and performed, yet fail to generate client satisfaction because the managers or entrepreneurs have failed to assess correctly the needs of the customer. In another situation, management may correctly identify customer needs, but incorrectly perceive the ability of staff to implement the specifications.

Lewis and Klein (1987) illustrated this process when they found that management tended to overestimate the level of service required by customers, but in doing so underestimated the importance of some individual factors, such as the need for quietness and staff friendliness. Parasuraman *et al.* (1988) comment:

> In essence, service firms' executives may not understand: (1) what features connote high quality to consumers in advance, (2) what features a service must have in order to meet customer needs, and (3) what levels of performance on those features are needed to deliver high quality service.

In short, while it is hypothesized that the nature of the interaction between client and the representative of the service provider does indeed generate critical incidents that determine satisfaction, such incidents occur within a context that is managed. Thus Boden (1990) comments that within the context of 'Cadbury World' it was deemed important that staff sought to speak to every visitor and so generate a 'golden moment'; this policy arose from an identification of higher than expected levels of dissatisfaction from the tourist visit.

From this perspective, the gap analysis suggested by Laws (1986), Parasuraman *et al.* (1988), Swartz and Brown (1989) and others provide the model to be followed. The gaps that the researchers sought to measure were:

1 Management perception of guest expectation versus guest expectation.
2 Guest expectation versus guest perception of service delivery.
3 Management perception of service delivery versus guest perception of service delivery.
4 Management perception of service delivery versus guest expectation.
5 Management perception of guest expectation versus management perception of service delivery.

In measuring such gaps, Swartz and Brown (1990) identified in the field of medical services three main sets of variables: competence, credibility and communication skills. Martin (1986) used a 40-item scale that covered tangibles, competence and interaction. The Servqual model utilized a 22-item, seven-point Likert scale and assessed responses in terms of the gaps identified above and the factors of tangibles, reliability, responsiveness, assurance and empathy. We thus sought to measure the five factors of the Servqual model and the gaps identified above, but to do so with variables specific to hotels. The resultant questionnaire was a 33-item, five-point Likert scale (the items are identified in Appendix 7.1). It comprised three sections. The first asked about expectations of service, the second about perceptions of quality, and the final section sought demographic information and data relating to length of stay and hotel usage rates. The items on the first and second sections of the questionnaire remained constant. The five-point scale ranged from 1 as the most positive response to 5 as the least satisfactory.

The sample consisted of 17 managers and 200 guests staying at a major hotel in a large western Canadian city. The levels of management ranged from supervisory level to chief executive and covered the functions of reception, catering, house-keeping, personnel and general administration, including accounting functions. As the hotel catered for business users, the sample of guests was characterized by above average earnings and qualifications. Forty-two per cent earned in excess of C$50 000 and approximately 60 per cent had university or postgraduate qualifications; 60 per cent were male; 42 per cent were staying for three or more nights, the remainder for less than three. The high percentage of long stays was because of conference business. The interviews were conducted in the late summer and early autumn, primarily in the evenings and over approximately a three-week period.

7.4 THE RESULTS

The first step was to assess the reliability of the data. Alpha coefficients were calculated as indicated in Appendix 7.2. As perhaps is the norm, the scores were high, over 0.8 generally. However, a difficulty became apparent in the guest sample in that the two factors of tangibles and reliability scored lower than anticipated (0.43 and 0.54 respectively). The reasons for this are discussed below, but when the items were merged the alpha coefficient became 0.7442. Another check was to utilize an item to dimension correlation. As might be expected from the respective sample sizes, the scores for the management sample held up well, whereas for two of the dimensions for the guests sample the results were low. Again this will be discussed below. However, in terms of analysing the gaps, the data did permit t tests to be used.

Appendix 7.1 shows the item-by-item gaps, and it can easily be seen that many of the gaps were at statistically significant levels. A summary of the results by the different dimensions is given in Table 7.1. The first brief comment to make is that guest perception of service quality was that it was moderately good, at 2.08 on the five-point scale. None the less, the dimension did indicate significant differences between the dimensions. Satisfaction was highest with the tangible components of the service, but lowest with the empathic and responsiveness elements. This would seem to confirm a general consensus of many commentators (Bateson, 1989) that the easiest management problems within services marketing relate to the tangible components, but the training, monitoring and evaluation of staff are more difficult.

The study supports the findings of Lewis and Klein (1987) in that there is a tendency for management to overestimate the expectations of guests, although there are many areas where the differences are not significant. Of the 33 separate items, management significantly overestimated guest expectation on 14, but with no significant difference on the remaining variables. What is interesting is that there was no pattern as to which variables management significantly overstated guest expectation on – as can be seen in Appendix 7.1 the items are not clustered into any one dimension.

Equally, the gap between consumer expectation and consumer perception of the quality of the service was relatively consistent across all the items, and naturally raises the question of why it is that, if management has a tendency to overestimate guest expectations, the actual quality of the service tendered fails to meet those expectations. Attention must therefore be paid to the service performance, and the specific question to be asked is whether or not management and guests are perceiving the same performance of service in different ways.

Lewis and Klein (1987) reported that on 29 of 44 functions, management maintained the stance that service delivery was good, while the guests responded with lower scores. This study reports a tendency in the same direction, in that of the 33 items, management scored 15 items higher than guests. But on the remaining factors, guests score service delivery higher than management. Again, there is no consistency across the dimensions, and on a dimension analysis the negative and positive gaps have a tendency to cancel each other out with the result, as shown in Table 7.1, that there is congruence between management and

Table 7.1 Gap analysis relating to client usage of hotels

	Tangibles	Reliability	Responsiveness	Assurance	Empathy
Gap 1: management perception of guest expectation versus guest expectation					
Management	1.349	1.240	1.465	1.403	1.452
Guest	1.450	1.418	1.774	1.623	1.817
Difference	−0.101	−0.178	−0.309	−0.220	−0.365
Significance	n.s.	0.10	0.01	0.05	0.01
Gap 2: guest expectation versus guest perception					
Expectation	1.450	1.418	1.774	1.623	1.817
Perception	1.768	2.118	2.278	1.971	2.272
Difference	−0.318	−0.700	−0.504	−0.348	−0.455
Significance	0.01	0.01	0.10	0.10	0.01
Gap 3: management perception of service delivery versus guest perception of service delivery					
Management	2.135	2.056	2.194	2.118	2.183
Guest	1.768	2.118	2.278	1.971	2.272
Difference	0.367	−0.062	−0.084	0.147	−0.089
Significance	0.01	n.s.	n.s.	n.s.	n.s.
Gap 4: management perception of service delivery versus guest expectation					
Management	2.135	2.056	2.194	2.118	2.183
Guest	1.450	1.418	1.774	1.623	1.817
Difference	0.685	0.838	0.420	0.495	0.365
Significance	0.01	0.01	0.01	0.01	0.01
Gap 5: management perception of guest expectation (a) versus management perception of service delivery (b)					
(a)	1.349	1.240	1.465	1.403	1.452
(b)	2.135	2.056	2.194	2.118	2.183
Difference	−0.786	−0.816	−0.729	−0.715	−0.731
Significance	0.01	0.01	0.01	0.01	0.01

guests. If there is agreement between management and guest perceptions of actual service delivery, but guests' expectations are not being met, then logically there would be a gap between management perception of the services and guests' expectations. This proves to be the case. Similarly, if management tend to overestimate guest expectations, but approximately shares guests' perceptions of services, then further gaps should emerge, and these are evident in Table 7.1.

7.5 DISCUSSION OF THE RESULTS

To summarize the above discussion, it can be argued that management overestimates guests' expectations, guests record their perceptions of service being below their expectations, and both management and guests share the same perceptions of service delivery. The implication of this is that management is involved in a process of condoning the provision of a service that is thought not to meet client needs. One possible explanation may be that management has to seek a series of second best solutions within the resource constraints that exist. The perception of guests' needs becomes the optimal target, the provision of a service that 'satisfies' exemplifying a process of target satisficing. The gap between guest expectation and guest perception of actual service might be part of the same process. Expectation might be partially based on a marketing message that is itself a representation of an ideal, while the actual experience is based on degrees of tolerance of service that is satisfactory, but that does not quite meet expectation.

This approach might indicate some problems in assessing levels of customer satisfaction. If customer tolerance of some deviation from expectation exists, and thus a level of service less than the ideal does not generate dissatisfaction, this implies that the boundary between that which is acceptable and that which is not is 'fuzzy'. It further implies that the analysis of client satisfaction has to be conducted in terms of what Laws (1990) has defined as 'the just noticeable difference'. There is evidence that 'the just noticeable difference' is a factor not only of past consumer experience, but also of structural components within the service delivery process. Outside the hotel industry, Quelch and Ash (1981) suggest that in cases where the service provider possesses high degrees of expert knowledge clients may be intimidated, may not possess sufficient knowledge to be aware of poor service or may have poor sets of reference within which to assess quality. Such factors are unlikely to apply to hotel users, particularly of the sort involved in the current sample. None the less, there was weak evidence to suggest that one structural component could increase levels of dissatisfaction. This was the size of the group. At levels of $P = 0.1$ (i.e. not particularly significant) it was found that guests who were part of larger groups were more likely to score perceived service levels slightly lower. It is hypothesized that the availability of someone within a party to confirm a perceived fault might set up a process of reinforcement.

A further factor that may be operating is a process akin to threshold effects. The presence of certain factors may be insufficient to raise levels of satisfaction because the client is habituated to them, or expects them. On the other hand, the very absence of those factors is quickly noticed by hotel guests. Equally, on the other hand, the performance of staff that is significantly above expectation, i.e. a level that is 'noticeable', becomes a significant determinant of satisfaction.

In this respect, the nature of the critical incident again plays an important role in the provision of hotel services. Bitner *et al.* (1990) report that of a total of 180 incidents they recorded in hotels, 38 per cent fell into the category of unprompted and unsolicited employee actions. These were situations where staff actions unrelated to technical failures or responses to specific client needs made a significant impact. This study also provides some evidence for the importance of the staff–client interaction. The responses to the 33 items were subjected to factor analysis, initially with the intention of confirming the five dimensions that prompted the structure of the questionnaire. Five factors did emerge with eigenvalues greater than 1, but the results were unexpected. While five factors explained 78.6 per cent of the variance, one factor alone accounted for 62.8 per cent. With heavy weighting from items such as trustworthiness, being polite, showing enthusiasm, being helpful even while busy, being reassuring and possessing good communication skills, this factor was entitled 'conviviality'.

Such a finding was both interesting and disturbing. It was disturbing in the sense that it called into question the five dimensions within which the questions had been initially categorized. A review of Appendix 7.1 will indicate that the distinctions are fine. One of the starting points of the study had been the acceptance of the point that client–service provider interaction was a key factor distinguishing between services and goods. Another influential factor was the work of Martin (1986) and Parasuraman *et al.* (1985), in that we wished to concentrate on service performance from the viewpoint of the expressive components of the hospitality industry. Hence, from this perspective the tangibles included not only the possession of up-to-date equipment, but also the tangible signs of service, such as staff being well dressed and being in uniform. In discussion with hotel management, in both the sample hotel and others, the distinctions were supported. However, the distinctions and definitions made by the researchers and management are not necessarily those made by clients. Equally, it can be contended that clients might utilize more holistic modes of assessment than is represented by this approach.

7.6 CONCLUSIONS

Nightingale (1985) comments that it is important for hotels to attempt to obtain periodic feedback from customers. However, in the conventional approach of using room questionnaires 'the response rate is generally low and probably unrepresentative' (Nightingale, 1985, p. 19). It can be further contended that such questionnaires tend to emphasize physical attributes of the hotels, but a more important determinant of satisfaction is the expressive performance of procedures and the quality of interaction between staff and guests. What emerges positively from this study is that gap analysis relating to such considerations generates a means of analysing the situation and generates data for management.

What also emerges from this study is not so much hypothesis testing, but a process of thesis creation. We have subsequently conducted research utilizing a multi-attribute approach, as it would seem that not all factors are of equal importance (Saleh and Ryan, 1991a, b). The relationship between guests' holistic assessments and attitudes towards components of hotel service has yet to be fully assessed. An important factor in the gap analysis has also to be researched: the perception not simply of management and guests, but also of employees. A methodological problem of asking respondents to state expectations even while they use the services and have experiences of them is obviously one that requires thought. Experience of the research would certainly support Foxall's (1990, p. 169) comment that

A comprehensive plurality of paradigms is inescapable if authentic understanding of consumer behaviour is preferable to the doctrinaire parochialism that would follow the domination of consumer research by one ontology and associated methodology.

Even with this important caveat, the findings support the contention that gap analysis oriented towards expressive performance is of help in understanding determinants of consumer satisfaction within services generally, and the hotel industry in particular.

Note

The following acknowledgements are made. For use of Appendices 7.1 and 7.2, *Service Industries Journal*, volume 11, number 3 (1991) to Frank Cass Ltd, London; and, for help in gathering data, to Wendy Welte and Gerard Merkovsky, College of Commerce, University of Saskatchewan.

References

Ajzen, I. (1988) *Attitudes, Personality and Behaviour*. Milton Keynes: Open University.

Bateson, J.E.G. (1989) *Managing Services Marketing*. Orlando, FL: Dryden Press.

Bitner, M.J., Booms, B.H. and Tetreault, M.S. (1990) The service encounter: diagnosing favorable and unfavorable incidents. *Journal of Marketing*, **54**, 71–84.

Boden, A. (1990) Requirements of quality service. Seminar paper, Centre for Urban and Rural Studies, University of Birmingham, 26 November.

Booms, B.H. and Nyquist, J. (1981) Analyzing the customer/firm communication component of the service marketing mix. In Donnelly, J.H. and George, W.R. (eds), *Marketing of Services*, pp. 172–7. Chicago: American Marketing.

Cadotte, E.R and Turgeon, N. (1988) Key factors in guest satisfaction. *Cornell Hotel and Restaurant Administration Quarterly*, **28**(4), 44–51.

Foxall, G. (1990) *Consumer Psychology in Behaviourial Perspective*. London: Routledge.

Gronroos, C. (1978) A service-oriented approach to the marketing of services. *European Journal of Marketing*, **12**(8), 588–601.

Laws, E. (1986) Identifying and managing the consumerist gap. *Service Industries Journal*, **6**(2), 131–43.

Laws, E. (1990) Effectiveness of airline responses to passengers during service interruptions – a consumerist gap analysis. Conference Paper, Tourism Research into the 1990s, Durham University.

Lehtinen, U. and Lehtinen, J.R. (1982) Service quality: a study of quality dimensions. Unpublished working paper. Helsinki: Service Management Institute. (Quoted by Swartz, T.A. and Brown, S.W. (1989) Consumer and provider expectations and experiences in evaluating professional service quality. *Journal of the Academy of Marketing Science*, **17**(2), 189–95.)

Lewis, R.C. (1983a) When guests complain. *Cornell Hotel and Restaurant Administration Quarterly*, **24**(2), 23–32.

Lewis, R.C. (1983b) Getting the most from marketing research. *Cornell Hotel and Restaurant Administration Quarterly*, **24**(3), 81–5.

Lewis, R.C. and Klein, D.M. (1987) The measurement of gaps in service quality. In Czepiel, J.A., Congram, C.A. and Shanahan, J. (eds) *The Services Challenge, Integrating for Competitive Advantage*, pp. 33–8. Chicago: American Marketing Association.

Lewis, R.C. and Pizam, A. (1981) Guest surveys – a missing opportunity. *Cornell Hotel and Restaurant Administration Quarterly*, **22**(3), 37–44.

Martin, W.B. (1986) *Quality Service: The Restaurant Manager's Bible*. New York: Brodock Press, Cornell University.

Nightingale, M. (1985) The hospitality industry: defining quality for a quality assurance programme – a study of perceptions. *Service Industries Journal* **5**(1), 9–22.

Parasuraman, A., Zeithaml, V.A. and Berry, L. (1985) A conceptual model of service quality and its implications for future research. *Journal of Marketing*, **49**(4), 41–50.

Parasuraman, A., Zeithaml, V.A. and Berry, L. (1988) SERVQUAL: a multiple-item scale for measuring consumer perceptions of service quality. *Journal of Retailing*, **64**(1), 12–37.

Quelch, J.A. and Ash, S.B. (1981) Consumer satisfaction with professional services. In Donnelly, J.H. and George, W.R. (eds) *Marketing of Services*, pp. 82–5. Chicago: American Marketing Association.

Saleh, F. and Ryan, C. (1991a) Analysing service quality in the hospitality industry using the Servqual model. *Service Industries Journal*, **11**(3), 352–73.

Saleh, F. and Ryan, C. (1991b) Client choice of hotels – a multi-attribute model. Paper presented at New Horizons in Tourism and Hospitality Education, Training and Research Conference, Calgary, 2–5 July.

Swartz, T.A. and Brown, S.W. (1989) Consumer and provider expectations and experiences in evaluating professional service quality. *Journal of the Academy of Marketing Science*, **17**(2), 189–95.

Zeithaml, V.A., Parasuraman, A. and Berry, L. (1985) Problems and strategies in services marketing. *Journal of Marketing*, **49**, 33–46.

Appendix 7.1 *T* test significant levels and mean differences of service attribute gaps

		Service attribute	A	B	C	D	1 AD	5 CD	6 BC	7 BD	8 AB
1.	T.	Well dressed and neat	1.50	1.94	1.59	1.36		*	**	*	**
2.	T.	Have up-to-date equipment	1.17	2.23	1.74	1.53	*	*	*	*	*
3.	R.	Sympathetic/reassuring	1.22	1.33	2.26	1.42		*		*	*
4.	T.	Exhibit good manners	1.44	2.56	1.72	1.26		*	*	*	*
5.	T.	Show enthusiasm at work	1.16	2.17	1.94	1.56	*	*		*	*
6.	T.	Smile at work	1.50	2.17	1.84	1.57		*	***	*	*
7.	T.	Avoid chewing gum	1.11	1.94	1.89	1.61	**	*			*
8.	Q.	Helpful even while busy	1.17	2.00	2.19	1.83	*	*			*
9.	T.	Not offensive/sarcastic	1.17	2.28	1.68	1.22		*	*	*	*
10.	R.	Dependable	1.39	1.83	1.86	1.42		*		*	**
11.	Q.	Inform about service	1.67	2.11	2.38	1.73		*		**	**
12.	R.	Service when promised	1.28	2.17	2.13	1.39		*		*	*
13.	Q.	Check guest satisfaction	1.50	2.33	2.35	1.98	**	*		***	*
14.	Q.	Greet guests ASAP	1.44	2.00	2.18	1.88	**	*		*	**
15.	Q.	Prompt service	1.44	2.22	2.02	1.51		*		*	*
16.	Q.	Solve complaints	1.11	2.17	2.36	1.57		*		*	*
17.	Q.	Cater services to guests	1.56	2.11	2.15	1.70		*		*	**
18.	Q.	Inform about activities	1.72	2.33	2.64	1.96		*		**	**
19.	A.	Trustworthy	1.39	1.83	1.94	1.33		*		*	**
20.	A.	Polite to guests	1.28	1.72	1.64	1.29		*		*	**
21.	A.	Communicate with guests	1.28	1.67	1.77	1.55		*			**
22.	A.	Kind and cordial tone	1.50	1.67	1.67	1.54		*			
23.	A.	Advise undecided guests	1.89	2.44	2.55	2.05		*		**	**
24.	E.	Individual attention	1.28	2.56	2.14	1.90	*	*	**	*	*
25.	A.	Knowledgeable	1.22	2.06	2.21	1.79	*	*			*
26.	E.	Anticipate guests' needs	1.39	3.00	2.39	2.05	*	*	*	*	*
27.	E.	Conscientious	1.50	2.28	1.97	1.61		*	***	*	*
28.	E.	Respect guests	1.44	2.33	1.87	1.43		*	*	*	*
29.	A.	Don't narrate problems	1.44	2.22	1.88	1.63		*	***	*	*
30.	A.	Communicate with staff	1.33	2.00	2.12	1.80	*	*			*
31.	E.	Serve individual needs	1.50	2.17	2.30	2.00	*	*			**
32.	E.	Address guests by name	1.67	2.44	2.86	2.47	*	*	***		**
33.	E.	Individual attention	1.28	1.94	2.43	1.65	*	*	**	**	*

T, tangibles; R, reliability; Q, responsiveness; A, assurance; E, empathy.

[a] Attribute means on a scale of 1 (high) to 5 (low): A, management's perceptions of guest expectations; B, management's perceptions of hotel service delivery; C, guest's perceived service; D, guest expectations.

[b] Gaps: 1, between A and D; 5, between C and D; 6, between B and C; 7, between B and D; 8 between A and B. Two-tail *t* test probabilities: * 0.01, ** 0.05, *** 0.10.

Appendix 7.2 Test results of surveys' internal reliability

Management responses (sample size = 18)

Dimension	Number of items	Item-to-total correlations	Alpha coefficient
Tangibles	7	0.3736	0.7342
		0.6347	
		0.5921	
		0.4249	
		0.6442	
		0.7358	
		0.4335	
Reliability	3	0.6289	0.5028
		0.6926	
		0.7345	
Responsiveness	8	0.5855	0.7545
		0.6980	
		0.5788	
		0.3666	
		0.5770	
		0.5451	
		0.5741	
		0.4617	

Guest responses (sample size = 200)

Dimension	Number of items	Item-to-total correlations	Alpha coefficient
Tangibles and reliability[a]	10	0.4852	0.7442
		0.3872	
		0.4718	
		0.5165	
		0.5244	
		0.4891	
		0.4314	
		0.4830	
		0.5145	
		0.5280	
Responsiveness	8	0.5326	0.9279
		0.5060	
		0.5761	
		0.4176	
		0.6021	
		0.4825	
		0.5591	
		0.5042	

Appendix 7.2 *continued*

Management responses (sample size = 18)

Dimension	Number of items	Item-to-total correlations	Alpha coefficient
Assurance	8	0.6235	0.7950
		0.8391	
		0.7429	
		0.5364	
		0.7612	
		0.6022	
		0.6236	
		0.4781	
Empathy	7	0.6378	0.7901
		0.7410	
		0.7596	
		0.5873	
		0.6724	
		0.5776	
		0.7149	
Total Test	33		0.7415

Guest responses (sample size = 200)

Dimension	Number of items	Item-to-total correlations	Alpha coefficient
Assurance	8	0.3759	0.8709
		0.5097	
		0.5539	
		0.5072	
		0.3735	
		0.4534	
		0.4406	
		0.3611	
Empathy[b]	6	0.4685	0.8565
		0.5944	
		0.3201	
		0.3690	
		0.4595	
		0.4380	
Total Test	32		0.7700

[a] Tangibles and reliability were statistically combined to improve reliability.
[b] Question 32 was removed in order to improve the accuracy of the Empathy dimension.

8 Price Competitiveness and Inclusive Tour Holidays in European Cities

Ann Clewer, Alan Pack and M. Thea Sinclair

8.1 INTRODUCTION

The nature of holiday choice has altered considerably during recent decades as large numbers of tourists have chosen to purchase inclusive tour 'package' holidays. Past attention has tended to focus on mass tourism involving inclusive tour (IT) holidays consumed in coastal areas (Gaviria *et al.*, 1974; Barke and France, 1986). However, consumers also purchase IT holidays in cities, and many local councils have become aware of the increasing purchasing power of both domestic and international tourists. This chapter will focus on city tourism and examine the competitiveness of IT holidays in London and Paris, available for consumption by tourists from the UK, France, Germany and Spain.

The demand for IT holidays depends upon, *inter alia*, the 'bundles' of characteristics of which the holidays consist, including the standard of accommodation and type of board. The characteristics of the IT city holidays are examined in the following section of this chapter. Comparison of the characteristics of the holidays purchased by tourists and supplied by tour operators from different European origins permits identification of the ways in which the holiday characteristics vary according to the individual tour operator selling the holiday, the different nationalities of the tour operators and the destinations where the holidays are provided. The mean unstandardized prices of IT holidays sold by different tour operators in different destinations are also compared. The subsequent section sets out the hedonic price model, which is used to compare the competitiveness of IT city holidays. The results obtained from estimating the model are then provided. The results are based upon both the demand and the supply conditions for IT city holidays, and the final section of the chapter considers the implications of the findings with respect to the relative importance of the characteristics of IT holiday packages and the competitiveness of individual tour operators and tour operators of different nationalities. The results are compared for the different city destinations.

Examination of intra-European Community (EC) tourism is of interest because intra-EC tourism constitutes the main component of total EC tourism. Of all expenditure on tourism by EC residents in the mid-1980s, approximately 60 per cent consisted of expenditure in other EC countries (O'Hagan et al., 1986), and over 80 per cent of total tourist arrivals originated from other EC countries (Jeffries, 1987; Withyman, 1987). City tourism is of growing importance within the EC and is also likely to expand in an East European context. The economic aspects of city tourism have, however, been relatively neglected, although some studies of the geographical and morphological aspects of urban tourism have been undertaken (Ashworth, 1989; Pearce, 1989).

Diversified preferences on the part of tourism consumers (Vellas, 1989) and strong competition between tour operators have encouraged tour operators to pursue a strategy of differentiating IT holiday packages in order to increase consumption by different segments of the holiday market. Thus different IT packages include a variety of combinations of characteristics, such as the type and category of accommodation and facilities including catering and entertainments. The availability of holidays in a range of destinations also increases the diversity of holiday products that can be purchased by the consumer. Most tour operators supply IT holidays to the national markets in the countries in which they are based, and hotels in given destinations accommodate clients from a variety of origin countries. This has important implications for EC competition policy. The Single European Market should, in theory, bring about the equalization of prices of the same products, as predicted by the factor price equalization theory (Samuelson, 1948, 1949). However, since IT holidays supplied by tour operators from both the same and differing national origins consist of a variety of combinations of characteristics without separate market prices, comparison of IT holiday price competitiveness using the prices at which the holidays are supplied is problematic.

Comparison of the price competitiveness of products consisting of packages of characteristics may be achieved using the hedonic price model, which allows for the estimation of the price differentials relating to variations in the packages of characteristics. The application of the model to IT holidays in European cities can provide a range of interesting information. Little research has been undertaken on price competitiveness within the tourism industry (Goodall *et al.*, 1989; Holloway, 1989; Stabler, 1989, 1990; Sinclair, 1991) and further work will contribute to filling this major gap in the literature. Research on the economics of city tourism is useful in the context of the relative past neglect of this type of tourism, and the examination of price competitiveness at the intra-European level is important in the context of the Single European Market.

8.2 CHARACTERISTICS OF INCLUSIVE TOUR CITY HOLIDAYS CONSUMED BY TOURISTS FROM DIFFERENT EUROPEAN COUNTRIES

Within the EC, the demand for IT holidays by UK residents has been relatively high and tour operators from the UK have played an important role in the promotion of IT holidays. This has resulted, in large part, from the UK's position as an island economy and the relatively high propensity of UK residents to travel to other EC countries by air. West Germany's position as the EC country with the highest level of expenditure on tourism (O'Hagan *et al.*, 1986; Drexl and Agel, 1987) has contributed to high German expenditure on IT holidays, and German tour operators have also played a large role in supplying IT holidays. It was therefore decided to examine IT holidays available for consumption by UK and German tourists and, in addition, to examine the holidays available to tourists from origin countries with very different characteristics, France and Spain. Although increasing in popularity, IT holidays are a less common form of holiday taking within the French market than within the UK and German markets, and are a rapidly increasing form of holiday taking for the Spanish. The European destinations considered are the traditionally popular cities of London and Paris. The percentage of overseas tourists including London in their stay in the UK was estimated to be around 60 per cent in the mid-1980s (McVey, 1986; London Tourist Board, 1987; McGuffie, 1987).

The data for the IT holidays were obtained from the holiday brochures of UK, French, German and Spanish tour operators for the first full seven days in August 1989. Owing to the limited amount of information about hotel facilities included in many of the brochures, additional information was obtained from the Michelin guides (used for the purpose of standardized cross-country comparability). The findings provided by this study cannot, therefore, be generalized to all tour operators. As the lowest category hotels were rarely used for IT city holidays and little information about them was available from the hotel guides, they were not considered in the study.

The hotels were classified into star ratings of between two and five stars, where two stars corresponds to the lowest category of hotel and five stars to the highest. The concentration of IT holidays supplied by tour operators from different origin countries by category of accommodation, in percentage terms, is of particular relevance, owing to the considerable differences in the absolute numbers of holidays supplied by different nationalities of tour operator. Most IT holidays for French tourists in London are supplied in two-star (45 per cent) and three-star (32 per cent) categories of accommodation. German tourists are offered more holidays in four-star (41 per cent) followed by two-star (30 per cent) accommodation, and Germany had the highest percentage of all origin nationalities in five-star hotels (11 per cent). Spanish tourists are offered most accommodation in four-star (40 per cent) and three-star (33 per cent) hotels. The distributions of accommodation which German and Spanish tour operators use in Paris are very similar to the distributions for London. Tour operators from the UK offer tourists in Paris a relatively high standard of accommodation in four-star (48 per cent), followed by three-star (23 per cent) and five-star (22 per cent) hotels.

There are considerable differences between the accommodation category mixes offered in the brochures of different tour operators, for all origin countries. The exceptions are the brochures for the German tour operators ADAC and Jet Reisen, which supply a similar accommodation mix. The Spanish brochures for Club de Vacaciones and Pullmantur (which belong to the organization OTA) offer a similar pattern of accommodation, although Iberojet and Mundicolor (which are owned by Iberia) supply differing accommodation distributions. Spanish tour operators contract with larger hotels in London than tour operators from other origins, the mean number of rooms being 363 for Spanish tour operators compared with 299 and 249 respectively for the

German and French operators. UK tour operators use larger hotels in Paris, with a mean room number of 409, compared to 275 for Spanish operators and 170 for German operators. The type of board most commonly offered within IT holiday packages for both London and Paris is bed and breakfast, which is provided for over 85 per cent of IT holidays for tourists from all origins.

Although all London hotels in which IT holidays are supplied have at least one restaurant, just over half of the Paris hotels in which German and Spanish tourists stay, and 70 per cent of the hotels in which UK tourists stay have a restaurant. All the hotels in London and virtually all hotels in Paris provide a telephone and television in the bedroom and most of the hotels in both cities have air-conditioning. The percentages of London hotels providing car parking facilities range from 31 to 48 per cent, in contrast to the Paris hotels, which provided no car parking. In most cases, therefore, the range of facilities that different European tour operators provide within IT city holiday packages are similar. The exception is the provision of 'freebies' by different tour operators in London and Paris.

'Freebies' are such incentives as a 'free' travelling bag (provided by some Spanish tour operators), a 'free' drink on arrival, and champagne and flowers for honeymoon couples, which are offered to tourists purchasing the IT holiday. Very high percentages of holidays supplied by UK (86 per cent) and German (97 per cent) tour operators offer freebies to tourists staying in Paris. However, only 38 per cent of IT holidays in London supplied by German tour operators and 45 per cent of London holidays supplied by French tour operators include freebies. Relatively small percentages of Spanish tour operators offer freebies to tourists purchasing holidays in either destination (20 per cent for London and 27 per cent for Paris).

The mean unstandardized prices of IT holidays included in tour operators' brochures (not weighted by the numbers of holidays demanded) vary considerably in relation to both the tour operator brochure and the destination, as is shown in Tables 8.1 and 8.2. The prices related to an IT holiday for a person staying in a double room in the first seven days of August 1989, and were converted into sterling using the spot exchange rates for July 1988. The July 1988 exchange rates were used because tour operators contract accommodation approximately 12 months in advance of the tourists' arrival. The resulting prices take account of the cost and profit conditions of the different European tour operators and exclude unanticipated exchange rate changes. They thus provide

Table 8.1 Mean unstandardized prices of IT holidays in London supplied by different European tour operators

Tour operator and origin	Price by hotel category				Overall mean
	2	3	4	5	
France					
Frantour Voyages	–	535	–	–	535
Republique Tours	401	556	520	870	502
Visit Europe	–	–	510	–	510
vps Voyages	395	553	–	–	454
Overall mean	398	549	515	870	489
Germany					
ADAC	398	438	–	–	418
Airtours	449	585	611	842	623
Dertour	375	426	528	–	460
Jet Reisen	321	544	–	–	432
Overall mean	402	515	580	842	546
Spain					
ABREU	387	393	–	–	391
Club de Vacaciones	381	462	484	–	456
Corte Ingles	436	479	464	709	484
Diamante Azul	–	–	515	–	515
Euro Este	387	–	532	–	496
Flytours	485	–	543	–	524
Iberojet	474	–	484	667	533
Londonow	406	478	500	–	469
Mundicolor Iberia	–	–	582	–	582
Puente del Mundo	455	524	672	699	552
Pullmantur	395	426	516	–	449
Super Viajes	384	450	430	–	414
Touring Club	454	501	542	801	575
Turavia	426	569	578	722	550
Overall mean	427	475	526	746	501

the basis for a more appropriate comparison of the cross-country price competitiveness of the IT holidays than would result from the use of the exchange rates for the subsequent year.

On average, tour operators based in Germany charge the highest prices for holidays in London, followed by Spanish and French tour operators. UK tour operators charge the highest prices for holidays in Paris, followed by tour operators from Spain and Germany. However, there are considerable differences in the mean unstandardized prices for holidays in a given category of accommodation and destination, both between tour operators

Table 8.2 Mean unstandardized prices of IT holidays in Paris supplied by different European tour operators

Tour operator and origin	Price by hotel category				Overall mean
	2	3	4	5	
UK					
French Travel Service	–	321	408	860	486
Sovereign	–	–	713	–	713
Taber	301	513	–	–	407
Take a Break	–	–	560	959	760
Overall mean	301	380	436	870	493
Germany					
ADAC	356	–	450	–	387
Adler	344	–	–	–	344
Airtours	345	317	502	783	517
Dertour	307	334	434	–	371
Jet Reisen	343	–	505	–	424
Overall mean	333	332	465	783	427
Spain					
Corte Ingles	382	419	584	–	489
Diamante Azul	–	412	451	643	448
Iberojet	360	382	416	–	379
Lugares	394	547	752	–	564
Mundicolor Iberia	392	437	451	905	508
Puente del Mundo	429	515	621	1010	648
Pullmantur	355	385	–	–	361
Turavia	339	387	425	–	404
Overall mean	371	418	487	866	465

from a given origin and between tour operators based in different European origins. Taking, for example, holidays in three-star hotels in London, the percentage difference between the mean prices charged by tour operators based in France is 4 per cent, compared with 34 per cent for German tour operators and 45 per cent for Spanish tour operators. The corresponding percentage differences in the prices of holidays in three-star hotels in Paris are 60 per cent for UK tour operators, 5 per cent for German tour operators and 43 per cent for Spanish tour operators. Moreover, not all tour operators offer accommodation in all categories of hotels; some only supply accommodation in lower- or medium-category hotels. Comparison of mean unstandardized prices by tour operator and destination may, however, be misleading since IT holiday packages are not homogeneous but consist of different mixes of characteristics. In a small number of cases, for example, the mean unstandardized prices charged for a holiday in a lower-category hotel exceed those for a higher-category establishment. This illustrates that the hotel category is not the only holiday characteristic which is of importance in price determination and strengthens the case for the standardization of prices undertaken in this chapter. The hedonic price model is therefore used to estimate the price differentials relating to the characteristics of IT city holiday packages supplied by the different European tour operators.

8.3 METHODOLOGY FOR EXAMINING THE COMPETITIVENESS OF INCLUSIVE TOUR HOLIDAYS

Following Rosen's (1974) model, an IT holiday is considered to consist of a package of heterogeneous characteristics. The implicit valuations of the characteristics on the part of consumers and the costs of supply contribute to the overall price of the holiday. The hedonic price model, based on competitive markets, is used to estimate the implicit equilibrium prices of each of the characteristics and to estimate the variations in the holiday price resulting from variations in the different characteristics included in the package and in the tour operator supplying the package.

An IT holiday A consisting of characteristics $A_1, \ldots, A_n$ can be written as

$$A = (A_1, A_2, A_3, \ldots, A_n)$$

where A_i is the quantity of the ith characteristic included in the IT package. The price of the IT holiday depends upon the characteristics of which it consists and the hedonic price function is written as

$$P(A) = A(A_1, A_2, A_3, \ldots, A_n)$$

Tourists' demand for the IT holiday depends upon the IT characteristics, A, income, Y, and preferences δ:

$$D(A) = D(A_1, A_2, A_3, \ldots, A_n, Y, \delta)$$

The amount that the tourist would be prepared to pay for a holiday with an additional unit of the ith characteristic is given by PD_i, the first partial derivative of D with respect to A_i.

Tour operators are willing to supply the IT holiday for prices that depend on the characteristics, A, the profit level, Π, and the costs of supplying the holiday, E:

$$S(A) = S(A_1, A_2, A_3, \ldots, A_n, \Pi, E)$$

Firms are assumed to maximize profits. The amount which the firm would charge for supplying a holiday with an additional unit of the ith characteristic is given by PS_i, the first partial derivative of S with respect to A_i.

In a competitive market, the market clearing price of IT holidays occurs when the quantity demanded is equal to the quantity supplied:

$$Q^D(A_i) = Q^S(A_i) \qquad \text{for all } i$$

and when

$$PD_i = PS_i \qquad \text{for all } i$$

Each type of IT holiday (i.e. each package of characteristics) has an equilibrium price, and the relationship between the equilibrium prices of all types of holidays and the different packages of characteristics supplied is given by the hedonic price function. The coefficients of the different characteristics included in the hedonic price equation are based on the equilibrium values of the (implicit) prices of the characteristics of the IT holiday, determined by the underlying demand and supply conditions for IT holidays. The coefficients show the variations in the holiday price resulting from variations in the characteristics in the package. The estimation of the hedonic price model has usually been carried out using multiple regression analysis, although the selection of the appropriate functional form for estimation has been contentious (Halvorsen and Pollakowski, 1981; Cassel and Mendelsohn, 1985). Most past studies have selected the functional form on an *ad hoc* or empirical basis.

The application of the hedonic price model to IT holidays requires information on the prices of IT holidays and the characteristics of the holiday packages. The holiday prices, converted into sterling using the July 1988 spot exchange rates, were obtained from tour operators' brochures from the UK, France, West Germany and Spain. The hotel characteristics considered were the hotel category (classified into star ratings of two to five), availability of one or more restaurants, a television in the room, a telephone in the room, air-conditioning, one or more swimming pools, car parking and freebies. Transport costs were not considered, although differences in transport costs may explain some of the overall differences between tour operators from different countries. Data on transport costs are extremely difficult to obtain as tour operators are not forthcoming in this respect.

The model was estimated by regressing the prices of the IT holidays (with separate equations for London and Paris), on dummy variables representing the different hotel characteristics and the tour operators from different origin countries. A non-linear functional form for the hedonic price equation was chosen following Rosen's (1974) argument that the non-linear form is appropriate in cases when consumers are unable to demand alternative packages of characteristics to those supplied (by repackaging characteristics) or when there is joint supply of characteristics by firms. A semi-logarithmic functional form was selected as appropriate in the context of explanatory variables taking the form of dummies, given the ease of interpretation of the coefficients; as Halvorsen and Pollakowski (1981) show, the effect on the price of the availability of a characteristic with a coefficient β is given by $(e^{\beta} - 1) \times 100$ per cent.

8.4 RESULTS

The tour operator and hotel characteristics variables provided a good explanation of the IT holiday prices; the coefficient of determination for the equation for London was $R^2 = 0.74$ and that for Paris was $R^2 = 0.87$. The effects of the variables on the IT city holiday prices are included in Table 8.3. The 'implied percentage effects' are the point estimates of the percentage differentials in the standardized prices of IT holidays resulting from a particular holiday characteristic or tour operator, *ceteris paribus*, and are calculated for those variables that have a significant effect upon the IT holiday price at the 10 per cent level.

Differences in the categories of hotel in which accommodation is provided have a very large and highly significant effect on price, particularly for five-star hotels. The point estimates of the percentage increases in the standardized prices of holidays in three-, four- and five-star hotels over and above the prices for two-star hotels were 23, 36 and 70 per cent for London, and 13, 36 and 140 per cent for Paris. Variations in the type of board supplied did not have a significant effect upon the price, owing to the fact that bed and breakfast was by far the most predominant type of board supplied in both destinations, and were not included as explanatory variables in the final equations. Other things being equal, the size of the hotel, measured by the number of rooms, was found to have a significant effect on the holiday price. A quadratic

Table 8.3 The effects of hotel characteristics and tour operators on IT holiday prices

Independent variables	London		Paris	
	Coefficient	Implied percentage effect	Coefficient	Implied percentage effect
Constant	5.878 (80.93)		5.824 (59.0)	
3 stars	0.207 (10.27)	23.0	0.125 (4.82)	13.3
4 stars	0.305 (14.25)	35.7	0.305 (8.81)	35.7
5 stars	0.533 (13.59)	70.2	0.874 (21.10)	139.6
No. rooms	−0.001 (−4.17)		−0.001 (−4.54)	
Rooms squared	5.19×10^{-7} (2.13)		5.80×10^{-7} (4.11)	
Restaurant			0.031 (1.14)	
TV			0.048 (0.77)	
Air-conditioning	0.061 (2.79)	6.3	0.071 (2.79)	7.4
Swimming pool	0.085 (2.13)	8.8		
Parking	0.061 (3.73)	6.3		
Freebies	0.199 (2.73)	22.0	0.051 (0.59)	

Tour operator and origin

UK

French Travel Service			−0.136 (−3.15)	−12.7
Sovereign			0.369 (4.22)	44.6
Taber			0.065 (0.74)	
Take a Break			0.142 (1.62)	

133

Table 8.3 *continued*

Independent variables	London		Paris	
	Coefficient	Implied percentage effect	Coefficient	Implied percentage effect
France				
Frantours Voyages	0.151 (1.65)	16.3		
Republique Tours	0.253 (3.24)	28.7		
Visit Europe	0.180 (1.70)	19.7		
vps Voyages	0.011 (0.18)			
Germany				
Airtours	0.368 (5.02)	44.5	−0.070 (−1.57)	
Dertour	0.006 (0.11)		−0.166 (−3.91)	−15.3
Spain				
ABREU	0.142 (1.58)			
Club de Vacaciones	0.230 (2.95)	25.9		
Corte Ingles	0.231 (3.14)	26.0	0.130 (1.53)	
Diamante Azul	0.204 (2.73)	22.6	0.014 (0.16)	
Euro Este	0.264 (3.43)	30.2		
Flytours	0.116 (2.01)	12.3		
Iberojet	0.248 (2.99)	28.1	0.011 (0.13)	
Londonow	0.231 (3.18)	26.0		
Lugares			0.312 (3.10)	36.6
Mundicolor Iberia	0.331 (3.40)	39.2	0.063 (0.77)	6.5

134

Table 8.3 *continued*

Independent variables	London		Paris	
	Coefficient	Implied percentage effect	Coefficient	Implied percentage effect
Puente del Mundo	0.348 (4.60)	41.6	0.280 (3.23)	32.3
Pullmantur	0.023 (0.42)		−0.016 (−0.32)	
Super Viajes	0.229 (2.72)	25.9		
Touring Club	0.326 (4.42)	38.5		
Turavia	0.133 (2.35)	14.2	−0.085 (−1.73)	−8.1
	$R^2 = 0.74$		$R^2 = 0.87$	

The *t* statistics are given in parentheses under the values of the corresponding coefficients.

term was included to allow for possible non-linearity due to economies of scale (lower unit prices in larger hotels). The coefficients for the number of rooms and number of rooms squared were statistically significant. In the case of London, the fitted quadratic had a minimum at 850 rooms, suggesting economies of scale up to this point; most of the London hotels considered in the study had less than 850 rooms. In the case of Paris, the minimum was at 603 rooms. There were a few large hotels in the Paris data, particularly in the higher star categories.

Virtually all the London hotels had a restaurant and provided a television in the bedrooms, and so these variables were not included in the equation for London. The availability of a restaurant and television had an insignificant effect on Paris holiday prices. However, the provision of air-conditioning had a significant effect upon the price in both destinations. The point estimate of the price difference associated with a swimming pool in London hotels was 9 per cent, and that for car parking facilities was 6 per cent, both variables being significant. Neither a swimming pool nor car parking was available in most Paris hotels considered. The effect of freebies was significant and equal to 22 per cent for holidays in London, but was insignificant for Paris.

The implied percentage effects for the tour operators demonstrate interesting variations both between tour operators from a given European origin and between tour operators from different origins. The standardized price charged by the German tour operators ADAC and Jet Reisen was considered as the base in relation to which the implied percentage price differences for other tour operators were calculated for London. The German tour operator Adler was also included in the base for Paris. All the implied percentage effects and t statistics refer to the differentials and statistical significance relative to the group of German operators; it is therefore not possible to make direct inferences about the statistical significance of the differences between coefficients of tour operators other than the base group. However, Table 8.3 does indicate the extent of the variations in the percentage effects associated with the different operators.

The point estimates of the differentials in prices charged by tour operators not in the base group compared with the prices charged by ADAC and Jet Reisen show that tour operators from France and Spain charge considerably higher prices for holidays in London, *ceteris paribus*, than these German tour operators. The implicit percentage differences between the prices charged by the French tour operators and this group of German operators are 16, 20 and 29 per cent. Of the 11 Spanish tour operators that set significantly higher prices than the German tour operators, ten charged prices that were over 22 per cent higher. However, the German tour operator Airtours appeared less competitive in supplying holidays in London than the French and Spanish operators.

In the case of IT holidays in Paris, the French Travel Service appeared more competitive in supplying holidays than the group of German tour operators. The French Travel Service supplies IT holidays to UK residents via brochure distribution to UK travel agents and, although included under the UK tour operator origin heading, is of French ownership. BA's Sovereign Holidays appeared to be less competitive than the German operators. The German tour operator Dertour was more competitive than the German group, as was the Spanish operator Turavia. However, the other three Spanish tour operators for which the coefficients were significantly different from zero were all less competitive, by over 30 per cent in two cases. It is interesting that although virtually all of the Spanish tour operators were less competitive in supplying IT holidays in London than the group of German operators, this conclusion did not apply to IT holidays in Paris.

8.5 IMPLICATIONS AND CONCLUSIONS

The application of the hedonic price model to IT city holidays demonstrated the importance of the hotel category, the availability of a small range of hotel facilities and, for London, the provision of freebies in affecting IT holiday prices. There were also considerable differences in the standardized prices of IT holidays charged by a number of the tour operators from different European origins. The high percentage increases in price associated with increases in the hotels' star ratings are related to the underlying demand and supply conditions for tourist accommodation in cities, and differ considerably from the case of coastal resort tourism (Sinclair *et al.*, 1990). Hotel accommodation in London has undergone considerable upgrading with the objective of capturing the increases in profitability associated with higher-category hotels (McVey, 1986). However, such upgrading has not been accompanied by a significant increase in the supply of hotel and non-hotel accommodation within the city and, in general, there is an excess demand for hotel accommodation (McVey, 1986; McGuffie, 1987).

In Paris, in contrast, the supply of accommodation in lower- and medium-category establishments, particularly three-star hotels, has increased, although the supply of accommodation in the highest category accommodation has remained approximately constant (McVey, 1986). The differences in the supply conditions for hotel accommodation in London and Paris are likely to constitute a partial explanation of the lower implied percentage price differentials for three-star hotels in Paris than in London, but the higher differential for five-star hotels. The fact that three- to five-star city hotels are the core accommodation demanded by business tourists (McGuffie, 1987) may help to explain the high values of the percentage differentials for these categories of hotels relative to, for example, the same categories of hotels in coastal resorts in Spain. The percentage increases in the prices of IT holidays in three-, four- and five-star hotels relative to the group of one- and two-star hotels in Malaga in 1988 were found to be 11, 28 and 108 per cent respectively (Sinclair *et al.*, 1990). The generally lower percentages for accommodation in the coastal resorts are also related to the excess supply of accommodation throughout most of the year, which has persisted as the rate of growth of demand has declined (Clewer *et al.*, 1991) and as the supply of non-hotel accommodation has increased (Valenzuela, 1988).

The considerable differences in the distribution of accommodation by hotel categories which different tour operators, including those of similar size, offer in both cities and coastal resorts (Barke and France, 1986) challenges Casini *et al.*'s (1985, p. 146) assertion of similarity in the products supplied by tour operators. In contrast to Casini *et al.*'s implicit view, competition between tour operators on the basis of product differentiation does appear to be important. Product differentiation between IT city holidays is particularly important in terms of the category of hotel accommodation supplied, since many other hotel characteristics are similar or have an insignificant effect upon the holiday price. The availability of a swimming pool and car parking facilities at hotels in London, and air-conditioning in hotels in both cities, does, however, have significant effects upon the price, although the car parking variable may constitute a proxy for hotel location, indicating the potential interest of further work on hotel location. The results for holidays in city hotels differ from those for coastal hotels, where a range of characteristics such as the type of board, availability of a nursery, money-changing facilities and a night-club were found to have a significant effect upon the holiday price (Sinclair *et al.*, 1990). The provision of freebies varies considerably between tour operators from different origins and between individual tour operators, indicating significant differences in marketing techniques between the different nationalities of tour operator. The result that freebies can be related to a considerable increase in the price of London holidays (also found for IT holidays in Spanish coastal resorts) indicates the potentially disadvantageous effect on the consumer of the inclusion of freebies in IT holidays.

The price effects associated with the provision of holidays by tour operators of both the same and different nationalities depend upon the demand and supply conditions that affect the holiday markets in different countries. The competitiveness of different tour operators relative to the base group is represented by the tour operator coefficients in Table 8.3 and, for ease of comparison, in Table 8.4 the regression equation has been used to estimate the prices of a standard holiday in three-star and four-star hotels. Comparison of the standardized prices with the unstandardized prices given in Tables 8.1 and 8.2 shows the importance of standardization for accurate comparison. In the case of London holidays, the rank order by price differs substantially between standardized and unstandardized prices, the rank correlation coefficients being only 0.41 for three-star hotels and 0.31 for

Table 8.4 Estimated standard holiday prices: London and Paris

	3-star hotel		4-star hotel	
Tour operator and origin	London	Paris	London	Paris
France				
Frantour Voyages	465	–	513	–
Republique Tours	514	–	567	–
Visit Europe	478	–	527	–
vps Voyages	404	–	446	–
UK				
French Travel Service	–	334	–	400
Sovereign	–	553	–	662
Taber	–	408		488
Take a Break	–	441	–	528
Germany				
Airtours	577	357	637	427
Dertour	397	324	438	388
Spain				
ABREU	461	–	508	–
Club de Vacaciones	503	–	555	–
Corte Ingles	503	435	555	521
Diamante Azul	490	387	541	464
Euro Este	520	–	574	–
Flytours	449	–	495	–
Iberojet	512	387	565	463
Londonow	504	–	555	–
Lugares	–	522	–	625
Mundicolor Iberia	556	407	614	488
Puente del Mundo	566	504	624	606
Pullmantur	409	376	451	451
Super Viajes	503	–	555	–
Touring Club	554	–	610	–
Turavia	457	351	504	420

The estimated prices quoted in the table are for a standard 'holiday package' in a 200-bedroomed hotel, with TV and air-conditioning.

four-star hotels. For example, the most competitive operator for IT holidays in four-star hotels on the basis of standardized prices (Dertour) would be ranked only tenth using unstandardized prices. For Paris the rank order shows greater, but not perfect, consistency with a rank correlation of approximately 0.87 for both categories. The most competitive operator for four-star hotels using standardized prices is also Dertour, which again would be judged slightly less competitive (ranked fourth) from an examination of unstandardized prices. The use of unstandardized prices does not allow for differences in the mixes of characteristics that are included in IT holidays and may produce misleading conclusions.

Using standardized prices for London holidays, the German operators used as the base for comparison appeared to be significantly more competitive, *ceteris paribus*, than 11 Spanish tour operators, three French operators and the German operator Airtours. (The use of mean unstandardized prices had shown the German tour operators to be most expensive, on average, followed by the Spanish and French.) The standardized results for holidays in Paris showed the base German group to be more competitive than the UK's Sovereign Holidays and three Spanish tour operators. The French Travel Service, the Spanish operator Turavia and the German operator Dertour were more competitive than the base group. The finding, based on standardized prices, that German tour operators are, on average, more competitive than tour operators in other countries is in line with Drexl and Agel's (1987) argument. Drexl and Agel concluded that while West Germans became more price conscious during the 1980s, they also became more critical of holiday characteristics such as the standard of accommodation.

Estimation of the point percentage price differentials for IT city holidays showed considerable differences both between tour operators of different nationalities and between tour operators from a given origin. It was also found that the prices of standard holidays in London exceeded the prices of standard holidays in Paris provided by the same tour operator, and that the prices of standard holidays for a given destination differed considerably between tour operators from the same and different origins. The findings are based on the underlying demand and supply conditions. Price differentials may be related, for example, to variations in the price elasticities of demand between different tourist origins and between different market segments within a given origin. Exclusive dealing arrangements which have existed between some tour operators and travel agents have deterred overseas competitors from entering some national markets, such as the German market, and the position of the major tour operators may be oligopolistic over the long run. The findings from the study contradict Casini *et al.*'s (1985) assertion of similarity in the prices charged by European tour operators and indicate an apparent absence of price convergence for IT holidays between and within EC member countries. Further research on the competitiveness of EC tour operators supplying IT holidays, using the hedonic price methodology, could trace the dynamics of the process of price competitiveness. Such research could indicate whether a process of convergence is occurring in line with the objectives of the Single European Market, or whether inter- and intra-national differences in price competitiveness within the EC tour operator sector will remain or increase.

Note

We would like to thank David Clewer, Cristina Lara, Betty Sinclair, Theodore Syriopoulos and Marion Wortman for their work on extracting the data. The support of the Research Committee of the University of Kent and the Spanish National Research Plan is gratefully acknowledged.

References

Ashworth, G. (1989) Urban tourism: an imbalance in attention. In Cooper, C.P. (ed.) *Progress in Tourism, Recreation and Hospitality Management*, Volume 1, pp. 33–45. London: Belhaven.

Barke, M. and France, L. (1986) The marketing of Spain as a holiday destination. *Tourist Review*, (3), 27–30.

Casini, S., Varaldo, R., Masetti, P., Dall'Ara, G., Bonini, A. and Ghirardelli, G. (1985) *The Tourism Sector in the Community. A Study of Competition and Competitiveness*. Brussels: Commission of the European Communities.

Cassel, E. and Mendelsohn, R. (1985) The choice of functional form for hedonic price equations. *Journal of Urban Economics*, **18**(2), 135–42.

Clewer, A., Pack, A. and Sinclair, M.T. (1991) Forecasting models for tourism demand in city-dominated and coastal areas. *European Papers of the Regional Science Association*, **69**, 31–42.

Drexl, C. and Agel, P. (1987) Tour operators in West Germany. Survey of the package tour market, the operators and how they sell. *Travel and Tourism Analyst*, May, 29–43.

Gaviria, M., Iribas, J.M., Monterde, M., Sabbah, F., Sanz, J.R. and Udina, E. (1974) *España a Go-Go*. Madrid: Ediciones Turner.

Goodall, B., Radburn, M. and Stabler, M. (1989) *Market Opportunity Sets for Tourism*. Geographical Papers no. 100, Tourism Series 1. Reading: University of Reading.

Halvorsen, R. and Pollakowski, H.O. (1981) The choice of functional form for hedonic price equations. *Journal of Urban Economics*, **10**(1), 37–49.

Holloway, J.C. (1989) *The Business of Tourism*, 3rd ed. Plymouth: Macdonald and Evans.

Jeffries, D. (1987) Selling Europe. Pan-European promotion and the European Travel Commission. *Travel and Tourism Analyst*, July, 17–28.

London Tourist Board (1987) *The Tourism Strategy for London*. London: London Tourist Board.

McGuffie, J. (1987) UK hotel industry. Revival for the chains at home and abroad. *Travel and Tourism Analyst*, September, 15–31.

McVey, M. (1986) International hotel chains in Europe. Survey of expansion plans as Europe is 'rediscovered'. *Travel and Tourism Analyst*, September, 3–23.

O'Hagan, J.W., Scott, Y. and Waldron, P. (1986) *The Tourism Industry and the Tourism Policies of the Twelve Member States of the Community*, Report commissioned by the Commission of the European Communities, Directorate General for Transport, Tourism Service, Brussels. Dublin: Trinity College.

Pearce, D.G. (1989) *Tourist Development*, 2nd edn. Harlow: Longman.

Rosen, S. (1974) Hedonic prices and implicit markets: product differentiation in pure competition. *Journal of Political Economy*, **82**(1), 34–55.

Samuelson, P.A. (1948) International trade and the equalization of factor prices. *Economic Journal*, **58**(230), 163–84.

Samuelson, P.A. (1949) International factor-price equalization once again. *Economic Journal*, **59**(234), 181–97.

Sinclair, M.T. (1991) The economics of tourism. In Cooper, C.P. (ed.) *Progress in Tourism, Recreation and Hospitality Management, Volume 3*, pp. 1–27. London: Belhaven.

Sinclair, M.T., Clewer, A. and Pack, A. (1990) Hedonic prices and the marketing of package holidays: the case of tourism resorts in Malaga. In Ashworth, G.J. and Goodall, B. (eds) *Marketing Tourism Places*, pp. 85–103. London: Routledge.

Stabler, M. (1989) Modelling the tourist industry: the concept of opportunity sets. *Leisure, Labour and Lifestyles: International Comparisons. Tourism and Leisure. Models and Theories*, Proceedings of the Leisure Studies Association 2nd International Conference, Conference Papers no. 39, volume 8 (1), pp. 60–76. Eastbourne: Leisure Studies Association.

Stabler, M. (1990) The concept of opportunity sets as a methodological framework for the analysis of selling tourism places: the industry view. In Ashworth, G.J. and Goodall, B. (eds) *Marketing Tourism Places*, pp. 23–41. London: Routledge.

Valenzuela, M. (1988) Spain: the phenomenon of mass tourism. In Williams, A.M. and Shaw, G. (eds) *Tourism and Economic Development. Western European Experiences*, pp. 39–57. London: Pinter.

Vellas, F. (1989) Tourisme et économie internationale. *Teoros,* **7**(5), 36–9.

Withyman, M. (1987) Destination Europe. Survey of European countries as destinations. *Travel and Tourism Analyst*, June, 15–31.

9 The Life Cycle Concept and Tourism

Chris Cooper

9.1 INTRODUCTION

The life cycle concept is rooted in the theories of population ecology and diffusion processes (Hannan and Freeman, 1977; Haywood, 1990). It has been a debating point in marketing for a number of years (see Kotler, 1980) and has been utilized in a number of disciplines to explain long-term change. For example, in industrial economics Vernon (1966, 1979) has used the life cycle of products to illustrate patterns of international investment and trade.

The life cycle approach is only now gaining attention in tourism and hospitality as an explanatory tool: in tourism it is seen as a useful conceptualization of destination area development (see Butler, 1980; Cooper and Jackson, 1989); in hospitality management it is beginning to be used as a guide for strategic planning (Tse and Elwood, 1990). Elsewhere, the life cycle has been used to explain the development of business organizations and of particular elements of an organization's functioning (Kwansa and Evans, 1988). It is the aim of this chapter to debate the utility of the life cycle approach in tourism and suggest an agenda for further research into the life cycle concept.

9.2 LIFE CYCLES AND TOURISM

In marketing, the product life cycle (PLC) describes the evolution of a product as it passes through various stages: introduction, growth, maturity and decline. On the one hand there is no doubt of the life cycle's intuitive appeal as a generalization of product sales. Indeed, there are many examples of classic empirically validated PLC curves. Yet while many comment upon this, few have tried to explain it (Vernon, 1979). Critics of the life cycle approach argue that plots of product sales made with hindsight are of little use in forecasting or product planning (Brownlie, 1985). The true value of the life cycle lies in the insights it can provide into the influences upon, and decisions taken about, the product at different stages in the life cycle. These arguments are largely played out in marketing, but in tourism and hospitality management they still have much to offer.

The debate began with Butler's (1980) paper, in which he argued that it is possible to trace a cycle of evolution for destinations that is similar to the PLC. Numbers of visitors replace sales of a product and it is possible to trace both the evolution of the market, in terms of type and number of visitors, and the development of the destination, in terms of such factors as physical facilities and administrative structures. The various stages were described by Butler (1980) as follows:

Exploration Here the destination is visited by small numbers of adventurous tourists who tend to shun institutionalized travel. The natural beauty or cultural characteristics at the destination are the main attraction, but visitor numbers are restricted by lack of access and facilities. At this stage the attraction of the destination is that it remains as yet unchanged by tourism, and contact with local people will be high.

Involvement At this stage local initiatives, to provide for visitors and later advertise the destination, result in increased and regular numbers of visitors. A tourist season and market area emerge and pressures may be placed on the public sector to provide infrastructure.

Development Once a destination moves into development, large numbers of visitors arrive and the organization of tourism begins to change as control is passed out of local hands and companies from outside the area (often national or multi-national) move in to provide up-to-date facilities. Control in the public sector can also be affected as regional and national planning may become necessary, in part to ameliorate problems but also to market to the international tourist-generating areas, as visitors become more dependent upon travel arrangements booked through the trade. This is a critical stage as these facilities, and the changing nature of tourism, can alter the very nature of the destination. Failure may therefore be sown in the seeds of success: with increasing numbers and popularity the destination may suffer a change in quality through problems of over-use and deterioration of facilities.

Consolidation By this stage the rate of increase of visitors is declining although total numbers are still increasing. The destination is now a fully fledged part of the tourism industry with an identifiable recreational business district.

Stagnation Peak numbers of visitors have now been reached and the destination is no longer fashionable. Repeat visits from more conservative travellers dominate in this stage. Business use of the resort's extensive facilities is also sought but generally major efforts are now needed to maintain the number of visits. The destination may by now have environmental, social and economic problems.

Decline Visitors are now being lost to newer resorts and the destination becomes dependent on a smaller geographical catchment for day trips and weekend visits. Alternatively, destination managers may recognize this stage and decide to 'rejuvenate'. The introduction of new types of facility such as a casino, as at Scheveningen, Netherlands (Weg, 1982) and Atlantic City, USA (Stansfield, 1978), is a common response. Alternatively destinations may capitalize on previously unused natural resources, such as winter sports, to extend the season and attract a new market.

The life cycle not only outlines the physical development of the destination but can also be used to examine market evolution. Changing provision of facilities and access is matched by an evolving clientele in both quantitative and qualitative terms. In fact a resort's market can be seen as the progressive adoption of that resort by consumers and will therefore display the classic S-shaped curve of diffusion theory (see, for example, Burns and Stalker, 1961; Clarke, 1985). Here the more adventurous tourists will visit – or adopt – the resort in its earlier years to be replaced by the laggards, or more conservative tourists, as the resort moves into the later stages of the life cycle. Cooper (1981) has examined the risk-taking behaviour of tourists in this adoption process. He found that while tourists minimize risk and maximize utility in resort choice, there are differences in the degree of risk avoidance, and thus the adoption of resorts in the early stages of the life cycle when they are perceived as a riskier investment of time and effort. Vernon (1966) also accepts that knowledge is not a free good and levels of information may be an independent variable in the decision process. Indeed, if, as Vernon suggests for products, destinations become increasingly standardized as they progress through the cycle, then they would be expected to appeal to the low risk taking, laggard tourists in the later stages of consolidation, maturity and decline.

Plog (1973) has similarly characterized tourists as allocentric (or adventurous innovators), ever seeking new destinations, or psychocentric (laggards) seeking familiar destinations and the security of the travel trade. Mid-centrics have some of both of these characteristics and represent the bulk of the market. Plog envisages a destination appealing to allocentrics in the early stages of evolution, to mid-centrics in the later stages of 'development' and 'consolidation' and to psychocentrics in 'stagnation' and 'decline'. Other typologies of tourists utilize the same dimensions. For example, Cohen's (1972) explorers will visit in the early stages of the cycle, followed by organized mass tourists in the latter stages. While this could be seen as simplistic, failing to take account of the mosaic of different types of tourists always present at a destination, the demonstration of successive waves of different numbers and types of tourists, with distinctive preferences, motivations and desires, populating the resort at each stage of the life cycle is useful.

9.3 UTILITY OF THE LIFE CYCLE

9.3.1 Calibration

There is increasing empirical evidence in the literature for the life cycle and a number of researchers have overtly used the cycle as a framework for analysing changing destinations (Stansfield, 1978; Hovinen, 1981; Meyer-Arendt, 1985; Oglethorpe, 1984; Wilkinson, 1987; Cooper and Jackson, 1989). However, few studies have actually attempted to develop the model, although Lundgren's (1982) examination of the spatial evolution of accommodation supply in the Laurentians, Nelson and Wall's (1986) analysis of the changing transport network on Vancouver Island, and Keller's (1987) development of the cycle in an examination of centre–periphery tourism do develop the concept of the life cycle.

Opponents of the cycle argue that, to date, empirical studies simply demonstrate that the shape of the curve varies depending upon supply factors (rate of development, access, government policy and competing destinations) and factors on the demand side (such as the changing nature of clientele) as the destination's market evolves hand in hand with supply-side developments. Clearly this demonstrates that the life cycle is destination-specific. Each stage varies in length and the curve displays differing shapes and patterns (Hovinen, 1981). The main problems are as follows.

IDENTIFYING TURNING POINTS
Turning points can be identified by the use of leading indicators, such as the growth rate of visits, the level of visits compared to market potential, the percentage of first-time visitors, the numbers of competitors, the levels of prices and profits, advertising, promotional and price elasticity, and the emergence of new destinations meeting customer needs more effectively (Doyle, 1976; Rink and Swan, 1979; Day, 1981; Haywood, 1986).

IDENTIFYING STAGES
The variety of possible shapes of the curve and acceleration or delay due to external factors make it difficult to identify the stage reached by a destination, although this can be done by plotting the rate of change of visitor numbers, visitor expenditure, type of tourist, market share or profitability. Jones and Lockwood (1990, p. 7) argue that shape is less relevant than different types of growth. They suggest that:

> irrespective of the shape, the PLC concept infers that at some time in their development all products will have a period of slow, medium or high growth, constant sales and declining sales. Where sales follow the suggested sequence, an S shaped curve will result, but where they do not, a different shape of curve will emerge.

Both Jones and Lockwood (1990) and Tse and Elwood (1990) utilize this approach to develop guidelines for strategy in hospitality management.

DIFFERING LENGTHS
The length of each stage, and therefore of the cycle itself, is variable. At one extreme instant resorts such as Cancún (Mexico)

or timeshare developments move almost immediately to growth; at the other extreme well-established resorts such as Brighton (England) have taken hundreds of years to move from exploration to rejuvenation. Equally there is a variety of types of cycle, such as the scalloped pattern where a sequence of developments at the destination prompts a revival of visitor arrivals (Buttle, 1986).

LEVEL OF AGGREGATION

The level of aggregation and geographical scale are important simply because the tourist area life cycle for each country is made up of a mosaic of resorts and tourist areas (which in turn contain life cycles for hotels, theme parks, etc.) (Rink and Swan, 1979; Kotler, 1980; Brownlie, 1985). Depending upon the scale taken, each element may be at a different stage in the cycle (compare for example the stage reached by differing islands in the Spanish Canary Islands). The unit of analysis is therefore crucial.

9.3.2 Forecasting

Use of the life cycle approach as a forecasting tool depends upon the ability to isolate and predict the forces driving it (Onkvisit and Shaw, 1986). Most forecasts have strict assumptions – a constraint on long-run growth, an S-shaped diffusion curve, homogeneity of customers – and give no explicit consideration of marketing decisions or the competition. If forecasts are to be successful, long runs of visitor arrivals data are needed to give stable parameter estimates (Brownlie, 1985). Commonly, only island destinations are able to provide such data sets. Dewar (1983) and Nelson and Wall (1986) consider alternative data sources, such as hotel registers, in an attempt to provide data for the cycle.

9.3.3 Strategy

At each stage in the life cycle, expected market growth, distribution of market shares, degree of competition and profitability vary. A different marketing mix may therefore be appropriate at each stage (Levitt, 1965; Hofer, 1975; Wind and Claycamp, 1976; Kotler, 1980; Onkvisit and Shaw, 1986; Kimberley and Miles, 1987). Both Tse and Elwood (1990) and Low and MacMillan (1988) take this one stage further by examining the different management styles and personalities required at differing stages of the life cycle. Haywood (1990) suggests that organizations in the early stages of life have distinctive characteristics – such as vulnerability, management by crisis and little delegation. While strategic options have received attention in tourism research, those of management style, personalities and the characteristics of leaders have received little attention. More work has been done to prescribe the strategic options at each stage of the life cycle.

At the involvement stage concern is with building up a strong market position before competitors enter. In the development stage emphasis changes to building market share through increased visitor numbers, pre-empting competitors' customers. As consolidation approaches, the defence of share against competitors becomes important, as does maintaining margins and cash flow by cost control and avoiding price wars. However, once visitor numbers stabilize, management should not await decline as inevitable but should seek to revitalize visits. At this stage, Levitt (1965) argues that it is important to utilize the stages of the life cycle to develop and evaluate marketing strategy by life extension – a planned series of actions to ensure that numbers of visitors and profitability are sustained for as long as possible.

Jones and Lockwood (1990) consider growth patterns of sales (or for destinations, visits) as the determinant of strategy. They suggest the following classification.

LAUNCH OR RELAUNCH

Innovation   To be used at launch or relaunch, this is a radical approach demanding decreased costs of inputs matched by increased volume of sales. In hospitality management this may involve a total change of the service delivery mechanism, perhaps by switching from serviced tables to counter service.

GROWTH

Sales development   This strategy is suited to early stages of growth when there are fewer competitors. Here inputs are kept constant but sales volume is increased by charging a premium price. This is a market-oriented approach.

Balanced growth   This strategy aims to expand the customer base in a period of rapid growth. It is accepted that in order to increase the value of sales both inputs and the volume of sales must increase. Here it is important to capitalize on any economies of scale.

MATURITY

Cost reduction   This strategy maintains the value of sales while the cost of inputs is reduced through gains in productivity.

DECLINE

Retrenchment Here it is recognized that in cutting costs there may be a reduction in sales volume but that margins can still be improved. Thus even with a diminishing customer base, productivity and profits can rise.

In practice, strategies for the decline stage are much more difficult when managers are dealing with the built fabric of tourist destinations. For example, many cold-water resorts in northern Europe and also on the eastern seaboard of the USA have reached the decline stage of the life cycle. At the strategic level, thinking on the scale of the life cycle can provide managers with a historical perspective and prompt a new scale of strategic thinking. Diamond (1988) suggests that four possible strategies are available to resorts.

Turnaround This represents a concerted public and private sector effort to reverse falling visitor numbers by investment in development and substantial planning and promotional efforts. Scheveningen (Netherlands) falls into this category.

Sustainable growth Here the resort's external conditions are unfavourable, perhaps in terms of access, and the strategy concentrates on maintaining existing markets and achieving a low level of growth by new recruitment of visitors to supplement a loyal repeat clientele. A number of small and medium-sized resorts in northern England fall into this category.

Incremental growth This strategy adopts a phased approach to resort development with limited use, by test marketing, of new products and phased development projects as the resort seeks new markets. In England, Bournemouth's strategy in the leisure segment of its market fits this category.

Selective tourism Here only certain market segments are targeted to capitalize on the resort's strengths. In England, Swanage, with a concentration on family holidays and the education market, is a good example.

9.4 THE TOURISM ISSUES RAISED BY REJUVENATION

One of the most pressing problems faced by coastal resorts in northern Europe is to overcome declining visitor numbers and to rejuvenate. Clearly these resorts are in the decline stage of the life cycle, partially because of the success of Mediterranean tourist destinations in meeting the demands of holiday-takers in the second half of the twentieth century. The strategic response to these problems is complex, as the resorts are major manifestations of Victorian and Edwardian capital investment in bricks and mortar. Often tourism is closely woven into the very way of life of the town and supports jobs, services and carriers (Cooper, 1990). The reduction of tourism thus places the architectural, economic and social future of these resorts in jeopardy (Smith, 1980) and it is therefore difficult to argue that such resorts have reached the end of their useful life.

The scale of the problem is exemplified by the variety of threats facing cold-water resorts. These threats can be summarized as: an eroding share and volume of the tourist market; low-status, low-quality tourism; a high degree of seasonality; a poor standard of tourist plant; short-term planning; inadequate financial and human resources; and local opposition to change. These problems prompted the English Tourist Board to stimulate strategic thinking in resorts through the Resort 2000 competition, launched in 1985 (English Tourist Board, 1985). Resorts were asked to submit strategies which would be judged on criteria including: degree of local authority commitment; level of political support; degree of 'corporate' thinking and evidence of partnerships with other public agencies, voluntary bodies and commercial interests; attitude and commitment of the local tourism industry; potential and ability to capitalize on strengths and opportunities; and tourist board involvement. The winners of the competition received Tourism Development Action Programme (TDAP) status. This is a means of focusing government aid to tourism, while involving the private sector, to act as a catalyst for future development and marketing of the resorts (English Tourist Board, 1987).

Not all resorts in decline are within the British statutory tourist board framework, but it is interesting that similar strategic initiatives have been carried out in the Channel Islands and on the Isle of Man. The Isle of Man in particular has suffered severe problems of decline in the post-war era and has required a tailor-made strategy to rejuvenate. While the island demonstrates all the problems identified above, it is seriously disadvantaged by its location in the Irish Sea. This location makes the island dependent upon the actions and prices of carriers and also denies it a large day trip or weekend catchment for short holiday breaks or the support for a major tourist attraction (Cooper and Jackson, 1985).

In common with most tourist islands, the Isle of Man has regular monitoring of both the volume and characteristics of visitors. In the post-war era tourist arrivals to the island have gradually declined, and as the competition from both the domestic and Mediterranean markets intensified in the 1970s and 1980s the island's tourism industry became demoralized and unprofitable (Figure 9.1).

In the 1980s the traditional long-holiday market continued to decline rapidly. These visitors demonstrate many of the features of unadventurous, laggard adopters of a resort. They are highly seasonal (47 per cent of all arrivals are in July and August), travel by sea, are low-spending and middle-aged, and display a high degree of repeat visiting. Length of stay is eroding and the geographical catchment is gradually reducing, and is now focused

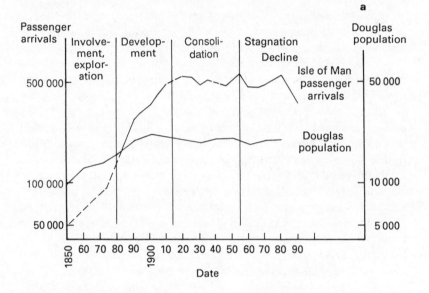

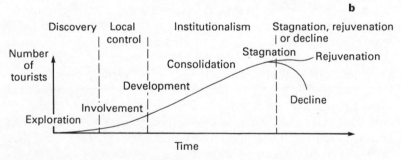

Figure 9.1 Actual and hypothetical life cycles.

a, *Passenger arrivals to the Isle of Man, and the Douglas population.* **b**, *Hypothetical tourist area life cycle.*

154

on northern England, southern Scotland, Eire and Northern Ireland (Economic Adviser's Office, 1987). Increasing air arrivals are explained by a flourishing off-shore finance industry which has boosted business tourism. However, although this trend is welcome, it is holiday arrivals that support much of the island's tourism plant – business tourism accounts for less than 10 per cent of bed-nights.

The island's tourism plant dates from the late nineteenth century. For example, the accommodation sector suffers from a lack of private investment since the 1920s and is now dominated by a legacy of inappropriate accommodation. The real problem is the combination of over-provision of small hotels (with large family-sized rooms and lacking en-suite bathrooms, lifts and toilets) with the small family businesses that dominate the guest-house sector. They cannot afford to invest in modernization and are seeking to change use from accommodation to residential, health or business premises as confidence in tourism diminishes. In addition, the high degree of seasonality prejudices their profitability and thus businesses cannot invest to upgrade tourist facilities. This weakens the Isle of Man's position in the UK domestic and overseas markets and threatens the viability of those enterprises that remain.

In the face of these problems the Isle of Man has decided to adopt a sustainable growth strategy (Diamond, 1988). The Isle of Man is administratively independent of the English system of tourist boards and can therefore design a strategy to target the particular problems of the Manx tourism industry. In 1986 a renewed political commitment to tourism led to the commissioning of a tourism strategy for the island to take it into the 1990s.

The sustainable growth strategy had three key elements. The first was to give the industry a public sector lead by strengthening the Isle of Man Tourist Board (IOMTB). The second was adoption of a disciplined market planning process. This was designed to protect the island's traditional market, to test-market in selected emergent market sectors and to provide the foundations for the 1990s by investing in research and computerized reservations, and by strengthening the tourist board's inclusive tour programme. Finally, a development plan for tourism addresses the need to update the island's tourist facilities. This is designed to support the marketing strategy with a programme of upgrading and new building of tourist plant to allow the island to attract new markets and compete in the tourism market-place of the 1990s. The development strategy is important as, in the past, the island has promoted but not developed tourism. A clear identification of the island's strong and weak tourist facilities was therefore required, matched by government aid to build on the island's rich natural and cultural heritage.

The sustainable growth strategy adopted by the Isle of Man is a practical example of a strategic option available to resorts in decline. It provides clear lessons for other resorts in a similar position – in particular the need for commitment on the part of the tourism industry, for professional leadership from the public sector, and for a co-ordinated promotion and development strategy over the medium rather than the short term in order to match the holiday product to the needs of emergent market segments.

9.5 CONCLUSIONS

Butler's original conceptualization of the tourist cycle did not envisage its use as a prescriptive tool and it is clear that problems emerge when the cycle is used in this way. Accurate forecasting demands long runs of data on visitor numbers, which are often lacking (Butler, 1980), and the cycle, at best, can assist general trend projection rather than causal forecasts. In terms of its use for strategic planning, some argue that rather than being an independent guide for strategy, or forecasting, the cycle is simply an outworking of management decisions and heavily dependent on external factors such as competition, the development of new destinations, swings in consumer taste, government legislation and regional policy (Dhalla and Yuspeh, 1976).

This is, in fact, the strength of the life cycle approach. If the life cycle is seen as integrating the disparate factors that are involved in developing a resort, then it is an excellent descriptive tool. This becomes more attractive when it is realized that all elements of tourism demand, supply and organization at destination level can be integrated within this one explanatory framework. In particular the integration of physical development factors (investment, organization, scale, impact, planning) with those of demand (changing market volume and characteristics as visitors adopt the destination) at each stage of the life cycle provides tourism researchers with a glimmer of the elusive unifying concept or generalization of tourism.

The life cycle approach has, therefore, much to offer tourism researchers and rather less to offer the tourist practitioner. Its logical and intuitive appeal deserves greater attention among tourism researchers, who should not be swayed by those who criticize the life cycle for its lack of operational value. By regarding destinations as dependent upon the actions of managers, the tourist industry and their markets, the life cycle provides an integrating medium for the study of tourism, a promising vehicle for future research, and a frame of reference for emergent themes in tourism, such as sustainable tourism.

It is therefore important to develop research into the life cycle concept. In particular there is a need for research in the following areas:

1 Examination of the historical context of resorts to elicit the activity of decision-makers at turning points and generalizations of the characteristics of resorts at each stage.
2 Examination of data sets, where they exist, to determine the nature of market segments at each stage, and the growth rates of visitors and turning points to allow initial calibration of the cycle.
3 Examination of the changing nature of variables such as organizational structure and functioning, investment, land use profits, seasonality and transportation in relation to the cycle.
4 Mathematical modelling of the curve and the factors influencing visitor adoption of resorts.

References

Brownlie, D. (1985) Strategic marketing concepts and models. *Journal of Marketing Management*, **1**, 157–94.

Burns, T. and Stalker, G.M. (1961) *The Management of Innovation.* London: Tavistock.

Butler, R.W. (1980) The concept of a tourist area cycle of evolution: implications for management of resources. *Canadian Geographer*, **24**, 5–12.

Buttle, F. (1986) *Hotel and Food Service Marketing.* London: Holt.

Clarke, R. (1985) *Industrial Economics.* Oxford: Blackwell.

Cohen, E. (1972) Towards a sociology of international tourism. *Social Research*, **39**, 164–82.

Cooper, C.P. (1981) The spatial and temporal behaviour of tourists. *Regional Studies*, **15**, 359–71.

Cooper, C.P. (1990) Resorts in decline. The management response. *Tourism Management*, **11**(1), 63-7.

Cooper, C.P. and Jackson, S. (1985) Changing patterns of Manx tourism. *Geography*, **70**, 74-6.

Cooper, C.P. and Jackson, S. (1989) Destination life cycle: the Isle of Man case study. *Annals of Tourism Research*, **16**(3), 377-98.

Day, G.S. (1981) The product life cycle: analysis and applications issues. *Journal of Marketing*, **45**, 60-7.

Dewar, K. (1983) Old hotel registers as a tool in analysing resort visitation and development. *Recreation Research Review*, **10**, 5-10.

Diamond, N.P. (1988) A strategy for cold water resorts into the year 2000. MSc thesis, University of Surrey.

Dhalla, N.K. and Yuspeh, S. (1976) Forget the product life cycle concept. *Harvard Business Review*, **54**, 102-10.

Doyle, P. (1976) The realities of the product life cycle. *Quarterly Review of Marketing*, **1**, 1-6.

Economic Adviser's Office (1987) *Isle of Man Passenger Survey 1986*. Douglas: Economic Adviser.

English Tourist Board (1985) *Resort 2000 Competition*. London: ETB.

English Tourist Board (1987) *Annual Report for the Year Ending 31 March 1987*. London: ETB.

Hannan, M.T. and Freeman, J. (1977) The population ecology of organizations. *American Journal of Sociology*, **82**(5), 929-64.

Haywood, K.M. (1986) Can the tourist area life cycle be made operational? *Tourism Management*, **7**, 154-67.

Haywood, K.M. (1990) Resort cycles: a commentary. Paper presented to the Association of American Geographers, Toronto.

Hofer, C.W. (1975) Toward a contingency theory of business strategy. *Academy of Management Journal*, **18**, 784-809.

Hovinen, G.R. (1981) A tourist cycle in Lancaster County, Pennsylvania. *Canadian Geographer*, **25**, 283-6.

Jones, P. and Lockwood, A. (1990) Productivity and the product life cycle in hospitality firms. Paper presented to Contemporary Hospitality Management Conference, Bournemouth.

Keller, C.P. (1987) Stages of peripheral tourism development – Canada's North West Territories. *Tourism Management*, **8**, 20-32.

Kimberley, J.R. and Miles, R.H. (1987) *The Organization Life Cycle*. San Francisco: Jossey-Bass.

Kotler, P. (1980) *Principles of Marketing*, 3rd edn. Englewood Cliffs, NJ: Prentice-Hall.

Kwansa, P. and Evans, M. (1988) Financial management in the context of the life cycle. *Hospitality Education Research Journal*, 12(2), 197–214.

Levitt, T. (1965) Exploit the product life cycle. *Harvard Business Review*, 43, 81–94.

Low, M. B. and MacMillan, I. C. (1988) Entrepreneurship: past research and future challenges. *Journal of Management*, 14, 139–61.

Lundgren, J. O. J. (1982) The development of tourist accommodation in the Montreal Laurentians. In Wall, G. and Marsh, J. (eds) *Recreational Land Use: Perspectives on its Evolution in Canada*, pp. 175–89. Ottawa: Carleton University Press.

Meyer-Arendt, K. J. (1985) The Grand Isle, Louisiana resort cycle. *Annals of Tourism Research*, 12, 449–66.

Nelson, R. and Wall, G. (1986) Transport and accommodation: changing interrelationships on Vancouver Island. *Annals of Tourism Research*, 13, 239–60.

Oglethorpe, M. (1984) Tourism in Malta. A crisis of dependence. *Leisure Studies*, 3, 147–62.

Onkvisit, S. and Shaw, J. J. (1986) Competition and product management: can the product life cycle help? *Business Horizons*, 29, 51–62.

Plog, S. C. (1973) Why destination areas rise and fall in popularity. *Cornell Hotel and Restaurant Association Quarterly*, 13, 13–16.

Rink, D. R. and Swan, J. E. (1979) Product life cycle research: literature review. *Journal of Business Research*, 78, 219–42.

Smith, S. J. C. (1980) Coastal planning: where next? *The Planner*, 66, 143–5.

Stansfield, C. A. (1978) Atlantic City and the resort cycle. Background to the legalization of gambling. *Annals of Tourism Research*, 5, 238–51.

Tse, E. C. and Elwood, C. M. (1990) Synthesis of the life cycle concept with strategy and management style: a case analysis in the hospitality industry. *International Journal of Hospitality Management*, 9(3), 223–36.

Vernon, R. (1966) International investment and international trade in the product cycle. *Quarterly Journal of Economics*, 80, 190–207.

Vernon, R. (1979) The product life cycle hypothesis in a new international environment. *Oxford Bulletin of Economics and Statistics*, **41**, 255-67.

Weg, H. van de (1982) Revitalization of traditional resorts. *Tourism Management*, **3**, 303-7.

Wilkinson, P.F. (1987) Tourism in small island nations: a fragile dependence. *Leisure Studies*, **6**, 127-46.

Wind, Y. and Claycamp, H.J. (1976) Planning product line strategy: a matrix approach. *Journal of Marketing*, **40**, 2-9.

10 Modelling Visitor Flows at the Beamish Museum

Adrian Darnell, Peter Johnson and Barry Thomas

10.1 INTRODUCTION

The formal econometric modelling of tourism demand between countries has received considerable research attention in recent years (see, for example, Little, 1980; Kliman, 1981; Loeb, 1982; Witt and Martin, 1985, 1987 – these and other studies are briefly surveyed in Johnson and Ashworth (1990) and Ashworth and Johnson (1990)). This study complements these 'macro' studies by formally modelling demand at the level of the individual tourist attraction. Such modelling may provide a better and more rigorous understanding of the underlying nature and determinants of demand and hence a sounder basis for forecasting. It is against this background that this chapter presents the results of an analysis of visitor flows to a major individual attraction, the North of England Open Air Museum at Beamish.[1]

Attention is focused on a single-equation demand model based on elementary economic theory. It is shown that such a model, despite its limitations, can provide some interesting insights and may be of value as a management tool. Decisions on pricing, investment, staffing, marketing and product development, for example, are likely to be affected by their implications for demand; moreover some of these decisions will be *a consequence* of past or forecast trends in demand. While the formal modelling of demand cannot be a substitute for the intimate intuitive knowledge of visitor flows that managers may have built up over many years – frequently, an econometric analysis cannot easily capture some of the more 'qualitative' factors that managers may think are important – it can nevertheless provide an appropriate base from which to work. It is thus a useful complement to managerial intuition and an aid to judgement.

The structure of this chapter is as follows: Section 10.2 provides a brief description of the development of Beamish, and of visitor trends since its formation; Section 10.3 outlines the methodology and results of the modelling exercise; Section 10.4 offers some discussion of the exercise; and Section 10.5 presents a summary and conclusion.

10.2 THE BACKGROUND TO BEAMISH

The idea of an open-air museum in the north of England was first formalized in 1958 when a proposal was put to Durham County Council's Bowes Museum Sub-Committee by Frank Atkinson, the then newly appointed Curator of the Bowes Museum.[2] Atkinson's ideas had originated from a visit to an open air museum in Scandinavia in the early 1950s. The proposal was eventually taken up by a consortium of local authorities in the North-East and an initial exhibition was opened in May 1971. The opening of the museum occurred a year later. The purpose of the museum was 'to study, collect, preserve and exhibit buildings, machinery, objects and information, illustrating the historical development of industry and the way of life of the North of England.'[3] It was to be a 'living' museum.

The museum was enthusiastically received in the region, with the opening exhibition – which ran for only 20 summer weekends in 1971 – attracting 50 000 visitors. As Figure 10.1 shows, visitor numbers rose substantially during the 1970s: the 1979–80 attendance was over six times that of 1971. During that period, a number of major exhibits (including the tram, track, station, pit cottages, signal box and drift mine) were opened. These developments were financed by the local authorities, grant-giving bodies and a trust fund set up to promote the development of the museum. The local authorities also provided a substantial contribution to revenue funding.

In the summer of 1980, the museum experienced its first ever downturn in visitor numbers. This fall created substantial financial pressures on the museum and led to some retrenchment. However, it also led to a new commitment to the marketing of the

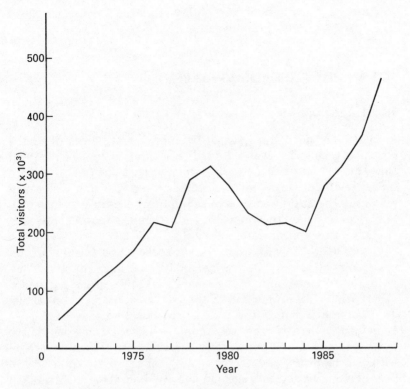

Figure 10.1 Total visitor numbers to Beamish Museum.

museum and to the introduction of much better budgetary and planning procedures. The decline eventually reversed in the summer of 1985, since when the trend has been upwards. The severity of the earlier downturn is shown by the fact that only in 1987 did the summer figures finally exceed those of 1979. In the mid-1980s, Beamish consolidated its position as a major museum. In 1985 a key new development, the Town Street, was opened at the museum. Then in 1986, the year a new Visitor Centre was opened, the museum received the Museum of the Year Award. In the following year it received the European Museum of the Year Award. The local authorities have continued to contribute to the revenue account, although their contribution has declined in real terms since 1974–5 and is now less than one-third of total income.

Although the museum was initially envisaged as meeting regional needs, over half of its visitors now come from outside the

North-East. Visitor flows are highly seasonal. This of course is largely attributable to the weather.

10.3 MODELLING THE DEMAND FOR BEAMISH

10.3.1 The Model

In modelling the visitor flows at Beamish the technique of single-equation estimation was adopted. Although it could be argued that there is an identification issue and that the quantities are influenced by price and vice versa, this is not relevant in this context since the 'supply' is treated as infinitely elastic at the prevailing price chosen by the museum. Thus a single-equation approach is likely to be appropriate.

The quarterly flows exhibit a clear seasonal pattern, which on a simple ratio to moving average analysis – which involves computing a 12-month moving average then expressing a particular observation as a proportion of the trend – appears to be stable. This pattern is not in the least surprising and may be wholly explained by correlating the monthly observations of visitor flows (expressed as a percentage of a 12-month moving average) with the monthly figures for average maximum temperature, average rainfall and average sun hours. Given the great stability in the distribution of visitors over the year the flows were modelled in a log-linear form, using simple shift dummy variables to capture the seasonality. There is also a need to model 'quality' changes as the nature of the museum's 'product' has changed significantly over the recent past with the opening of the Town Street and the new Visitor Centre. Again, dummies were introduced to capture this effect, although they were introduced in a manner that allows a 'decay' in the effect: both dummies take the value 1 in the quarter of introduction, but then the dummies each decline so that in the next period they take the value 0.9, 0.8 and so on to a value of 0.1, which is then maintained. This is a rather crude attempt to capture the likely decline of the influence of such quality changes. The timing of Easter is also likely to have an impact, and Easter may fall in either the first or the second quarter. Two dummies were introduced to capture the effect, one taking the value 1 in quarter 1 if Easter Sunday falls in that quarter and 0 otherwise, and a second taking the value 1 in quarter 2 if Easter Sunday falls in that quarter and 0 otherwise; this allows there to be a differential impact upon visitor flows, depending upon the quarter in which Easter falls.

The equation that was first examined therefore included the above dummies, and included as 'economic variables' the entry price to Beamish,[4] disposable personal income and the retail price index (as an index of the price of other goods); these variables were included in accordance with standard economic theory. When estimated in this fashion, the equation showed marked autocorrelation in the residuals, which was interpreted as an indicator of misspecification. Any regression equation is necessarily characterized by errors, omissions and approxima-tions; however, a well-specified equation will have residuals that are consistent with a non-systematic error structure, and the presence of autocorrelation indicates that the error contains some systematic components. This clearly indicates that the specifica-tion is deficient in some way, and further analysis is required. The deficiencies may arise, *inter alia*, from the use of an incorrect func-tional form, a misspecified set of regressors or data that are inade-quate proxies for their theoretical counterparts.

In a simple equation which seeks to explain visitor flows by a set of dummies (thought *a priori* to be important and having theoretical justification) and a set of contemporaneous economic variables, it is recognized that a number of salient variables may have been omitted or may have been misspecified. For example, the role of advertising is not included, nor is the important effect of information 'trickling down' through the potential population of visitors: visitors tell others of Beamish and this leads to increased demand as awareness of the museum becomes more widespread. Furthermore, there is no attempt to model the com-position of demand in terms of first-time and repeat visits. (The frequency of visits will depend, *inter alia*, on the rate of decay of the initial experience.) Again, there is no explicit recognition of the fact that continued growth in demand entails drawing visitors from more and more distant locations. Travel costs thus increase and the price of the 'day out' (rather than simply the admission price) increases *pari passu*. There may be several complex inter-actions: for example, repeat visits are more likely for visitors who live nearer, and the attraction's marketing strategies may influence and be influenced by the geographical source of visitors. Finally, possible supply constraints and the role of competitors have not been examined.

These issues, which perhaps require the direct modelling of the individual consumer's decisions and of supply, may be of impor-tance but need not be considered here. However, account has been taken of the possibility that, in making consumption decisions, individuals may react to previous values of the admission price, of their own disposable income and of the general price level. Specifically, the rate of change of the admission price may be salient, as may the rate of growth of their income and the rate of growth of the retail price index (RPI). In order to examine these possibilities, the original specification was expanded to include the lagged values of the entry price, disposable income, RPI and visitor flows as additional explanatory variables. The inclusion of the lagged dependent variable allows for the 'trickle down' effect referred to earlier and for habit persistence. The latter effect implies that individuals will repeat visits: *ceteris paribus*, an individual who has made a visit in period t is more likely to do so in period $t + 1$.

These additions result in a well-specified regression equation which successfully passes all diagnostic tests (see below), and the estimated equation may be written in a somewhat simplified form. The coefficients on the current and lagged entry price are not significantly different in size, but are of opposite sign, and this allows us to combine the two independent variables of current and lagged price in difference form. It is also possible to combine the disposable income variables with the general price level and to write the equation in terms of current deflated disposable income and its rate of growth. These changes are data-based simplifications of a general equation whose specification is determined by theoretical considerations. This equation, estimated over the period from 1975, second quarter (1975Q2), to 1988, third quarter (1988Q3), may then be written in the following terms:

$$\ln(V) = -13.53 + 0.64Q_1 + 3.20Q_2 + 2.71Q_3 + 0.91E_1 + 0.69E_2$$
$$ (4.65) \quad (0.28) \quad (0.29) \quad (0.09) \quad (0.14) \quad (0.16)$$

$$+ 0.08X_1 + 0.22X_2 - 0.91S - 0.54\ln\left(P/P_{-1}\right) + 3.10\ln(\text{rpdi})$$
$$ (0.11) \quad (0.13) \quad (0.18) \quad (0.17) \quad (0.90)$$

$$+ 1.21\ln\left(\text{rpdi}/\text{rpdi}_{-1}\right) - 0.55\ln\left(\text{RPI}\right) + 0.45\ln V_{-1}$$
$$ (1.27) \quad (0.17) \quad (0.11)$$

(standard errors are in parentheses)
$R^2 = 0.9880$; $F(13, 40) = 253.0602$;
$\bar{R}^2 = 0.9841$; s.e. of regression $= 0.1641$;
Durbin–Watson (DW) statistic $= 1.7834$;
Durbin's $h = 1.3412$

where V is the visitor flow; Q_i is 1 in quarter i, 0 otherwise; E_i is 1 if Easter Sunday falls in quarter i, 0 otherwise; X_1 is the product quality dummy for the Town Street (see text); X_2 is the product quality dummy for the Visitor Centre (see text); S is the exceptional weather dummy (see text), 1 in 1979Q1, 0 otherwise; P is the full admission price (average for the quarter); rpdi is real personal disposable income; and RPI is the Retail Price Index. The following diagnostic tests are reported:

Serial correlation: $\chi^2(4) = 7.2690$; $F(4, 36) = 1.4000$
Functional form: $\chi^2(1) = 1.6640$; $F(1, 39) = 1.2400$
Normality: $\chi^2(2) = 0.9387$; F statistic not applicable
Heteroscedasticity: $\chi^2(1) = 2.5583$; $F(1, 52) = 2.5861$

The 5 per cent critical values are as follows:

$\chi^2(1) = 3.84$; $\chi^2(2) = 5.99$; $\chi^2(4) = 9.49$
$F(4, 36) = 2.86$; $F(1, 39) = 4.09$; $F(1, 52) = 4.03$

The four tests reported are, respectively, the Lagrange multiplier test of residual serial correlation, Ramsey's RESET test using the square of the fitted values, a test of the skewness and kurtosis of residuals and a test based on the regression of squared residuals on squared fitted values.

This equation was also subjected to a test of stability, estimating it over the period 1975Q1 to 1987Q1 and examining the predictions over the next six quarters with respect to the known outcomes; not only are the estimated coefficients little different from those from the full sample, but using Chow's second test for predictive failure, the hypothesis of stability cannot be rejected. The observed test statistics are $\chi^2(6) = 8.0188$; $F(6, 34) = 1.3365$, which are to be compared with critical values (using a 5 per cent significance level) of 12.59 and 2.38 respectively.

It is important to note that the lagged variables, although included in a general way, may be written in the specific form as above: the estimated equation allows the current and lagged admission price to be written as the logarithm of the ratio of current to last period's price; this is (approximately) the percentage increase in the admission price and, as predicted by theory, has a significant negative sign. The estimated equation also indicates that the role of the general price level is felt through the variable rpdi, which is nominal personal disposable income deflated by the RPI, through the logarithm of the ratio of current to last period's 'real' personal disposable income (which is, approximately, the percentage rate of growth of 'real' personal disposable income) and through the term in the RPI itself. The last period's visitor flows have a significant positive effect on the current flows. This latter variable may be explained by reference to the role of potentially important, though unmeasurable, variables: as information on the museum percolates through the potential visitor population this increases visitor flows further, many visitors repeat their visits and direct advertising (such as that through car stickers displayed by previous visitors) also acts to increase the number of visitors. This lagged flow variable may be interpreted as catching the aggregation of such effects.

As a test of economic theory, this equation performs as predicted by theory: the role of admission prices is significant and negative, and the current demand for admission would appear to be price-inelastic (a 1 per cent rise in the current admission price appears to reduce current demand by about 0.5 per cent, *ceteris paribus*). The influence of current 'real' personal disposable income is significant and positive, and indicates a relatively large short-run elasticity of 4.31. However, not only does the level of income matter, but so does the direction of growth: growth in income increases demand. (This coefficient on the growth of rpdi is not well defined, but its deletion produces autocorrelation in the residuals, indicating that excluding this variable results in some misspecification, and on this criterion its inclusion is justified.) The general price level has a further role to play, in addition to deflating nominal incomes: even if incomes and prices were to rise in the same proportion this equation indicates that demand for museum admission would fall. This suggests that, even if real incomes were maintained, general inflation results in consumers switching demand away from such leisure activities as museums. The role of the last period's visitor numbers is, as predicted, significant and positive, and this must be interpreted as catching a large number of omitted, non-measurable influences.

The estimated equation also indicates that the quarterly effects are all significant, as is to be expected, and the quality changes both have positive impacts, although the coefficient on the Town Street dummy is not well defined. The effect of Easter is positive, and significant, with the size of the impact depending upon the quarter in which Easter falls. The dummy variable S takes account of the exceptional weather of quarter 1, 1979, during which the North-East suffered very badly from snow conditions.[5]

10.3.2 Forecasts

The equation can be used for forecasting demand on the basis of different assumptions about the growth in admission prices and in real personal disposable income. As an example, the visitor numbers for 1989 and the subsequent five years were forecast. This exercise was undertaken at the end of 1988 and used the then available UK Treasury estimates, adjusted where appropriate, of future likely trends in prices and incomes. The forecasts incorporated the price increases already agreed for 1989. Specifically, it was assumed that:

1 Prices would rise at 5 per cent per annum after 1989.
2 The RPI would grow at 7.5 per cent in quarters 1 and 2 of 1989, would rise to 8.0 per cent in quarter 3 and would then fall back to 7.0 per cent in quarter 4; during 1990, the assumption was that inflation would be 6.0 per cent and in all future years 4.0 per cent. (All the percentage figures are annualized rates.[6])
3 The growth in personal disposable income, deflated by the price level, would grow at 2.5 per cent, 3.0 per cent or 3.5 per cent per annum.[7]

Each of these scenarios was considered, and the results are shown in Figure 10.2. The lowest growth path is that associated with real growth of income at 2.5 per cent per annum, the middle growth path is that associated with real growth of income at 3.0 per cent per annum and the highest growth path is that associated with real growth of income at 3.5 per cent per annum. Whichever scenario is considered, the general path is upwards from 1989; the dip between 1988 and 1989 is largely a consequence of the known increases in admission prices[8] and the acceleration of the general price index. The forecasts suggest that the number of visitors may exceed 500 000 by 1991.

It is not realistic to use the model for longer-term forecasts but the forecasts for the years up to 1995 have been presented in Figure 10.2 simply to indicate the growth paths if there were no changes in environment or operating constraints. It cannot be emphasized too strongly that such long-term forecasts cannot be taken at their face value. However, while they may be seriously inaccurate they may nevertheless be of some use for planning, by providing a benchmark that can be modified (almost certainly downwards) in the light of managers' views of specific factors

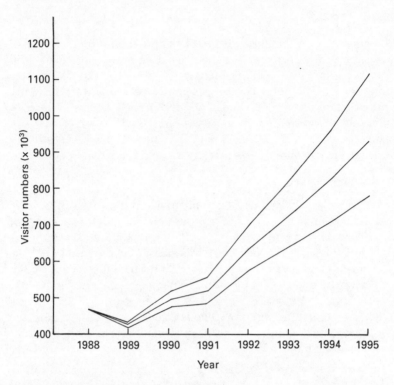

Figure 10.2 Annual forecasts up to 1995.

influencing the demand for the museum, its competitive position and its capacity. Various limitations of this forecasting exercise are considered in the next section.

10.4 DISCUSSION AND REVIEW

This modelling and forecasting exercise provides some useful results, summarized in the final section of the chapter, but it is proper to recognize that it has a number of limitations.

The forecasts are, of course, subject to error.[9] There are three sources of potential error. The first is the unexplained component of the estimated equation. The equation fits the data extremely well but it is, of course, not an exact fit and the consequent forecasting error will become larger as the period of the forecasts increases, because any error in a forecast in one period feeds into the forecasts of future periods.

A second source of error is the uncertainty over the future path of disposable income, the general price level and admission prices. The paths drawn in Figure 10.2 were based on 'intelligent guesses' about the movements of these variables.

A third source of error is that the forecasts are made on the assumption that the future will be an extrapolation of the past. Simple extrapolation takes no account, for example, of 'shocks' that may occur. An obvious instance in the case of Beamish Museum was the effect of the National Garden Festival held nearby in Gateshead in 1990. This was a major tourist attraction, but it was not clear in advance what its impact on Beamish would be. As it turned out, the festival probably had a favourable effect: the number of visitors to Beamish increased, and it seems likely that this increase was partly attributable to the festival. This example raises the more general question of the significance of factors like the competitive interaction of different tourist attractions and the role played by marketing, which are not explicitly modelled. The effect of changes in competitors' products and prices may influence the business strategies adopted by Beamish and the flow of visitors. The marketing strategies adopted by the museum may also be affected, as noted earlier, by the need to entice more visitors from distant locations, which may raise the museum's costs. Exceptionally good or bad weather represents another type of 'shock'.

The possible dangers of extrapolation from the demand model presented above are also evident from the fact that supply was assumed to be infinitely elastic, so there are no supply constraints on the flow of visitors. However, at some point in the growth of visitors it is likely that the capacity of the museum would be reached. The measurement of capacity might not be straightforward because the daily physical capacity varies across different parts of the museum and the issue of whether or not the product – 'the Beamish Experience' – comprises the option of visiting *all* parts of the museum becomes relevant. In any event the existence of capacity constraints could impose a ceiling on the growth of visitors from the supply side, which would operate separately from any demand side ceiling attributable to such factors as saturation, frequencies of repeat visits and eventually prohibitive travel costs as the market is extended geographically.

10.5 SUMMARY

This chapter has developed an econometric model of visitor flows to a single tourist attraction. It complements the work on aggregate studies of tourism demand. The single-equation model used is subject to a number of limitations, discussed in Section 10.4, but nevertheless provides some clear results which are of interest both as a test of economic theory and as a potentially useful management tool that may be applicable *mutatis mutandis* to other individual attractions.

The model shows the relevance of admission prices and of real personal disposable income as determinants of demand. In the short run, price elasticity over the range experienced is low (about − 0.5) and income elasticity is high (about + 4.3). These results are robust and suggest that a simple model of this kind can be of considerable value. This is not to deny that more sophisticated modelling, taking account of some of the issues raised in this paper, would not be desirable. The possibility of there being some ceiling to the forecasts might be considered but in fact, in this case study, the fit of a log-linear model to the sample data is extremely good and experiments with variable elasticities did not perform well.

The strength of the estimated equation permits a modest measure of confidence that the model may be of some value in aiding the formation of managerial judgements, for example about the size of the elasticities and the trends in visitor flows. Other findings are also potentially significant. The remarkable stability in the distribution of demand across the four quarters suggests, for instance, that it might be difficult to alter this pattern. Thus redistributing the summer peak might be possible but is likely to require substantial effort. The role of certain product developments is also highlighted, as are the carry-over effects from one period to the next.

As a short-run forecasting tool the model appears to have some predictive ability,[10] although for the longer term it could only be used as a basis for modifying projections in the light of judgements about qualitative aspects of the operating environment. The appropriate way to use the model for forecasting would thus be in the form of a rolling review with continual updating as estimates of future admission prices and real personal disposable income are revised.

Notes

This chapter is reprinted, with permission, from *Tourism Management*, volume 11, number 3, 1990. Minor amendments have been made.

1 It might be argued that Beamish is a museum first and a tourist attraction second. It is not, however, necessary to enter this debate. Whatever the status assigned to Beamish, the determinants of its visitor flows remain of considerable management interest. For a history of the museum, see Johnson and Thomas (1989).

2 Minutes of Durham County Council's Education Committee's Sub-Committee on Further Education, 10 December 1958.

3 *First Development Plan* presented to the Joint Committee for the North of England Open Air Museum, 11 December 1970.

4 It can be argued that the relevant price is the cost of the whole outing, and should therefore include travel costs and possibly the cost of meals out (bought either inside or outside the museum) and other shopping. This raises questions about the definition of the product demanded, i.e. whether it is admission to the museum or some wider experience, which might include visits to other tourist attractions.

5 In the first quarter of 1979 there were 22 days with one or more inches of snow lying at 9 a.m. in January, 12 such days in February and 13 such days in March. This was far greater than for any other year since the early 1960s.

6 The Treasury's forecast in *The Financial Statement and Budget Report*, March 1989, of the annual rise in the RPI was 5.5 per cent for 1989 and 4.5 per cent for 1990, but these figures were thought to be too low.

7 This range of figures was chosen on the basis of the Treasury's forecasts for the growth of GDP (1989, 2.5 per cent; 1990, 2.5 per cent) and consumer spending (1989, 3.5 per cent; 1990, 2.5 per cent).

8 The admission price increases in 1989 were substantial. They were well over 20 per cent.

9 It is unlikely that the error will exceed ±15 per cent for the earliest forecasts.

10 It was noted in Section 10.3 that 'within sample' forecasts were convincing. Forecasts of rpdi are not easily available but there are many good proxies, such as GDP and consumers' expenditure. Had forecasts of GDP, which were available in 1978 and 1979, been used the model would *at that time* have correctly forecast the downturn in the number of visitors in the early 1980s. Treasury forecasts of GDP growth a year ahead had been non-negative since 1959, but in 1978 the forecast for 1980 was for a substantial fall in GDP (which did

occur). By 1979 all the principal economic forecasting models of the economy were publishing forecasts of a fall in GDP.

References

Ashworth, J. and Johnson, P.S. (1990) Holiday tourism expenditure: some preliminary econometric results. *Tourist Review*, (3), 12–20.

Johnson, P.S. and Ashworth, J. (1990) Modelling tourism demand: a summary review. *Leisure Studies*, 9, 145–60.

Kliman, M.L. (1981) A qualitative analysis of Canadian overseas tourism. *Transportation Research*, **15A**(6), 487–97.

Little, J.S. (1980) International travel in the US balance of payments. *New England Economic Review*, May/June, 45–55.

Loeb, P. (1982) International travel to the United States: an econometric evaluation. *Annals of Tourism Research*, 9(1), 7–20.

Witt, S.F. and Martin, C.A. (1985) Forecasting future trends in European tourist demand. *Tourist Review*, (4), 12–19.

Witt, S.F. and Martin, C.A. (1987) International tourism demand models – inclusion of marketing variables. *Tourism Management*, March, 33–40.

11 International Tourism Demand: A Meta-analytical Integration of Research Findings

Geoffrey I. Crouch and Robin N. Shaw

11.1 INTRODUCTION

International travel and tourism is a substantial and rapidly growing segment of international trade. It is now highly competitive and often constitutes an important component of a country's balance of payments. The need to enhance our understanding of the determinants of international tourist flows is therefore considerable for both government and private enterprises engaged in the travel and tourism industry.

Although there exists a growing body of research literature on this topic, the number of studies is not particularly large given the importance of this sector of the global economy. Furthermore, the existing *ad hoc* studies have yielded little in the way of generalized conclusions, and have only touched on some of the potential determinants of international tourist flows (for a comprehensive summary of studies, see Crouch and Shaw, 1990). Each new attempt to undertake further primary research has, by itself, often contributed only marginally to our understanding of the issue. Research conditions, methodologies, results and objects often vary considerably from one study to another, making it difficult to induce general laws.

Few reviews of past studies which have researched this topic have been undertaken, and those that have attempted to integrate findings have generally adopted the traditional narrative approach. This approach has some major limitations, particularly when the number of studies to be integrated is large. The vagaries of the approach provide enough slack to allow different reviewers to extract their own opinions. It therefore becomes difficult to distinguish opinion from review conclusion.

This chapter addresses this situation by presenting some preliminary results of ongoing research that uses meta-analytical techniques to integrate research findings. Meta-analysis is an approach that employs statistical methods to extract information from large masses of data that are nearly incomprehensible by other means. It does not prejudge research findings in terms of research quality. Rather, inter-study differences, which might be important indicators as to why findings vary, form the bases of hypotheses to be tested through meta-analysis. The study integrates the empirical findings of 44 previous studies. In particular, this work focuses on income and price elasticities of demand. Based on 777 suitable income elasticities, the results indicate that income elasticity is significantly positive and, in value, is significantly influenced by several substantive and methodological study characteristics. In contrast, based on 1227 suitable price elasticities, fewer factors among those investigated seemed to explain the inter-study variation between estimated relative price elasticities.

11.2 PREVIOUS RESEARCH

Since the early 1960s, numerous empirical studies have been undertaken in order to develop an understanding of the factors that affect the flows of international tourism. To our knowledge, no published study has ever attempted to integrate comprehensively these research findings. Table 11.1 identifies the majority of previous studies together with details concerning the type of dependent and independent variables that have been examined. This list of studies, although not complete, does, as far as we know, include almost all published and unpublished studies that have reached the public domain.[1]

Nearly all the studies have employed regression analysis, and all but a few have yielded demand elasticities of some form. Most of the resulting elasticities have been estimated directly by employing a log-linear (multiplicative) functional form. Other estimates indirectly result from the regression coefficients of a linear (additive) functional form. The majority of studies have used the number of tourist visits as the measure of demand. A

Table 11.1 Previous empirical studies

Authors	Dependent variables				Independent variables																					
	1	2	3	4	1	2	3	4	5	6	7	8	9	10	11	12	13	14	15	16	17	18	19	20	21	22
Anastasopoulos (1984)			•		•	•						•				•	•	•		•						
Armstrong (1972)					•	•						•														
Artus (1970)		•	•		•	•	•					•														
Artus (1972)	•	•	•		•	•	•	•	•		•															
Askari (1973)		•	•	•	•	•	•	•		•			•	•									•			
Barry and O'Hagan (1972)					•	•				•																
Bechdolt (1973)					•																					
Blackwell (1970)	•	•	•		•	•				•																
Bond and Ladman (1972)		•	•	•	•		•		•	•																
Chadee and Mieczkowski (1987)					•	•				•																
Cigliano (1980)					•														•							
Clarke (1978)			•	•	•	•	•																			
Cleverdon and Edwards (1982)		•			•	•				•																
Crampon and Tan (1973)					•					•						•										
Diamond (1977)					•	•		•	•	•		•	•		•	•		•								
Fujii and Mak (1981)		•		•	•		•			•																
Gerakis (1965)		•	•		•					•																
Gray (1966)			•		•		•			•																
Guthrie (1961)			•		•	•				•																
Hollander (1982)			•		•	•			•	•			•				•			•						
IAC (1989)	•	•	•		•	•				•		•	•							•						
Jud (1971)			•		•	•				•																
Jud (1974)			•		•	•				•																
Jud and Joseph (1974)	•	•	•		•	•				•					•											

177

Table 11.1 *continued*

Authors	Dependent variables				Independent variables																					
	1	2	3	4	1	2	3	4	5	6	7	8	9	10	11	12	13	14	15	16	17	18	19	20	21	22
Kanafani (1980)			●		●	●				●						●	●									
Kliman (1981)		●	●		●	●				●							●									
Kwack (1972)	●	●			●	●																				
Laber (1969)					●																					
Little (1980)		●		●	●	●	●	●	●				●													
Loeb (1982)	●	●	●	●	●	●	●	●		●			●					●								
Mak *et al.* (1977)					●	●						●	●				●	●					●		●	●
Martin and Witt (1987)			●		●			●		●			●													
Martin and Witt (1988)				●	●	●		●		●			●													
Mutti and Murai (1977)					●								●													
Noval (1975)	●		●		●	●		●		●		●	●													
O'Hagan and Harrison (1984)					●	●							●			●			●							
Oliver (1971)					●								●													
Papadopoulos and Witt (1985)					●					●		●	●	●												
Papadopoulos (1987)					●					●			●	●												
Quayson and Var (1982)		●		●	●			●		●			●													
Rojwannasin (1982)					●	●				●			●													●
Rugg (1971)					●								●								●	●	●	●		
Schulmeister (1979)		●	●	●	●	●	●			●			●		●	●	●	●			●					
Smeral (1988)					●											●	●								●	
Smith and Toms (1978)		●			●	●		●		●		●	●				●									
Strazheim (1978)					●	●				●			●													
Stronge and Redman (1982)					●			●		●			●						●							
Summary (1987)					●																					

178

Study	1	2	3	4	5	6	7	8	9	10	11	12	13	14	15	16	17	18	19	20	21	22
Sunday (1978)	●	●			●	●							●									
Taplin (1980)					●	●																
Tremblay (1989)	●		●		●	●		●														
Truett and Truett (1982)	●	●	●		●	●		●														
Truett and Truett (1987)	●	●	●		●	●																
Uysal (1983)			●		●	●																
Uysal and Crompton (1984)					●	●	●															
Uysal and O'Leary (1986)					●	●	●															
White and Walker (1982)	●	●			●	●		●														
White (1985)	●		●		●	●		●														
Williams and Zelinsky (1970)														●								
Witt (1980a)	●				●	●		●					●					●				
Witt (1980b)	●				●	●		●					●									
Witt and Martin (1985)	●				●	●				●			●									
Witt and Martin (1987)	●				●	●				●			●									
Zeitoun (1978)					●	●							●									
Number of studies	26	25	44	6	58	46	6	20	2	39	1	11	29	7	2	9	7	10	3	2	2	5
Percentage of studies	41	39	69	9	91	72	9	31	3	61	2	17	45	11	3	14	11	16	5	3	3	8

Dependent variables:
1, tourist expenditures; 2, tourist receipts; 3, tourist numbers; 4, length of stay.

Independent variables:
1, income (ability to pay/unemployment/economic activity); 2, relative prices; 3, lagged relative prices; 4, exchange rates; 5, lagged exchange rates; 6, transportation costs; 7, lagged transportation costs; 8, trends; 9, disturbance factors (dummy variables); 10, marketing expenditure; 11, weather index; 12, population; 13, ethnic attraction/cultural ties; 14, distance/travel time; 15, total tourist expenditure; 16, supply factors (hotel rooms, government assistance); 17, trade/business links; 18, travel restrictions; 19, tourist appeal; 20, explanatory variables are hypothesized but are not tested empirically; 21, demographic factors; 22, previous visits.

substantial portion of studies have also examined tourist receipts and/or expenditure. In addition, a small number have investigated 'length of stay' as the dependent variable. The most frequently employed independent variables (income, relative prices, cost of transportation and exchange rates) reflect both the preponderance of econometric approaches and limitations concerning the availability of data. In addition, however, numerous other independent variable types have been examined. Many of these other variables indicate an attempt to incorporate *marketing* factors with the customary *economic* factors.

Although the studies span approximately 100 countries, the findings are dominated by Western European and North American travel. The majority of studies have analysed data in the form of a time series. Several studies, however, have used cross-sectional analysis and a small number have pooled data in order to increase the variation in some of the variables. The data employed range from the early 1950s to the late 1980s, although the 1960s and 1970s are the most heavily represented periods.

A cursory inspection of the findings of these studies (see Crouch and Shaw, 1990, Table 7) reveals that empirical results vary considerably, and that generalizations will not be possible without a detailed and comprehensive statistical analysis. Many of the hypothesized determinants of international tourist flows have been found to be significant under a variety of conditions. However, the magnitude of the influence of each factor might vary as a function of both *substantive* factors (i.e. factors which characterize the circumstances of each study) and *methodological* factors (i.e. factors which characterize the different research procedures employed). Such inter-study differences form the bases of hypotheses that might explain why findings vary from one study to another. The general approach to the statistical testing of such hypotheses is known as meta-analysis.

As already indicated, this chapter reports some preliminary meta-analytical results of an ongoing study. Several studies are still to be coded for inclusion in the complete meta-analysis, and the resulting coded information is to undergo more comprehensive analysis and hypothesis testing. For the purposes of this particular study, income and price elasticities have been selected for an exploratory meta-analysis. These two independent variables have been the most widely examined in previous research.

Table 11.2 summarizes, for each of the 44 completed coded studies to date, details concerning the number of usable income and price elasticity estimates. In total, the coded data set at

Table 11.2 Available elasticity estimates

Study	Usable income elasticities		Usable relative price elasticities		Total regression coefficients	
	Frequency	%	Frequency	%	Frequency	%
Anastasopoulos (1984)	120	15.4	738	60.1	1042	18.6
Artus (1970)	4	0.5	2	0.2	20	0.4
Artus (1972)	30	3.9	35	2.9	285	5.1
Askari (1973)	8	1.0	–	–	113	2.0
Barry and O'Hagan	18	2.3	5	0.4	79	1.4
Bechdolt (1973)	22	2.8	–	–	132	2.4
Blackwell (1970)	3	0.4	–	–	40	0.7
Bond and Ladman (1972)	3	0.4	–	–	101	1.8
Chadee and Mieczkowski	2	0.3	2	0.2	16	0.3
Cigliano (1980)	5	0.6	–	–	17	0.3
Clarke (1978)	64	8.2	96	7.8	352	6.3
Diamond (1977)	10	1.3	–	–	40	0.7
Fujii and Mak (1981)	7	0.9	–	–	27	0.5
Gerakis (1965)	–	–	–	–	7	0.1
Gray (1966)	19	2.4	–	–	53	0.9
Guthrie (1961)	2	0.3	–	–	18	0.3
Jud (1971)	58	7.5	19	1.5	141	2.5
Jud and Joseph (1974)	–	–	–	–	91	1.6
Kliman (1981)	18	2.3	18	1.5	301	5.4
Kwack (1972)	10	1.3	6	0.5	61	1.1
Laber (1969)	4	0.5	–	–	19	0.3
Little (1980)	11	1.4	–	–	62	1.1
Loeb (1982)	14	1.8	14	1.1	60	1.1
Martin and Witt (1988)	36	4.6	36	2.9	195	3.5
Mutti and Murai (1977)	–	–	–	–	49	0.9
Noval (1975)	8	1.0	–	–	161	2.9
Oliver (1971)	4	0.5	1	0.1	18	0.3
Papadopoulos and Witt (1985)	36	4.6	36	2.9	216	3.9
Rojwannasin (1982)	42	5.4	42	3.4	252	4.5
Rugg (1971)	26	3.3	16	1.3	267	4.8
Smeral (1988)	14	1.8	6	0.5	58	1.0
Smith and Toms (1978)	21	2.7	–	–	93	1.7
Strazheim (1978)	1	0.1	–	–	23	0.4
Stronge and Redman (1982)	37	4.8	39	3.2	185	3.3
Summary (1987)	10	1.3	10	0.8	53	0.9
Sunday (1978)	–	–	–	–	48	0.9
Tremblay (1989)	21	2.7	21	1.7	109	1.9
Truett and Truett (1982)	4	0.5	8	0.7	44	0.8
Truett and Truett (1987)	11	1.4	9	0.7	37	0.7
Uysal (1983)	22	2.8	22	1.8	118	2.1
Uysal and Crompton (1984)	–	–	–	–	111	2.0
White and Walker (1982)	4	0.5	4	0.3	18	0.3
White (1985)	–	–	–	–	232	4.1
Witt and Martin (1987)	48	6.2	42	3.4	238	4.2
Total	777	100	1227	100	5602	100

Table 11.3 Coded regression coefficients

Variable type	Frequency	Percent
Regression constant	1056	18.9
Lagged dependent variable	62	1.1
Income	955	17.0
Lagged income	13	0.2
Relative prices	1299	23.2
Lagged relative prices	48	0.9
AIDS[a] own-price	23	0.4
AIDS[a] cross-price	171	3.1
AIDS[a] expenditure	14	0.2
Exchange rates	237	4.2
Lagged exchange rates	29	0.5
Transportation cost	450	8.0
Lagged transportation cost	10	0.2
Business activity	14	0.2
Market share	36	0.6
Lagged market share	2	0.0
Marketing expenditure	148	2.6
Weather	62	1.1
Travel distance	34	0.6
Cultural ties	27	0.5
Population	83	1.5
Supply constraints	6	0.1
Lagged supply constraints	4	0.1
Trend	80	1.4
Disturbances	640	11.4
Other	99	1.8
Total	5602	100.0

[a]Almost ideal demand system.

present amounts to 5602 separate regression coefficients or elasticities. Table 11.3 summarizes the type of variable associated with each of these elasticities. Apart from the regression constant (intercept), the most frequently examined variables are income and relative prices, followed by disturbances (i.e. dummy variables), cost of transportation, exchange rates and marketing expenditure.

11.3 META-ANALYSIS

The traditional narrative review of the literature is the oldest and most frequently employed procedure. The scope, methodology, findings, limitations and assumptions of each piece of work are described and critically appraised in non-quantitative or verbal terms. 'In this procedure the reviewer takes each study at face value and attempts to find an overarching theory that reconciles the findings' (Hunter *et al.*, 1982, p. 129). This is not a difficult task when the number of individual studies to be reviewed is small. However, when a large number of previous studies are available, it becomes extremely difficult to generalize the overall findings, other than in a superficial way.

Hunter *et al.* (1982, p. 129) suggest that frequently the result of an information-processing task that is too taxing for the human mind is usually one of three outcomes. Firstly, the reviewer may give up on any attempt to integrate findings across studies, relying instead on only a long list of verbal synopses of studies. Secondly, the reviewer may get around the problem by selecting a small subset of the studies on which to attempt an integration of the findings. This is often rationalized by rejecting studies from the analysis based on the view that they are deficient in some way and are therefore not worthy of further consideration. The risk in this outcome is that conclusions may be biased because some valuable information will be discarded in the process. That is, studies are either 'good' or 'bad', and if they are 'bad' then all information arising from them is useless.

Finally, if an attempt to integrate mentally the findings of all studies is made, an inadequate job is performed. It has been shown that 'even when the number of studies reviewed is as small as seven, reviewers who use narrative-discursive methods and reviewers who use quantitative methods reach different conclusions' (Hunter *et al.*, 1982, p. 130). The primary failing of the narrative review is that it is highly subjective and therefore it usually fails to exploit fully the knowledge contained in a body of literature. The following discussion (from Farley and Lehmann, 1986, p. 1), is typical of many literature reviews:

> In 1957, Smith said the effect of income on purchase was A. In 1961, Jones said B. In 1964, Baker replicated both Smith and Jones but subsequently (1967) argued for C. Since the methods used were not identical, we cannot be sure whether A, B or C is true.

This situation has unfortunately, but understandably, raised doubts about the value of such research and whether additional empirical studies are likely to expand our knowledge much further. Should we be making more use of the studies we already have? Gene Glass, a researcher who has contemplated this question more than anyone else, believes we should. Glass has noted (as reported in Hunter *et al.*, 1982, p. 26) that

> such studies collectively contain much more information than we have been able to extract from them to date. He points out that because we have not exploited these gold-mines of information, 'we know much less than we have proven'. What is needed are methods that will integrate results from existing studies to reveal patterns of relatively invariant underlying relations and casualties, the establishment of which will constitute general principles and cumulative knowledge.... In many areas of research, the need today is not additional empirical data but some means of making sense of the vast amounts of data that have accumulated ... it is likely that methods for doing this will attain increasing importance in the future.

Meta-analysis involves the application of statistical methods to the findings of a body of empirical studies. As Glass *et al.* (1981, p. 21) point out, 'it is not a technique; rather it is a perspective that uses many techniques of measurement and statistical analysis'. The prefix *meta* means of a higher or second-order kind, reflecting the fact that meta-analysis involves the analysis of secondary data. The use of the word 'analysis', however, is perhaps unfortunate as it implies the resolution of a problem into simpler elements. The opposite of analysis, that is, synthesis, is perhaps more appropriate as it involves a combination or composition of separate elements, especially of conception, propositions or facts, into a connected whole or generalization. Farley and Lehmann (1986, p. 54) liken the analysis to that of the archaeologist, who uses 'a few important clues and some general notions' to 'construct an admittedly incomplete understanding of a situation'.

The most important stage of the meta-analytical process involves coding. Coding requires the tabulation of all factors that characterize inter-study differences. Essentially, this involves a tabulation of all substantive and methodological differences. Hunter *et al.* (1982) suggest that this process occupies by far the major component of any meta-analysis. It involves going through each study in detail in order to extract all information relevant to the meta-analysis. This can be very time-consuming because: the number of studies involved may be quite large; coding requires great care as the value of the meta-analysis often hinges on good coding; it is often tedious and frustrating because most studies do not report all the information required; the information required is often not in a concise, easily identifiable form; and it is often good practice for two or more coders to complete the coding independently as a check for reliability and consistency.

11.4 METHODOLOGY

11.4.1 Selection of Studies

Only studies that provide empirical evidence of the relationship between certain factors and the pattern of international tourist flows are of interest in this study. Studies of a theoretical or conceptual nature (e.g. Culpan, 1987) and studies that have discussed tourism forecasting (see Calantone *et al.*, 1987) or examined the geography of international tourism (e.g. Husbands, 1983) but do not contain any empirical evidence, have been excluded from the review in order to focus on what is *known* as opposed to what is *thought* about the forces which shape international tourist flows.

The studies identified have been obtained from: a computer search of *Sociological Abstracts*, *Foreign Trade and Econ Abstracts*, *Economic Literature Index*, *Geobase*, *ABI/Inform*, *Management Contents*, *National Technical Information Service* (*NTIS*), *LC MARC – Books* (Library of Congress Machine Readable Cataloging) and *British Books in Print* databases; a manual search of *Leisure, Recreation and Tourism Abstracts*; an examination of several bibliographies; personal queries of some relevant researchers; the assistance of the Travel and Tourism Research Association's Travel Reference Center; and a search for references cited in the literature obtained from the other efforts.

11.4.2 Coding of Studies

With the assistance of a multi-dimensional relational database software system known as pcExpress, the findings and substantive and methodological characteristics of each study were coded.

Each study yielded results from numerous regression equations, which generally varied as a function of the variables included in the equation, the countries studied and the functional form of the regression model. As a result, the regression estimates include both independent and interdependent data. When the data on which the estimates are based are independent (such as when the same regression model is fitted to tourism data pertaining to different pairs of origin and destination countries) the regression estimates are effectively independent. Regression estimates are interdependent when the data on which they are based are in some way related (typically when a different regression model is fitted to the same data). The coding system employed therefore also identifies dependencies between regression equations.

In most cases, although several regression equations may be interdependent, the additional equations are not redundant and should therefore not be excluded from the meta-analysis. In this study, the problem was handled by duplicating each meta-analysis so that results were obtained for the full set of regression estimates (as though all estimates were independent) and from a reduced set of regression estimates which were effectively independent with regard to their data set. The results were then compared to evaluate the sensitivity of the conclusions to the way in which interdependence was handled.

11.4.3 Dependent Variables

Estimated income and price elasticities were selected as the dependent variables in this meta-analysis. Depending on the form of the regression equation, the value of the regression coefficient may be a function of the units used to measure tourism demand, income and price. Therefore, the regression coefficient is not suitable when comparing findings across studies. The t statistic and significance level for each regression coefficient also provide useful information, but these values in themselves only give an indication of whether tourism demand is income or price sensitive. They do not indicate the *extent* to which tourism demand is sensitive to income or prices. Estimated elasticities, however, indicate the percentage change in tourism demand for a 1 per cent change in income or prices.

11.4.4 Independent Variables

The independent variables in the meta-analysis include all potentially relevant substantive and methodological characteristics, which might explain why findings vary over the regression equations, both within and across studies. Tables 11.5 and 11.6 identify the independent variables examined in this study. They are grouped into classes of factors which relate to model specification, environmental characteristics, data characteristics and estimation method. The general approach employed is similar to that of Tellis (1988).

11.5 HYPOTHESES

11.5.1 Model Specification

The models used in previous research have varied considerably in terms of the variables included in, and omitted from, each regression equation. The respective estimated income and/or price elasticity from each regression may be affected by the presence or absence of other variables if such other variables are significantly related to both the tourism demand variable and the respective income or price variable. The bias in the estimated elasticity due to the omission of a significant explanatory variable can be measured (see Kmenta, 1986, pp. 443–6) from

$$\beta_1^* = \beta_1 + \beta_2 f(r_{12})$$

where β_1 is the regression coefficient of variable 1 with variable 2 included; β_1^* is the regression coefficient of variable 1 with variable 2 excluded; β_2 is the regression coefficient of variable 2 if included in the model; $f(r_{12})$ is some function of the covariance between variables 1 and 2.[2]

Using this relationship, the hypotheses shown in Table 11.4 are made with respect to income elasticities. Most of the expected signs of β_2 and r_{12} are reasonably self-evident, but some require elaboration. Increased business activity between countries ought to increase the demand for both business and pleasure travel. Business activity should also be positively correlated with income. The relationship between marketing expenditure and income is unclear but it is reasonable to assume that higher income is likely to attract higher marketing expenditure targeted at the higher-potential tourist markets.

For time series analyses real incomes have increased over time and real transportation costs have decreased (i.e. a negative correlation). However, for cross-sectional studies the correlation between income and transportation cost will depend on the particular origin and destination countries concerned. Hence, the expected relationship between income and transportation costs,

Table 11.4 Hypotheses with respect to income and price elasticities

Variable	Expected sign of β_2		Expected sign of r_{12}	Expected direction of bias	Hypotheses
Income elasticities					
Lagged income	+		+	+	H1
Lagged demand	+		+	+	H2
Price	−	depends on countries			
Transportation costs	−	depends on data structure			
Business activity	+	depends on countries			
Marketing expenditure	+		+	+	H4
Travel distance	−	depends on data structure			
Price elasticities					
Lagged price	−		+	−	H5
Lagged demand	+		−	−	H6
Income	+	depends on countries			
Transportation costs	−	depends on countries			
Business activity	+	depends on countries			
Marketing expenditure	+		+	+	H7
Travel distance	−	depends on countries			

and therefore between income and travel distance, depends on the type of data structure used. There is also no clear relationship between relative prices and income as both are a function of the particular origin and destination countries involved.

The hypotheses with respect to price elasticities are also shown in Table 11.4. Fewer hypotheses are possible in this case because the expected sign of r_{12} depends on the respective countries concerned and because the majority of studies measured price in relative terms. It has been assumed that marketing expenditure and relative prices are likely to be positively correlated if countries increase their marketing efforts in order to offset an unfavourable change in their relative price position. However, a country might react by shifting marketing resources to countries where it remains more price competitive.

Other differences between regression equations in terms of the definition of variables employed and the functional form of the equation may also contribute to an explanation of the variation in the estimated elasticities. Per capita measures of income ought to be associated with higher income elasticities as the influence of a country's increasing population on travel demand is controlled by per capita measures (hypothesis H8). Relative prices measured as the ratio of destination prices to prices in alternative destinations ought to be associated with lower price elasticities as some alternative destinations may be complements rather than substitutes (Anastasopoulos, 1984) (hypothesis H9).

11.5.2 Environmental Characteristics

It is conceivable that estimated income and price elasticities may vary over time or as a function of the origin and destination of the tourists concerned. With regard to the time period studied, it is generally considered that price sensitivity increases as a market matures. If this hypothesis holds for the tourism industry then one would expect price elasticities to increase in absolute magnitude for the more recent time periods (H10). It could also be argued that income elasticities ought to have increased over time. Today, international tourism is within the financial reach of the lower socio-economic groups by comparison to the situation that existed 20–30 years ago. It is therefore likely that international tourism demand has become more income sensitive over time (H11). For this purpose, the mid-point of each time series was used to identify the decade most closely associated with the estimated elasticity.

Origin and destination characteristics were measured both by country and by continent. There appears to be no basis *a priori* for assuming that income and price elasticity ought to be homogeneous across origin or destination countries. Some nationalities may be more income or price sensitive than others. Variations in price elasticity by destination should reflect the extent to which substitute destinations exist. The more unusual the destination the less price sensitive tourists ought to be towards that destination. Similarly, income elasticity ought to increase as a function of the extent to which the destination represents a 'luxury' good.

11.5.3 Data Characteristics

Previous studies have varied in the way in which tourist demand has been measured. The majority of studies have employed either the number of tourist visits or the value of tourist expenditure or receipts. It has been suggested, in the literature, that income and price elasticities ought to increase in absolute magnitude when expenditure or receipts are used instead of tourist numbers (H12 and H13, respectively). The basis for this argument is that tourists are more likely to vary their length of stay or average daily expenditure than to alter their decision to visit a country.

A further variation across studies occurs in the form of the tourism demand investigated. In this respect, regression equations fall into four categories: (1) those that model total travel *to* a particular country; (2) those that model total travel *from* a particular country; (3) those that model travel *between* a pair of countries; and (4) those that model travel involving certain *groups* of countries. Categories (1) and (4) involve tourists at a higher level of aggregation than categories (2) and (3), in which tourists originate from a single country. Hence, there ought to be a greater degree of variability exhibited in the elasticities of categories (2) and (3) compared to categories (1) and (4).

The data structure was examined at three levels (time series, cross-sectional and pooled time series × cross-sectional). How the data structure might affect estimated elasticities is not clear. Tellis (1988, p. 336) argued that price elasticity from time series data should be more negative than that from cross-sectional data. For both types of data structure causality between price and demand can be in either direction (although for international tourism it is usually argued that the price of tourist services is not substantially influenced by demand from international tourists, as such demand represents only a small portion of total demand for such services). For cross-sectional data, however, large-share destinations may charge higher prices, because of their superior name recognition or some other competitive advantage (H14).

11.5.4 Estimation Method

Ordinary least squares regression (OLS) and regression using the Cochrane–Orcutt procedure (CO) have been the most frequently employed techniques. Elasticity estimates were examined for any method-induced bias.

11.6 RESULTS

11.6.1 Income Elasticity

Figure 11.1 illustrates the frequency distribution of income elasticities. The two distributions represent the full set of estimates and a reduced set which includes only independent estimates, as discussed earlier. It is interesting to note that there is little difference between the two distributions. The mean income elasticity is 1.758 and is significantly different from zero

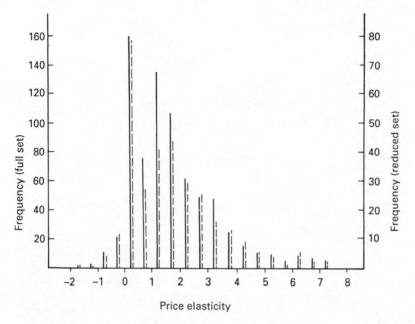

Figure 11.1 Frequency distribution of income elasticities.

———, *full set; - - -, reduced set. Statistics (figures in parentheses relate to the reduced set): mean = 1.758 (1.799); standard deviation = 1.799 (1.959); t = 27.3 (16.8) for hypothesis that mean = 0; t probability = 0.000 (0.000); degrees of freedom = 776 (332).*

(probability = 0.000). Thus, on average, a 1 per cent change in the income of tourists results in a 1.76 per cent change in tourism demand in the same direction.

Table 11.5 summarizes the results of the analysis of variance (ANOVA) tests for each of the independent variables of the meta-analysis. Again, generally the results do not vary substantially between the full and reduced sets. The F statistic values are significant at the 5 per cent level in both sets for exchange rates, transportation costs, income definition 1, time period, destination of tourists by country, destination of tourists by continent, demand measure and demand form. Other variables that achieve this level of significance for only one of the two sets include price, marketing expenditure, other variables, income definition 2, nationality of tourists by country, nationality of tourists by continent and technique. Table 11.6 summarizes the results in terms of the income elasticity hypotheses.

Table 11.5 ANOVA results – income elasticity

Variable class	Variable	Level	Mean elasticity	Standard deviation	No of cases	F	Significance level[a]	Scheffé test[b]
Model specification	Lagged income	included	1.228 (–)	1.242 (–)	6 (–)	(–)	(–)	
		omitted	1.763 (1.799)	1.802 (1.959)	771 (333)	0.525	0.469	
	Lagged demand	included	1.879 (2.190)	1.162 (1.103)	60 (27)	(1.17)	(0.280)	
		omitted	1.748 (1.765)	1.842 (2.015)	717 (306)	0.295	0.587	
	Price	included	1.665 (1.751)	1.912 (2.119)	569 (254)	(0.657)	(0.418)	
		omitted	2.014 (1.955)	1.417 (1.320)	208 (79)	5.78	0.0164	
	Exchange rates	included	2.369 (2.233)	1.946 (2.114)	191 (99)	(7.03)	(0.0084)	
		omitted	1.559 (1.616)	1.703 (1.864)	586 (234)	30.3	0.0000	
	Transportation costs	included	2.112 (2.236)	1.939 (2.126)	356 (154)	(14.8)	(0.0001)	
		omitted	1.460 (1.424)	1.613 (1.723)	421 (179)	26.2	0.0000	
	Trend	included	2.169 (2.764)	1.484 (1.372)	29 (14)	(3.57)	(0.0596)	
		omitted	1.743 (1.757)	1.809 (1.972)	748 (319)	1.57	0.211	
	Business activity	included	1.429 (1.210)	1.012 (0.780)	7 (3)	(0.273)	(0.6015)	
		omitted	1.761 (1.805)	1.804 (1.966)	770 (330)	0.237	0.626	
	Marketing expenditure	included	2.094 (2.497)	2.122 (2.289)	124 (24)	(3.30)	(0.0701)	
		omitted	1.695 (1.745)	1.725 (1.925)	653 (309)	5.15	0.0235	
	Travel distance	included	1.098 (0.810)	0.382 (0.385)	25 (5)	(1.30)	(0.256)	
		omitted	1.780 (1.814)	1.823 (1.970)	752 (328)	3.49	0.0621	
	Other variables	included	1.973 (1.730)	2.060 (2.130)	325 (164)	(0.405)	(0.525)	
		omitted	1.604 (1.867)	1.569 (1.782)	452 (169)	7.99	0.0048	
	Income definition 1	disposable income	1.446 (1.507)	1.453 (1.633)	427 (208)	(6.70)	(0.0014)	*–*
		production index	2.169 (2.551)	2.006 (2.254)	185 (56)	12.3	0.0000	*–*
		other	1.459 (1.935)	2.087 (2.905)	63 (28)			(–)
	Income definition 2	per capita measure	1.856 (1.819)	1.863 (1.864)	612 (297)	(3.30)	(0.0704)	
		total measure	1.340 (0.870)	0.994 (1.233)	118 (13)	8.58	0.0035	

Equation form	linear	1.671 (1.635)	0.767 (0.725)	18 (14)	(0.102)	(0.749)
	log-linear	1.760 (1.807)	1.816 (1.996)	759 (319)	0.043	0.836
Environmental characteristics						
Time period	1950s	2.565 (2.899)	1.543 (1.628)	40 (11)		
	1960s	1.159 (1.212)	1.499 (1.901)	411 (143)		
	1970s	2.434 (2.230)	1.890 (1.867)	324 (178)	(11.2)	(0.0000)
	1980s	−0.690 (−2.900)	3.125 (0.00)	2 (1)	39.5	0.0000
Nationality of tourists by country	Austria	1.458 (0.885)	1.697 (1.657)	22 (9)		
	France	2.508 (1.934)	2.582 (1.766)	29 (16)		
	W. Germany	2.020 (2.026)	1.629 (1.632)	42 (29)		
	Italy	1.717 (1.301)	1.619 (1.339)	24 (11)		
	Netherlands	0.520 (0.427)	0.631 (0.637)	14 (7)		
	Switzerland	1.629 (1.396)	2.396 (2.173)	21 (10)		
	UK	1.969 (2.112)	1.491 (1.592)	113 (58)		
	USA	1.618 (1.835)	1.252 (1.499)	195 (57)		
	Canada	1.039 (0.934)	1.738 (2.292)	48 (25)		
	Japan	1.149 (1.537)	1.254 (1.621)	14 (3)		
	Australia–NZ	2.258 (2.162)	1.193 (1.122)	20 (10)		
	W. Indies–Central–Sth America	0.198 (1.425)	0.995 (0.749)	18 (2)		
	Asia (ex. Japan)	1.417 (1.650)	0.617 (0.891)	7 (2)		
	Other Europe–Nth America[c]	1.717 (1.288)	1.981 (1.735)	62 (25)		
	Other[d]	2.083 (1.847)	2.245 (2.669)	92 (44)	(1.67)	(0.0555)
	Whole world[e]	2.379 (2.958)	2.530 (2.753)	56 (25)	3.52	0.0000
Nationality of tourists by continent	Europe	1.824 (1.714)	1.823 (1.686)	318 (162)		
	Nth America	1.539 (1.582)	1.390 (1.812)	249 (83)		
	W. Indies–Central–Sth America	0.198 (1.425)	0.995 (0.749)	18 (2)		
	Asia–Pacific	1.779 (1.966)	1.305 (1.194)	35 (14)		
	Other[d]	2.020 (1.828)	2.157 (2.583)	101 (47)	(2.08)	(0.0669)
	Whole world[e]	2.379 (2.958)	2.530 (2.753)	56 (25)	5.45	0.001

193

Table 11.5 *continued*

Variable class	Variable	Level	Mean elasticity	Standard deviation	No of cases	F	Significance level[a]	Scheffé test[b]
Destination of tourists by country		Austria	2.125 (2.441)	1.682 (1.825)	12 (9)			
		France	1.868 (1.751)	1.369 (1.484)	14 (11)			
		W. Germany	1.583 (1.615)	1.401 (1.265)	19 (13)			
		Italy	1.071 (1.169)	1.590 (1.585)	33 (22)			
		Netherlands	1.874 (1.874)	0.853 (0.853)	6 (6)			
		Switzerland	2.302 (2.302)	1.309 (1.309)	9 (9)			
		UK	2.422 (2.429)	1.152 (1.224)	9 (7)			
		USA	1.981 (1.952)	1.378 (1.130)	37 (23)			
		Canada	1.762 (1.338)	2.158 (2.171)	20 (12)			
		Greece	2.322 (1.903)	2.510 (2.301)	75 (28)			
		Spain	1.236 (1.290)	1.270 (1.422)	36 (22)			
		Mexico	1.093 (1.940)	0.952 (1.109)	54 (8)			
		Turkey	1.195 (0.668)	1.819 (1.769)	39 (23)			
		Yugoslavia	0.449 (0.639)	0.938 (1.209)	24 (14)			
		Portugal	0.600 (0.957)	2.196 (2.919)	23 (13)			
		Australia–NZ	2.607 (2.607)	1.490 (1.490)	7 (7)			
		W. Indies–Central –Sth America	1.876 (3.364)	2.099 (2.577)	103 (24)			
		Asia	3.148 (3.075)	1.843 (1.923)	46 (11)			
		Other Europe– Nth America[c]	1.511 (1.659)	0.829 (0.759)	45 (14)			
		Other[d]	1.977 (1.841)	1.843 (2.690)	114 (39)	(2.39)	(0.0009)	
		Whole world[e]	1.700 (2.195)	0.768 (0.710)	52 (18)	4.60	0.0000	

194

Destination of tourists by continent	Europe	1.594	(1.568)	1.838	(1.757)	295	(164)		
	North America	1.904	(1.741)	1.677	(1.562)	57	(35)		
	W. Indies–Central –Sth America	1.607	(3.008)	1.824	(2.366)	157	(32)		
	Asia–Pacific	2.748	(2.911)	1.624	(1.689)	82	(19)		
	Middle East	1.195	(0.668)	1.819	(1.769)	39	(23)		
	Other[d]	1.842	(1.776)	1.970	(2.587)	95	(42)	(5.20)	(0.0000)
	Whole world[e]	1.700	(2.195)	0.768	(0.710)	52	(18)	5.67	0.0000
Data characteristics	Demand measure								
	expend–receipts	1.992	(2.319)	1.795	(2.170)	271	(106)	(11.3)	(0.0009)
	tourist numbers	1.636	(1.557)	1.793	(1.807)	504	(227)	6.93	0.0086
Demand form	to a country	1.720	(2.359)	2.125	(2.635)	159	(62)		
	from a country	2.042	(2.216)	1.299	(1.190)	91	(39)		
	country pairs	1.576	(1.478)	1.750	(1.784)	449	(218)	(6.86)	(0.0002)
	others	2.554	(3.170)	1.617	(1.558)	78	(14)	7.59	0.0001
Data structure	time series	1.792	(1.856)	1.812	(1.888)	669	(286)		
	cross-sectional	1.626	(1.185)	0.897	(0.432)	65	(14)	(1.04)	(0.356)
	pooled	1.432	(1.569)	2.488	(2.783)	43	(33)	1.00	0.3673
Estimation method	Technique								
	OLS	1.606	(1.647)	1.793	(2.078)	639	(241)		
	CO	2.505	(2.225)	1.746	(1.616)	118	(83)	(2.75)	(0.0651)
	Other	2.216	(1.964)	0.959	(0.630)	20	(9)	13.5	0.0000

Results in parentheses relate to the reduced set of elasticities.

[a] Two-tailed test.

[b] *,* Indicate pair differences at the 0.05 level.

[c] To represent other European countries or for Europe or North America as a whole.

[d] To represent all other nationality or destination classes with the exception of 'whole world'.

[e] 'Whole world' was used when total travel from the whole world to a country or total travel from a country to the whole world was modelled.

Table 11.6 Hypothesis results – income elasticities

Hypothesis	Outcome	ANOVA significant at 5%
H1: Omission of lagged income: +ve bias	−ve bias	No
H2: Omission of lagged demand: +ve bias	−ve bias	No
H3: Omission of business activity: +ve bias	+ve bias	No
H4: Omission of marketing: +ve bias	−ve bias	Yes, full set only
H8: Per capita measures: +ve bias	+ve bias	Yes, full set only
H11: Increased elasticity over time: +ve bias	no clear trend	Yes
H12: Demand measured in terms of expenditure/receipts: +ve bias	+ve bias	Yes

11.6.2 Price Elasticity

The frequency distribution of price elasticities is illustrated in Figure 11.2. The mean price elasticity is −0.39 and is significantly different from zero (probability = 0.000). Thus, on average, a 1 per cent change in the relative price of tourism services at a destination results in a 0.39 per cent change in tourism demand in the opposite direction. The frequency distributions do not differ substantially between the full and reduced sets of estimates.

The ANOVA results are summarized in Table 11.7. By comparison to the income elasticity results, the price elasticity results indicate that few of the independent variables of the meta-analysis appear to explain the variation in price elasticities. F statistic values are significant at the 5 per cent level in both sets for exchange rates, demand measure and demand form variables. Destination of tourists by continent and price definition 1 are significant at the 5 per cent level for the full set only. Table 11.8 summarizes the results in terms of the price elasticity hypotheses.

11.7 CONCLUSION

The results of this exploratory meta-analysis indicate some promising findings in some areas but also point to the need for considerable further investigation in others. The meta-analysis performed on the set of estimated income elasticities indicates that many of the variables examined appear to explain some of the variation in the elasticities. The high levels of statistical significance are encouraging, but it must also be recognized that a number of the hypotheses were not supported by the results.

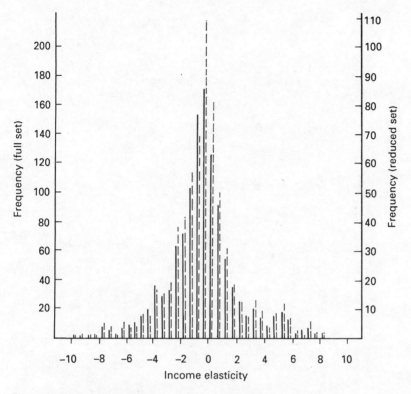

Figure 11.2 Frequency distribution of price elasticities.

————, full set; - - -, reduced set. Statistics (figures in parentheses relate to the reduced set); mean = −0.386 (−0.338); standard deviation = 3.698 (3.862); t = −3.65 (−2.30) for hypothesis that mean = 0, t probability = 0.000 (0.022); degrees of freedom = 1226 (693).

The results for the estimated price elasticities are not so encouraging. Few of the variables appear to explain the variation in price elasticity, suggesting that perhaps some important explanatory variables have been omitted from the meta-analysis. In one sense, these results are not surprising as, in contrast to income, the definition of relative prices varied considerably across studies. For example, some studies related price levels at the destination to price levels in the tourist's origin country. Others, however, related prices to those in alternative destinations. Anastasopoulos (1984) clearly demonstrated that alternative destinations need not be substitutes as has often, at least implicitly, been assumed. Where alternative destinations are complementary instead of competing, the expected sign of the

Table 11.7 ANOVA results – price elasticity

Variable class	Variable	Level	Mean elasticity	Standard deviation	No. of cases	F	Significance level[a]	Scheffé test[b]
Model specification	Lagged price	included	−1.008 (−1.880)	1.180 (1.849)	16 (5)	(0.803)	(0.371)	
		omitted	−0.378 (−0.326)	3.720 (3.871)	1211 (689)	0.459	0.498	
	Lagged demand	included	−0.335 (−0.357)	0.361 (0.248)	44 (22)	(0.0006)	(0.981)	
		omitted	−0.388 (−0.337)	3.766 (3.924)	1183 (672)	0.0088	0.925	
	Income	included	−0.412 (−0.347)	3.357 (3.857)	1093 (637)	(0.0425)	(0.837)	
		omitted	−0.174 (−0.237)	5.788 (3.948)	134 (57)	0.493	0.483	
	Exchange rates	included	−1.249 (−1.330)	2.066 (2.066)	168 (82)	(6.19)	(0.0131)	
		omitted	−0.249 (−0.205)	3.878 (4.025)	1059 (612)	10.7	0.0011	
	Transportation costs	included	−0.562 (−0.744)	1.485 (1.950)	302 (111)	1.46	(0.227)	
		omitted	−0.328 (−0.260)	4.173 (4.123)	925 (583)	0.910	0.340	
	Trend	included	−1.419 (−0.957)	2.147 (2.199)	42 (24)	(0.639)	(0.424)	
		omitted	−0.349 (−0.315)	3.74 (3.908)	1185 (670)	3.40	0.0655	
	Business activity	included	−0.607 (−0.557)	1.023 (0.553)	7 (3)	(0.0097)	(0.922)	
		omitted	−0.385 (−0.337)	3.708 (3.870)	1220 (691)	0.025	0.874	
	Marketing expenditure	included	−0.406 (−0.523)	1.034 (1.083)	154 (28)	(0.0672)	(0.796)	
		omitted	−0.383 (−0.330)	3.94 (3.936)	1073 (666)	0.005	0.944	
	Travel distance	included	−0.721 (−0.865)	0.289 (0.205)	10 (2)	(0.0374)	(0.847)	
		omitted	−0.383 (−0.336)	3.713 (3.867)	1217 (692)	0.083	0.774	
	Other variables	included	−0.474 (−0.420)	3.109 (3.648)	479 (303)	(0.242)	(0.623)	
		omitted	−0.329 (−0.274)	4.032 (4.023)	748 (391)	0.448	0.503	
	Price definition 1	destination/origin	−0.870 (−0.826)	3.780 (2.988)	361 (193)			
		dest/alt.dest	−0.161 (−0.146)	3.890 (4.202)	744 (479)			
		dest/alt.dest & origin	−1.598 (−1.898)	2.249 (2.302)	14 (7)			
		destination only	−0.102 (−0.830)	1.324 (2.190)	76 (11)	(1.61)	(0.170)	

Price definition 2								
alt. destination only	−0.289	(−0.234)	1.059	(1.265)	32	(4)	2.74	0.0276
exchange rate corrected	−0.885	(−1.377)	2.112	(3.055)	187	(67)	(0.405)	(0.526)
not ex.rate corrected	−1.042	(−1.028)	4.197	(3.768)	282	(106)	0.224	0.636
Equation form								
linear	1.720	(−)	0.981	(−)	3	(−)	(−)	(−)
log-linear	−0.391	(−0.338)	3.701	(3.862)	1224	(694)	0.975	0.324
Environmental characteristics — Time period								
1950s	−0.984	(−)	0.00	(−)	1	(−)		
1960s	−0.304	(−0.247)	4.049	(4.193)	981	(566)	(0.858)	(0.424)
1970s	−0.716	(−0.730)	1.663	(1.728)	243	(127)	0.814	0.486
1980s	−0.315	(−1.520)	1.704	(0.00)	2	(1)		
Nationality of tourists by country								
Austria	−0.174	(−0.181)	2.727	(2.953)	62	(41)		
France	−0.051	(−0.053)	3.492	(3.714)	81	(54)		
W. Germany	−0.415	(−0.322)	4.024	(4.310)	85	(61)		
Italy	−0.589	(−0.491)	4.127	(4.488)	68	(39)		
Netherlands	−0.187	(−0.189)	3.752	(3.565)	66	(43)		
Switzerland	−0.142	(−0.126)	3.350	(3.588)	64	(42)		
UK	−0.421	(−0.374)	4.678	(3.181)	162	(92)		
USA	−0.399	(−0.275)	4.031	(5.950)	156	(61)		
Canada	−0.288	(−0.267)	3.067	(3.418)	110	(60)		
Japan	0.113	(0.145)	4.264	(4.173)	78	(48)		
Australia–NZ	0.090	(0.170)	0.539	(0.00)	8	(1)		
W. Indies–Central –Sth America	−0.234	(−0.970)	1.120	(2.043)	26	(3)		
Asia (ex. Japan)	−1.608	(−1.120)	1.015	(0.00)	6	(1)		
Other Europe –Nth America[c]	−0.337	(−0.227)	3.277	(3.021)	155	(99)		
Other*[d]	−1.018	(−1.285)	2.265	(3.012)	49	(23)	(0.690)	(0.796)
Whole world[e]	−1.788	(−2.363)	3.571	(4.487)	51	(26)	0.844	0.629

Table 11.7 *continued*

Variable class	Variable	Level	Mean elasticity		Standard deviation		No. of cases		F	Significance level[a]	Scheffé test[b]
Nationality of tourists by continent		Europe	-0.315	(-0.241)	3.824	(3.535)	736	(469)			
		North America	-0.349	(-0.273)	3.617	(4.822)	272	(122)	(1.93)	(0.0876)	
		W. Indies–Central –Sth America	-0.234	(-0.970)	1.120	(2.043)	26	(3)	1.995	0.0768	
	Destination of tourists by country	Asia–Pacific	0.005	(0.120)	3.997	(4.091)	90	(50)			
		Other[d]	-0.959	(-1.242)	2.210	(2.953)	52	(24)			
		Whole world[e]	-1.788	(-2.363)	3.571	(4.487)	51	(26)			
		Austria	-0.199	(-0.361)	1.232	(0.304)	11	(7)			
		France	-0.135	(-0.308)	1.926	(1.994)	14	(11)			
		West Germany	-0.585	(-0.697)	0.713	(0.574)	14	(9)			
		Italy	0.115	(0.112)	2.814	(2.623)	125	(84)			
		Netherlands	-1.710	(-1.087)	2.428	(1.804)	8	(7)			
		Switzerland	-0.666	(-0.666)	0.879	(0.879)	10	(10)			
		UK	-0.765	(-0.558)	0.615	(0.557)	4	(3)			
		USA	-1.573	(-1.545)	2.380	(2.114)	20	(9)			
		Canada	-1.211	(-1.271)	1.721	(1.471)	10	(5)			
		Greece	-0.860	(-0.758)	2.118	(1.997)	176	(96)			
		Spain	0.068	(-0.026)	7.839	(7.539)	136	(99)			
		Mexico	-0.475	(-0.919)	0.929	(0.856)	48	(4)			
		Turkey	-0.167	(-0.135)	3.235	(2.689)	134	(88)			
		Yugoslavia	0.050	(0.104)	3.206	(3.001)	138	(96)			
		Portugal	0.017	(-0.005)	4.103	(3.651)	131	(91)			
		W. Indies–Central –Sth America	-0.694	(-1.777)	2.392	(4.789)	112	(24)			
		Asia	-0.456	(-0.351)	1.175	(0.661)	43	(8)			
		Other Europe– Nth America	-0.949	(-0.922)	0.818	(0.813)	19	(10)			

Category	Subcategory	Class	Elasticity 1 (reduced)	Elasticity 2 (reduced)	n (reduced)	[*] [=] [*]	
Destination of tourists by continent		Other[d]	−1.362 (−1.518)	2.516 (2.971)	47 (26)		
		Whole world[e]	−1.888 (−2.833)	1.956 (1.941)	27 (7)	1.27 (0.822)	0.196 (0.681)
		Europe	−0.218 (−0.178)	4.222 (4.091)	783 (522)		
		North America	−1.452 (−1.477)	2.159 (1.853)	30 (14)		
		W. Indies–Central –Sth America	−0.628 (−1.655)	2.064 (4.440)	160 (28)		
		Asia–Pacific	−0.456 (−0.351)	1.175 (0.661)	43 (8)		
		Middle East	−0.167 (−0.135)	3.235 (2.689)	134 (88)		
		Other[d]	−1.306 (−1.481)	2.448 (2.919)	50 (27)		
		Whole world[e]	−1.888 (−2.833)	1.956 (1.941)	27 (7)	2.149 (1.82)	0.0455 (0.0931)
Data characteristics	Demand measure	expend–receipts	−1.523 (−2.011)	2.549 (3.419)	170 (68)		
		tourist numbers	−0.203 (−0.156)	3.821 (3.866)	1057 (626)	18.9 (14.4)	0.0000 (0.0002)
	Demand form	to a country	−1.008 (−1.768)	2.413 (3.685)	175 (56)		
		from a country	−1.957 (−2.732)	1.965 (1.824)	34 (9)		
		country pairs	−0.217 (−0.175)	3.973 (3.886)	976 (622)		
		others	−0.446 (−0.273)	1.187 (0.674)	42 (7)	4.415 (4.14)	0.0043 (0.0064)
	Data structure	time series	−0.365 (−0.305)	3.739 (3.886)	1184 (671)		
		cross-sectional	−0.551 (−0.557)	0.865 (0.553)	16 (3)		
		pooled	−1.221 (−1.405)	2.789 (3.214)	27 (20)	0.723 (0.792)	0.486 (0.453)
Estimation method	Technique	OLS	−0.372 (−0.327)	3.831 (4.022)	1125 (634)		
		CO	−0.429 (−0.450)	1.474 (1.303)	94 (58)		
		other	−1.894 (−0.604)	2.674 (0.404)	8 (2)	0.679 (0.0317)	0.507 (0.969)

Results in parentheses relate to the reduced set of elasticities.

[a] Two-tailed test.

[b] * Indicate pair differences at the 0.05 level.

[c] To represent other European countries or for Europe or North America as a whole.

[d] To represent all other nationality or destination classes with the exception of 'whole world'.

[e] 'Whole world' was used when total travel from the whole world to a country or total travel from a country to the whole world was modelled.

Table 11.8 Hypothesis results – price elasticities

Hypothesis	Outcome	ANOVA significant at 5%
H5: Omission of lagged price: − ve bias	+ ve bias	No
H6: Omission of lagged demand: − ve bias	− ve bias	No
H7: Omission of marketing: + ve bias	+ ve bias	No
H9: Price measured relative to price in alternative destinations: + ve bias	+ ve bias	full set only
H10: Increased elasticity over time: − ve bias	no clear trend	No
H13: Demand measured in terms of expenditure/receipts: − ve bias	− ve bias	Yes
H14: Time series data: − ve bias	+ ve bias	No

price elasticity variable changes. Figure 11.2 illustrates the extent to which many of the estimated price elasticities had a positive sign. The high statistical significance of the demand measures and demand form variables also supports the view that, if the variation in price elasticities is to be better understood, it will be necessary to begin by re-examining the *meaning* of the price variable.

The findings of this study point to considerable scope for further research. A number of further empirical studies could also be coded for inclusion in the meta-analysis. This would increase the number of degrees of freedom of the analysis, and would permit further meta-analytical integration of findings, beyond the income and price variables, to include many of the other independent variables listed in Table 11.1.[3] It is also possible to employ dummy variable regression over the complete set of meta-analytical variables in order to estimate the individual impact of each variable on estimated elasticities.[4]

Notes

1 The authors are aware of a few other relevant studies, which they are currently gathering and examining, and they would greatly appreciate hearing from anyone who is able to add to the bibliography.

2 If the omitted variable 2 is not related to the dependent variable ($\beta_2 = 0$) or if it is uncorrelated with variable 1 ($r_{12} = 0$), its omission does not bias β_1. If β_2 and r_{12} are of the same sign, the bias is positive; otherwise it is negative.

3 The authors are currently coding further studies in order to extend the meta-analysis.

4 The authors have undertaken a dummy variable regression as described. The results of this further work will be reported elsewhere.

References

Anastasopoulos, P.G. (1984) Interdependencies in international travel: the role of relative prices. A case study of the Mediterranean region. PhD dissertation, New School for Social Research.

Armstrong, C.W.G. (1972) International tourism: coming or going. The methodological problems of forecasting. *Futures*, 4(2), 115-25.

Artus, J.R. (1970) The effect of revaluation on the foreign travel balance of Germany. *International Monetary Fund Staff Papers*, 17, 602-19.

Artus, J.R. (1972) An econometric analysis of international travel. *International Monetary Fund Staff Papers*, 19(3), 579-614.

Askari, H. (1973) Demand for travel to Europe by American citizens. *Economia Internazionale*, 26(May), 305-17.

Barry, K. and O'Hagan, J. (1972) An econometric study of British tourist expenditure in Ireland. *Economic and Social Review*, 3(2), 143-61.

Bechdolt, B.V. (1973) Cross-sectional travel demand functions: US visitors to Hawaii, 1961-1970. *Quarterly Review of Economics and Business*, 13(4), 37-47.

Blackwell, J. (1970) Tourist traffic and the demand for accommodation: some projections. *Economic and Social Review*, 1(3), 323-43.

Bond, M.E. and Ladman, J.R. (1972) International tourism and economic development: a special case for Latin America. *Mississippi Valley Journal of Business and Economics*, 8(Fall), 43-55.

Calantone, R.J., di Benedetto, C.A. and Bojanic, D. (1987) A comprehensive review of the tourism forecasting literature. *Journal of Travel Research*, 26(2), 28-39.

Chadee, D. and Mieczkowski, Z. (1987) An empirical analysis of the effects of the exchange rate on Canadian tourism. *Journal of Travel Research*, 26(1), 13-17.

Cigliano, J.M. (1980) Price and income elasticities for airline travel: the North Atlantic market. *Business Economics*, 15(4), 17-21.

Clarke, C.D. (1978) An analysis of the determinants of demand for tourism in Barbados. PhD dissertation, Fordham University.

Cleverdon, R. and Edwards, A. (1982) *International Tourism to 1990.* Cambridge, MA: Abt Books.

Crampon, L.J. and Tan, K.T. (1973) A model of tourism flow into the Pacific. *Revue de Tourisme*, **28**, 98–104.

Crouch, G.I. and Shaw, R.N. (1990) Determinants of international tourist flows: findings from 30 years of empirical research. *Proceedings of 21st Annual Conference of the Travel and Tourism Research Association*, pp. 45–60. New Orleans, 10–14 June.

Culpan, R. (1987) International tourism model for developing economies. *Annals of Tourism Research*, **14**(4), 541–52.

Diamond, J. (1977) Tourism's role in economic development: the case re-examined. *Economic Development and Cultural Change*, **25**(3), 539–53.

Farley, J.U. and Lehmann, D.R. (1986) Meta-analysis in marketing: generalization of response models. Lexington, MA: Lexington Books/D.C. Heath.

Fujii, E.T. and Mak, J. (1981) Forecasting tourism demand: some methodological issues. *Annals of Regional Science*, **15**(2), 72–82.

Gerakis, A.S. (1965) Effects of exchange-rate devaluations and revaluations on receipts from tourism. *International Monetary Fund Staff Papers*, **12**(3), 365–84.

Glass, G.V., McGaw, B. and Smith, M.L. (1981) *Meta-Analysis in Social Research.* Beverly Hills, CA: Sage Publications.

Gray, H.P. (1966) The demand for international travel by the United States and Canada. *International Economic Review*, **7**(1), 83–92.

Guthrie, H.W. (1961) Demand for tourists' goods and services in a world market. *Papers and Proceedings of the Regional Science Association*, **7**, 159–75.

Hollander, G. (1982) *Determinants of Demand for Travel to and from Australia.* Bureau of Industry Economics, Australia, working paper no. 26.

Hunter, J.E., Schmidt, F.L. and Jackson, G.B. (1982) *Meta-analysis: Cumulating Research Findings across Studies.* Beverly Hills, CA: Sage Publications.

Husbands, W.C. (1983) Tourist space and tourist attraction: an analysis of destination choices of European travelers. *Leisure Sciences*, **5**(4), 289–307.

IAC (Industries Assistance Commission) (1989) *Some Economic Implications of Tourism Expansion*, Inquiry into Travel and Tourism, discussion paper no. 2. Canberra: Australian Government Publishing Service.

Jud, G.D. (1971) The demand for tourism: the case of Latin America. PhD dissertation, University of Iowa.

Jud, G.D. (1974) Tourism and economic growth in Mexico since 1950. *Inter-American Economic Affairs*, 28(1), 19–43.

Jud, G.D. and Joseph, H. (1974) International demand for Latin American tourism. *Growth and Change*, 5(1), 25–31.

Kanafani, A. (1980) Price elasticities of nonbusiness air travel demand. *Transportation Engineering Journal*, 106(TE2), 217–25.

Kliman, M.L. (1981) A quantitative analysis of Canadian overseas tourism. *Transportation Research*, 15A(6), 487–97.

Kwack, S.Y. (1972) Effects of income and prices on travel spending abroad, 1960 III–1967 IV. *International Economic Review*, 13(2), 245–56.

Kmenta, J. (1986) *Elements of Econometrics*. New York: Macmillan.

Laber, G. (1969) Determinants of international travel between Canada and the United States. *Geographical Analysis*, 1(4), 329–36.

Little, J.S. (1980) International travel in the US balance of payments. *New England Economic Review*, May/June, 42–55.

Loeb, P.D. (1982) International travel to the United States: an econometric evaluation. *Annals of Tourism Research*, 9(1), 7–20.

Mak, J., Moncur, J. and Yonamine, D. (1977) Determinants of visitor expenditures and visitor lengths of stay: a cross-section analysis of US visitors to Hawaii. *Journal of Travel Research*, 15(3), 5–8.

Martin, C.A. and Witt, S.F. (1987) Tourism demand forecasting models: choice of appropriate variable to represent tourists' cost of living. *Tourism Management*, 8(3) 223–45.

Martin, C.A. and Witt, S.F. (1988) Substitute prices in models of tourism demand. *Annals of Tourism Research*, 15(2), 255–68.

Mutti, J. and Murai, Y. (1977) Airline travel on the North Atlantic. *Journal of Transport Economics and Policy*, 11(1), 45–53.

Noval, S. (1975) The demand for international tourism and travel: theory and measurement. PhD dissertation, Princeton University.

O'Hagan, J.W. and Harrison, M.J. (1984) Market shares of US tourist expenditures in Europe: an econometric analysis. *Applied Economics*, 16(6), 919–31.

Oliver, F.R. (1971) The effectiveness of the UK travel allowance. *Applied Economics*, **3**, 219–26.

Papadopoulos, S.I. (1987) Strategic marketing techniques in international tourism. *International Marketing Review*, Summer, 71–84.

Papadopoulos, S.I. and Witt, S.F. (1985) A marketing analysis of foreign tourism in Greece. In Shaw, S., Sparks, L. and Kaynak, E. (eds) *Proceedings of Second World Marketing Congress*, pp. 628–93. Stirling: University of Stirling.

Quayson, J. and Var, T. (1982) A tourism demand function for the Okanagan, BC. *Tourism Management*, **3**(June), 108–15.

Rojwannasin, B. -O. (1982) *Determinants of international tourist flows to Thailand*. PhD dissertation, Faculty of Economics, Thammasat University, Thailand.

Rugg, D.D. (1971) The demand for foreign travel. PhD dissertation, University of California, Los Angeles.

Schulmeister, S. (1979) *Tourism and the Business Cycle: Econometric Models for the Purpose of Analysis and Forecasting of Short-term Changes in the Demand for Tourism*. Vienna: Austrian Institute for Economic Research.

Smeral, E. (1988) Tourism demand, economic theory and econometrics: an integrated approach. *Journal of Travel Research*, **26**(4), 38–42.

Smith, A.B. and Toms, J.N. (1978) *Factors Affecting Demand for International Travel to and from Australia*. Bureau of Transport Economics. Canberra: Australian Government Publishing Service.

Strazheim, M.R. (1978) Airline demand functions in the North Atlantic and their pricing implications. *Journal of Transport Economics and Policy*, **12**(2), 179–95.

Stronge, W.B. and Redman, M. (1982) US tourism in Mexico: an empirical analysis. *Annals of Tourism Research*, **9**(1), 21–35.

Summary, R. (1987) Estimation of tourism demand by multivariable regression analysis: evidence from Kenya. *Tourism Management*, **8**(4), 317–22.

Sunday, A.A. (1978) Foreign travel & tourism prices and demand. *Annals of Tourism Research*, **5**(2), 268–73.

Taplin, J.H.E. (1980) A coherence approach to estimates of price elasticities in the vacation travel market. *Journal of Transport Economics and Policy*, **14**(1), 19–35.

Tellis, G.J. (1988) The price elasticity of selective demand: a meta-analysis of econometric models of sales. *Journal of Marketing Research*, **25**(4), 331–41.

Tremblay, P. (1989) Pooling international tourism in Western Europe. *Annals of Tourism Research*, **16**(4), 477–91.

Truett, D.B. and Truett, L.J. (1987) The response of tourism to international economic conditions: Greece, Mexico and Spain. *Journal of Developing Areas*, **21**(2), 177–90.

Truett, L.J. and Truett, D.B. (1982) Public policy and the growth of the Mexican tourism industry, 1970–1979. *Journal of Travel Research*, **20**(3), 11–19.

Uysal, M. (1983) Construction of a model which investigates the impact of selected variables on international tourist flows to Turkey. PhD dissertation, Texas A & M University.

Uysal, M. and Crompton, J.L. (1984) Determinants of demand for international tourist flows to Turkey. *Tourism Management*, **5**(4), 288–97.

Uysal, M. and O'Leary, J.T. (1986) A canonical analysis of international tourism demand. *Annals of Tourism Research*, **13**(4), 651–5.

White, K.J. (1985) An international travel demand model: US travel to Western Europe. *Annals of Tourism Research*, **12**(4), 529–45.

White, K.J. and Walker, M.B. (1982) Trouble in the travel account. *Annals of Tourism Research*, **9**(1), 1–24.

Williams, A.V. and Zelinsky, W. (1970) On some patterns in international tourist flows. *Economic Geography*, **46**(4) 549–67.

Witt, S.F. (1980a) An abstract mode-abstract (destination) node model of foreign holiday demand. *Applied Economics*, **12**(2), 163–80.

Witt, S.F. (1980b) An econometric comparison of UK and German foreign holiday behaviour. *Managerial and Decision Economics*, **1**(3), 123–31.

Witt, S.F. and Martin, C.A. (1985) Forecasting future trends in European tourist demand. *Revue de Tourisme*, **40**(4), 12–20.

Witt, S.F. and Martin, C.A. (1987) Econometric models for forecasting international tourism demand. *Journal of Travel Research*, **25**(3), 23–30.

Zeitoun, M. (1978) Some economic aspects influencing international tourism. *Travel Research Journal*, **2**, 25–31.

12 The Track Records of Tourism Forecasting Services

Stephen F. Witt

12.1 INTRODUCTION

Accurate forecasts are required if managers are to plan efficiently. As Archer (1987, p. 77) points out:

> Forecasting should be an essential element in the process of management ... a manager must plan for the future.... In order to plan, he must use forecasts ... the accuracy of the forecasts will affect the quality of the management decision.

For managers operating in tourism-related industries, such as airlines, shipping companies, coach operators, hoteliers, tour operators and food and catering establishments, the accuracy of the forecasts is especially important because of the perishable nature of the product; for example, unused hotel rooms cannot be stockpiled – the lost revenue is lost forever.

If forecasts of tourism demand are too high, then it is likely that in general capital investment will be excessive, the labour force will be too big and excess stocks will be held of goods normally sold directly to, or used by, tourists. Thus, for example, there may be empty seats on aeroplanes and coaches, unoccupied apartments and hotel rooms, and unused hire cars. If, on the other hand, forecasts of tourism demand are too low, then firms will lose opportunities; for example, there may be insufficient hotel accommodation or too few flights to cater for all those wishing to visit a certain area at a given time. Even if supply can be expanded to a limited extent at short notice, this is likely to impose additional costs on firms as, say, less efficient aircraft are used and excessive overtime is worked.

Various organizations have attempted to generate forecasts of international tourism demand, which they have then sold to the tourism industry on a commercial basis. This chapter examines two such forecasting services: the *International Travel and Tourism Forecast* by Brooke *et al.*, which was published as a one-off by Industry Forecasts Limited in 1985 and sold for UK£95.00; and the TRAM (Travel Analysis Model) forecasts, which were produced by Coopers & Lybrand and published by the American Express Publishing Corporation in the *World Travel Overview* in 1986, 1987 and 1988 for US$95.00 per annual issue. It would appear that since the *International Travel and Tourism Forecast* only appeared as one issue and the TRAM only appeared in three issues of the *World Travel Overview*, neither of the forecasting services was viewed as a commercial success by the publishers. The necessity to generate *accurate* forecasts of tourism demand has already been stressed, and it could be the case that the records of forecasting accuracy achieved by the two commercial tourism demand forecasting services did not justify the price charged for the forecasts in the view of managers in tourism-related industries. In both cases, fairly complex tourism forecasting methods were used and hence the cost of generating the forecasts was high. A combination of high production costs with low utility to the final consumer and hence low sales would result in the financial non-viability of the tourism forecasting services. This study seeks to assess the accuracy and hence usefulness of the forecasts published in the *International Travel and Tourism Forecast* and the *World Travel Overview*.

12.2 THE TOURISM DEMAND FORECASTING SERVICES

12.2.1 International Travel and Tourism Forecast

The *International Travel and Tourism Forecast* (ITTF) (Brooke *et al.*, 1985) gives forecasts of UK outward tourism to 12 destination countries or country groups: Austria; Belgium and Luxembourg; France; German Federal Republic; Gibraltar, Malta and Cyprus; Greece; Italy; the Netherlands; Portugal; Spain;

Switzerland; and the USA. The forecast number of holiday visits from the UK to each of these countries is split into air independent holidays, air inclusive tours, surface independent holidays and surface inclusive tours. Thus four series are provided for each destination, giving a total of 48 forecast series. The ITTF was published in early 1985, and gives annual forecasts of holiday demand for the years 1985 to 1988.

The forecasting methodology used to generate the (future) values produced in the ITTF is a combination of multivariate state-space forecasting and econometrics.

12.2.2 The TRAM Forecast

The *World Travel Overview* (Means and Avila, 1986, 1987, 1988) gives forecasts of USA outbound tourism to the following set of destinations: Canada; Mexico; 16 destinations in Western Europe; four destinations in the Middle East; five destinations in South America; nine destinations in the Asia and Pacific region; and seven destinations in the Caribbean and Central America. The forecasts are annual and in the 1986/7 issue of the *World Travel Overview*, which was published in September 1986, forecasts are given for the years 1986 to 1990. The 1987/8 issue gives forecasts for 1987 to 1991, and the 1988/9 issue gives forecasts for 1988 to 1992.

The TRAM forecasts of international tourism demand are generated using econometric techniques.

12.3 ASSESSMENT OF FORECASTING ACCURACY

In order to assess the forecasting performance of the two organizations under consideration, it is necessary to select particular measures of accuracy. As the forecasting tests are carried out on data series of origin–destination tourist flows of widely differing sizes, it is essential to use criteria of forecast accuracy that are measured in unit-free terms. Thus absolute percentage error figures are calculated for each forecast value considered in this study; where average error values are required, the mean absolute percentage error (MAPE) is calculated.

The error (e) is defined as

$$e_t = \hat{V} - V_t \tag{12.1}$$

where V_t denotes the number of tourist visits in period t and $\hat{V}_t$ denotes the forecast value. If there are n forecasts, then

$$\text{MAPE} = \frac{1}{n} \sum_{t=1}^{n} \frac{|e_t|}{V_t} \times 100 \qquad (12.2)$$

where $|e_t|$ denotes the absolute value of the error. Lewis (1982, p. 40) suggests that the following classification of MAPEs is applicable to industrial and business data: <10 per cent, highly accurate forecasting; 10–20 per cent, good forecasting; 20–50 per cent, reasonable forecasting; >50 per cent, inaccurate forecasting. These ranges of values can be used to assess the forecasting performances of the ITTF and TRAM in absolute terms.

In addition to examining forecasting performance as above, it may be of interest to see how well the complex (expensive) models used by the two forecasting organizations perform relative to simple (cheap) models. Given the considerable time, effort and expense necessarily incurred in the development of the state-space and econometric models, it would be expected that there would be a corresponding improvement in the accuracy of forecasts generated by these models compared with the forecasts generated by 'naive' models. Two simple models are used to generate forecasts for comparison purposes.

Naive 1 The forecast for period $t + 1$ is equal to the actual number of visits in period t:

$$\hat{V}_{t+1} = V_t \qquad (12.3)$$

This is the 'random walk' model.

Naive 2 The forecast for period $t + 1$ is equal to the actual number of visits in period t multiplied by the growth rate over the previous period:

$$\hat{V}_{t+1} = V_t \left[1 + \frac{V_t - V_{t-1}}{V_{t-1}} \right] \qquad (12.4)$$

This model incorporates the assumption of no change in the growth rate.

The ITTF and TRAM forecast values are given to the nearest thousand, but sampling inaccuracies taken together with rounding to the nearest thousand can give totally unreliable indications of forecasting performance when considering very small series. For example, if the actual number of holiday visits abroad is 510 (i.e. one thousand) and the forecast number is 490 (i.e. zero thousand), then the absolute forecast error is 100 per cent; and if the actual number is 490 and the forecast number is 510, the error is infinite. Hence, attention is restricted to those ITTF and TRAM series in which the actual number of visits abroad is a minimum of 10 000.

In this study, the performances of the ITTF and TRAM are assessed for one-year-ahead forecasts only, and the data sets used relate to the only (ITTF) or first (TRAM) sets of forecasts produced. Thus, the accuracy of UK outbound tourism forecasts for 1985 is examined, together with the accuracy of USA outbound tourism forecasts for 1986.

12.4 EMPIRICAL RESULTS

12.4.1 The International Travel and Tourism Forecast

Table 12.1 presents the absolute percentage error figures for UK travel by independent air to each of the 12 destinations considered for the ITTF, naive 1 (N1) and naive 2 (N2) forecasting models, together with the MAPEs corresponding to each approach. Tables 12.2, 12.3 and 12.4 present similar data for inclusive tour air, independent surface and inclusive tour surface, respectively. Using the Lewis (1982) classification for MAPEs discussed earlier, it can be seen that in absolute terms the ITTF model generates 'good' forecasts of tourism demand for UK outbound independent holidays (both air and surface), but only 'reasonable' forecasts of UK outbound inclusive tour holiday demand (both air and surface).

When considered relative to the 'no change value' random walk model, the ITTF model is clearly superior in the case of independent air holidays (83 per cent of cases). For independent surface and inclusive tour surface holidays, the ITTF forecasts are more accurate than the N1 forecasts in only 50 per cent of cases. The ITTF model performs particularly badly for inclusive tour air holidays, only beating the random walk model in 36 per cent of cases. In aggregate, the ITTF model out-performs N1 in 56 per cent of cases. Examination of the MAPEs for the ITTF and N1 forecasts shows that only in the case of independent air holidays does the ITTF model out-perform N1. In the other three cases the MAPE corresponding to ITTF is larger than the MAPE corresponding to N1.

Table 12.1 ITTF forecasting performance relative to N1 and N2: independent air

Destination	Absolute percentage error		
	ITTF	N1	N2
Austria	10.3	10.3	58.0
Belgium/Luxembourg	7.7	30.8	147.0
France	7.0	14.9	21.8
Germany (FRG)	30.0	36.7	44.7
Gibraltar/Malta/Cyprus	0.8	7.3	12.6
Greece	3.9	9.4	3.9
Italy	17.7	8.2	38.7
Netherlands	42.3	45.1	40.5
Portugal	18.4	27.6	17.1
Spain	3.6	12.4	1.5
Switzerland	14.1	17.4	9.0
USA	2.4	4.1	8.1
MAPE	13.2	18.7	33.6

Source: derived from Brooke *et al.* (1985).

Table 12.2 ITTF forecasting performance relative to N1 and N2: inclusive tour air

Destination	Absolute percentage error		
	ITTF	N1	N2
Austria	3.0	1.5	31.3
Belgium/Luxembourg	–	–	–
France	15.3	22.2	24.3
Germany (FRG)	56.0	48.0	69.0
Gibraltar/Malta/Cyprus	12.9	2.4	21.2
Greece	22.4	25.2	6.5
Italy	31.8	27.0	45.2
Netherlands	14.8	25.9	9.8
Portugal	21.4	16.7	17.7
Spain	48.7	37.0	70.3
Switzerland	8.1	10.5	3.7
USA	45.0	27.5	4.4
MAPE	25.4	22.2	27.6

–, denotes actual value <10 000 visits.
Source: derived from Brooke *et al.* (1985).

Table 12.3   ITTF forecasting performance relative to N1 and N2: independent surface

Destination	Absolute percentage error		
	ITTF	N1	N2
Austria	17.4	17.4	4.9
Belgium/Luxembourg	46.2	30.3	22.2
France	1.9	4.9	15.3
Germany (FRG)	0.0	4.6	25.0
Gibraltar/Malta/Cyprus	–	–	–
Greece	47.4	26.3	8.1
Italy	9.1	20.8	20.8
Netherlands	9.1	7.6	22.7
Portugal	10.0	20.0	16.4
Spain	25.9	25.2	49.8
Switzerland	1.7	5.0	5.0
USA	–	–	–
MAPE	16.9	16.2	19.0

–, denotes actual value < 10 000 visits.
Source: derived from Brooke *et al* (1985).

Table 12.4   ITTF forecasting performance relative to N1 and N2: inclusive tour surface

Destination	Absolute percentage error		
	ITTF	N1	N2
Austria	94.9	47.4	83.9
Belgium/Luxembourg	4.8	27.3	47.4
France	1.9	5.3	18.9
Germany (FRG)	22.2	19.8	76.1
Gibraltar/Malta/Cyprus	–	–	–
Greece	–	–	–
Italy	6.3	0.8	33.3
Netherlands	16.2	26.3	28.2
Portugal	–	–	–
Spain	40.0	36.3	50.7
Switzerland	27.9	30.9	68.8
USA	–	–	–
MAPE	26.8	24.3	50.9

–, denotes actual value < 10 000 visits.
Source: derived from Brooke *et al*. (1985).

A comparison of the ITTF forecasting model with the 'no change growth rate' N2 model shows that the forecasting performance of the ITTF model is relatively good. The ITTF outperforms N2 for each of the four categories of holiday.

The forecasting ability of the ITTF model appears to be similar to that of the random walk model. The ITTF model outperforms N1 in 56 per cent of cases, but the MAPE for the ITTF model is smaller than the MAPE for N1 in only one out of four cases. The high expense incurred in generating the ITTF forecasts using state-space and econometric models is not justified by the forecasting performance achieved relative to the random walk model.

12.4.2 The TRAM Forecast

Table 12.5 presents the absolute percentage error figures for US travel to various destinations for the TRAM, N1 and N2 forecasting models. On examining the regional MAPE values, it can be seen that the TRAM model yields 'highly accurate' forecasts of US travel to the Caribbean and Central America, 'reasonable' forecasts of US travel to the Asia and Pacific region and Western Europe, and 'inaccurate' forecasts of US travel to the Middle East and South America.

The forecasting ability of the TRAM model relative to N1 may be assessed by examining the percentage of destinations for which the TRAM model yields more accurate forecasts than the no change N1 model. It can be seen that the TRAM econometric model out-performs the random walk in 13 cases out of 42 (i.e. 31 per cent of cases): Canada, Mexico, three of 16 European destinations, none of three Middle Eastern destinations, one of five South American destinations, three of nine destinations in the Asia and Pacific region and four of seven destinations in the Caribbean and Central America. The fact that the random walk model out-performs the TRAM model for 69 per cent of the destinations is a poor reflection on the forecasting accuracy of the latter model. The regional MAPEs corresponding to the TRAM and N1 models may also be compared. Table 12.5 shows that for the five regions considered, the econometric model only out-performs the random walk model for the Caribbean and Central America, and even in this case the improvement over N1 is marginal.

The TRAM model out-performs N2 in terms of absolute percentage errors for individual destinations in 67 per cent of cases.

Table 12.5 TRAM forecasting performance relative to N1 and N2

Destination	Absolute percentage error		
	TRAM	N1	N2
Canada	10.2	12.1	6.5
Mexico	4.4	8.8	17.9
Western Europe			
United Kingdom	0.9	5.6	35.3
France	28.3	23.9	31.5
Italy	65.4	50.1	33.2
Switzerland	33.7	35.1	51.5
Germany (FRG)	14.1	14.6	33.3
Austria	54.7	49.5	52.4
Denmark	20.7	11.5	26.9
Sweden	2.7	1.2	16.5
Norway	31.0	22.9	52.9
Netherlands	49.5	39.8	69.6
Belgium/Luxembourg	13.0	5.2	15.5
Spain	118.3	83.6	38.9
Portugal	43.5	17.4	10.8
Ireland	8.0	6.7	45.6
Greece	179.7	149.6	144.5
Finland	17.6	9.4	23.5
MAPE	42.6	32.9	42.6
Middle East			
Israel	99.9	89.3	119.5
Egypt	83.2	76.2	80.9
Saudi Arabia	22.7	13.0	25.1
MAPE	68.6	59.5	75.2
South America			
Argentina	22.7	10.2	32.3
Brazil	38.6	13.1	45.2
Colombia	24.5	8.6	31.2
Peru	585.9	537.5	662.0
Venezuela	8.4	26.7	0.5
MAPE	136.0	119.2	154.2
Asia/Pacific			
Japan	36.5	32.1	46.1
Hong Kong	16.6	17.1	11.9
Australia	28.5	36.1	27.0
New Zealand	24.8	33.6	22.4
Korea	18.4	4.6	23.2
Singapore	26.5	33.5	22.3
Philippines	3.3	0.0	8.7
Malaysia	108.5	100.0	112.7
India	43.3	32.0	48.9
MAPE	34.0	32.1	35.9

Table 12.5 *continued*

| | Absolute percentage error | | |
Destination	TRAM	N1	N2
Caribbean and Central America			
Bermuda	1.9	1.5	12.7
Bahamas	4.1	5.9	4.9
Jamaica	4.6	5.5	5.7
Other British West Indies	22.1	23.0	22.6
Netherlands West Indies	1.9	3.0	2.3
French West Indies	7.8	6.8	6.8
Other W. Indies/C. America	18.6	17.4	18.2
MAPE	8.7	9.0	10.5

Source: derived from Means and Avila (1986, 1987).

When regional MAPEs are considered, it is also clear that the TRAM model out-performs N2. The TRAM MAPE is lower than the N2 MAPE in every case, with the exception of Western Europe where the MAPEs are equal.

It is very clear that the considerable expense incurred in generating the TRAM econometric forecasts is not justified in terms of the forecasting accuracy achieved. In general, the (no cost) random walk model is more accurate.

12.5 CONCLUSIONS

The track records of two tourism forecasting services have been examined in terms of one-year-ahead forecasts for the only (ITTF) or first (TRAM) set of forecasts produced by the forecasting organizations. Although each of the forecasting organizations provides forecasts for several years ahead, as forecasts are made further into the future more uncertainty is likely to be present, and therefore a lower level of forecasting accuracy is likely. It would be expected, however, that *one-year-ahead* forecasts could be generated with a reasonable level of accuracy, particularly given the sophisticated nature of the forecasting techniques used. In fact, Means and Avila (1987, p. 120), when assessing the performance of the TRAM model in generating one-year-ahead forecasts for 1986, point out that:

> In reviewing an econometric forecasting model such as TRAM, it is a fair question for travel industry analysts to ask how the model performed in predicting travel behavior ... it is

inescapable that many analysts will want to use TRAM for short-term, one-year forecasts as part of their planning processes.

The empirical results presented in this paper have shown that the forecasts of international tourism demand published by the two tourism forecasting services considered are at best of a similar level of accuracy to those produced by a random walk model, and may be considerably worse. The commercial non-viability of the *International Travel and Tourism Forecast* and the TRAM model which appeared in the *World Travel Overview* is therefore hardly surprising. The empirical results obtained support previous findings by Martin and Witt (1989a, b) which show that the random walk model is ranked more highly in terms of forecasting accuracy than causal models in the context of international tourism demand.

In spite of the poor forecasting ability of the TRAM model, in both absolute and relative terms, Means and Avila (1987, p. 112) are optimistic about the value of TRAM:

> Simple extrapolations of past growth rates in travel are useless given the kinds of dramatic growth and decline experienced by the industry over the past few years. As the data available improves, and experience with TRAM increases, the importance of this model for planning and analysis will only increase.

They also point out (1987, p. 120) that the absolute percentage error

> is not the per cent by which TRAM was 'wrong', but rather this difference between TRAM and the actuals represents two factors:
> - The degree to which factors other than economics . . . may have influenced travel . . . ;
> - The degree to which new economic forces . . . distorted the economic results of the model.

While unforeseen events which impact upon international travel patterns are likely to increase the absolute forecast error of any model, the relative forecasting ability of different models is not likely to change particularly markedly if the event has not been accounted for in any of the models. The poor performance of

TRAM compared with N1 is therefore still a major cause of concern, as is the mediocre performance of the ITTF.

Possible avenues for further research into the track records of tourism forecasting services include examining forecasts for time horizons greater than one year, examining forecasts made for different time periods, and broadening the scope to include additional organizations that publish forecasts of tourism demand.

References

Archer, B.H. (1987) Demand forecasting and estimation. In Ritchie, J.R.B. and Goeldner, C.R. (eds) *Travel, Tourism and Hospitality Research*, pp. 77–85. New York: John Wiley & Sons.

Brooke, M.Z., Buckley, P.J. and Witt, S.F. (1985) *International Travel and Tourism Forecast*. London: Industry Forecasts.

Lewis, C.D. (1982) *Industrial and Business Forecasting Methods*. London: Butterworths.

Martin, C.A. and Witt, S.F. (1989a) Accuracy of econometric forecasts of tourism. *Annals of Tourism Research*, **16**(3), 407–28.

Martin, C.A. and Witt, S.F. (1989b) Forecasting tourism demand: a comparison of the accuracy of several quantitative methods. *International Journal of Forecasting*, 5(1), 7–19.

Means, G. and Avila, R. (1986) Econometric analysis and forecasts of US international travel: using the new TRAM model. *World Travel Overview 1986/87*, pp. 90–107. New York: American Express.

Means, G. and Avila, R. (1987) An econometric analysis and forecast of US travel and the 1987 TRAM model update. *World Travel Overview 1987/88*, pp. 102–23. New York: American Express.

Means, G. and Avila, R. (1988) Globalization redirects the travel industry: the 1988 TRAM analysis. *World Travel Overview 1988/89*, pp. 86–100. New York: American Express.

Author Index

Subject Index